Mel Bay Presents

A Concise

History

of the *Classic Guitar*

by Graham Wade

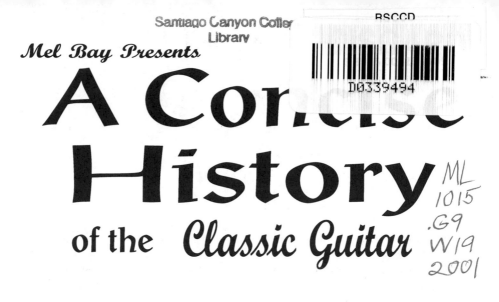

1 2 3 4 5 6 7 8 9 0

ocm 48749459

Visit us on the Web at www.melbay.com — E-mail us at email@melbay.com

Graham Wade, General Editor of the Mel Bay 'All About Music' Series, is Tutor in Classic Guitar for the Universities of Leeds and York and was formerly Head of Strings at the Leeds College of Music, England. A contributor for *The New Grove Dictionary of Music and Musicians*, he has written for various periodicals including *Soundboard, Guitar Review, Classical Guitar, Guitar International, Il Fronimo, The Strad, Musical Times, The Times*, etc. His previous books include: *A New Look at Segovia, His Life, His Music, Vols 1 & 2* (with Gerard Garno), *Segovia-A Celebration of the Man and His Music, Maestro Segovia, Traditions of the Classical Guitar, Joaquín Rodrigo-Concierto de Aranjuez, Distant Sarabandes-The Solo Guitar Music of Joaquín Rodrigo, Your Book of the Guitar, A Guitarist's Guide to Bach*, and *Gina Bachauer-A Pianist's Odyssey*.

Contents

PART I: THE RENAISSANCE

PART II: THE BAROQUE

PART III: THE CLASSIC GUITAR

PART IV: THE 20th CENTURY

LIST OF ILLUSTRATIONS

FOREWORD

This book, intended for both the general public and guitar students of all ages, explores the history of the guitar from the 16th century to the beginning of the 21st century.

In writing this concise guide, I owe, first and foremost, my grateful acknowledgements to the many scholars who over recent decades have researched seemingly almost every aspect of five hundred years of fretted instrument history. The footnotes and bibliographies will indicate the vast and amazing reservoirs of information now available to those who wish to explore individual areas in finer detail.

Classic guitar history is divided here into these categories:

1500-1600:	The evolution of music printing
	The vihuela in Spain
	The four-course guitar
1600-1750:	The five-course Baroque guitar in Spain, Italy, France, etc.
1750-1850:	Developments in the six string guitar
c.1850 onwards:	The Torres and post-Torres six string guitar

Between 1500 and 1900, the central issues involve:

a) The surviving music and sources of each period
b) Types of guitar used
c) Composers/performers
d) Recent research into the above areas (including relevant editions and recordings)

Moving past 1900, as sources of information multiply towards saturation point, emphasis has been placed on the following:

a) The international expansion of concert activities by leading artists
b) The content and development of guitar recitals
c) New compositions and editions
d) The work of luthiers
e) Recordings

In my first general history of the instrument, *Traditions of the Classical Guitar* (1980), I wrote in the Preface:

In a noisy and raucous age the simple voice of the classical guitar takes the listener back to an intimate, personal musical environment. The guitar's natural sound, being unamplified, corresponds to the dynamics of the speaking human voice; its simple directness appeals immensely in the somewhat dehumanized context of industrial society. For this reason the instrument has become popular in a great many countries, often cutting across traditional cultural boundaries.

Since these words were written we have all experienced many changes whatever country we live in. But my personal credo about the classic guitar has not significantly altered.

This book could not have been written without the help of a number of people. In particular, I owe an immense debt of gratitude to the following: to Julian Bream, for his wisdom and inspirational guidance over the years, to Catherine Dickinson and Andrew Liepins of the Spanish Guitar Center, Nottingham, UK, for infallible assistance in the provision of essential music, editions, recordings, etc., to Don Alberto López Poveda, of Linares, Spain, for material, information and enlightenment on Andrés Segovia and Spanish culture, and to William Bay, for his support, encouragement and patience at all times.

Above all, I am indebted to my wife, Elizabeth, for her extended and patient editorial work, for her determination, resilience and scholarly acumen.

G.W.
May, 2001

Grateful acknowledgement is due to the following for the use of copyright material or for providing specific and invaluable sources of information:

V.H.H. Green, Edward Arnold; Howard Mayer Brown, Prentice-Hall Inc., Harvard University Press; Guy Bourligueux, Thomas F. Heck, Volkmar Köhler, Martin Pickles, Robert Strizich, *The New Grove Dictionary of Music and Musicians,* Macmillan; Hutchinson; Gerardo Arriaga, Egberto Bermudez, Christina Bordas, The Metropolitan Museum of Art; Antonio Corona-Alcalde,*The Lute Society Journal;* Leo Schrade, Georg Olms, Breitkopf & Härtel; William Kinderman, James Tyler, Philip Ward, Simon Wright, Oxford University Press; Tom and Mary Anne Evans, Paddington Press; Manfred F. Bukofzer, J.M. Dent;

Victor Rangel-Ribeiro, Schirmer; Rudesindo F. Soutelo, Arte Tripharia; Monica Hall, Ronald C. Purcell, Simon Wynberg, Editions Chanterelle; Richard Hudson, Richard T. Pinnell, Neil D. Pennington, UMI Research Press; Claude Chauvel, Minkoff Reprint; Harvey Hope, Response Records; Carlo Andrea Giorgetti, Jakob Lindberg, Grammofon AB BIS; Glossa; Heugel; Alvaro Company, Vincenzo Saldarelli, Suvini Zerboni; Paulo Paolini, Ricordi; *Journal of the Lute Society of America;* Brian Jeffery, Tecla (www.tecla.com); Ralph Kirkpatrick, Princeton University Press; Luc Benoist, Thames and Hudson; Harvey Turnbull, Batsford; Craig H. Russell, University of Illinois Press; Douglas Alton Smith, Instrumenta Antiqua Publications; Hans T. David and Arthur Mendel, Norton; José L. Romanillos, Element Books; Victor Anand Coelho, Richard Savino, Cambridge University Press; Franco Colombo Publications/Belwin-Mills; Da Capo Press; François Lesure, Collection Eurydice; Stewart Button, Garland Publishing; Miguel Alcázar, Peter Segal, Thomas F. Heck, Anthony Weller, Matanya Ophee, Editions Orphée; Antonio Martín Moreno, Alianza Editorial; Paul Cox, Indiana University; *Guitar Review;* Schott & Co. Ltd; Charles Osborne, Weidenfeld & Nicolson; Mario Torta, Libreria Musicale Italiana; Studio per Edizioni Scelte; Julian Bream, Faber Music; Jim Ferguson, Guitar Solo Publications; Marc Van de Cruys, John Wager-Schneider, *Soundboard;* Chandos; Márta Sz. Farkas, Hungaroton; Melchor Rodríguez, Soneto; Alberto López Poveda; Bruno Tonazzi, Edizioni Bèrben; Richard D. Stover, Querico Publications; Juan Riera, Instituto de Estudios Ilerdenses; the Estate of Andrés Segovia; H.H. Stuckenschmidt, John Calder; *Gramophone; The* Estate of Emilio Pujol, Ricordi Americana; Jan J. de Kloe, David F. Marriott; Mervyn Cooke, *The Musical Times;* Corazón Otero, Ediciones Musicales Yolotl; Paloma Sáinz de la Maza, Ayuntamiento de Burgos; Fritz Jahnel, Verlag Das Musikinstrument; John Morrish, Balafon; Tony Palmer, Macdonald; The Estate of Victoria and Joaquín Rodrigo, Latin American Literary Review Press; Richard Burbank; Maurice Summerfield, Ashley Mark Publishing Company; British Broadcasting Corporation; Robert Offergeld, RCA; Reginald Smith Brindle; Enrique Franco, Deutsche Grammophon; John W. Duarte; Anthony Gishford; The Estate of José Ramírez III; Kay Jafee, John Williams, CBS Records, Sony; Martin Bookspan, Ross Yockey, Hamish Hamilton; The Estate of Alberto Ginastera, Boosey & Hawkes; J.M. Thomson, *Early Music;* Nikita Koshkin, Gendai Guitar; Sharon Isbin, Virgin Classics; Leo Brouwer, GHA; Peter Maxwell Davies; Chester Music; Augustin Wiedemann, Arte Nova Classics; Naxos; Elliott Carter, Hendon Music/Boosey & Hawkes; *Classical Guitar;* Lance Bosman, *Guitar International;* Yukiko Sawabe; Gareth Walters, EMI Classics; Noriko Ohtake, Scolar Press; Seppo Siirala, Minima Mini; Paul Griffiths; Eliot Fisk, Music Masters Classics; Ricardo Iznaola, IGW; Angelo Gilardino; Juan José Sáenz Gallego; Julian Byzantine; Allan Kozinn.

Photocredits: Henry E. Huntington Library and Art Gallery, p. 15; Musée Jacquemart-André, Paris, p. 22; Iveagh Bequest, Kenwood, p. 29; The British Library, p. 40; Bibliothèque Nationale, Paris, pp. 61, 75, 85; Biblioteca Nacional, Madrid, p. 81; New York Public Library, p. 79; Royal Library, Copenhagen, p. 90; José Mª López de la Osa, p. 93; Don Alberto López Poveda, pp. 106, 127; Basil Douglas Artists' Management, pp. 123, 181; Ediciones Joaquín Rodrigo, Madrid, p. 129; Deutsche Grammophon, p. 137; Julian Bream, p. 139; Harold Holt Limited, p. 160; José Romanillos, p. 163; Hazard Chase, p. 189; Asgerdur Sigurdardottir, p. 191; Music examples and other illustrations drawn by Peter Burke.

9

INTRODUCTION

What is a Guitar?

So many types of guitar-like instruments have been played over the centuries that it may be useful to define what is meant by the term *guitar*. This definition would help to clarify the characteristics of instruments designated as *guitars,* distinguishing between them and similar stringed instruments such as lutes, ukuleles or banjos.

Even defining what constitutes a *musical instrument* can be problematical. A tune can be coaxed from comb and paper and the resulting sound might be given a percussive accompaniment by banging on a tin can. Does this mean that 'comb and paper' or 'tin can' can be classified as *musical instruments*? E.M. Hornbostel, a leading expert in the field of instrumental definitions, came to the conclusion that every artifact 'with which sound can be produced intentionally'[1] should be defined as a musical instrument.

In partnership with Carl Sachs, he formulated a detailed list of instrumental types.[2] They decided that the main families of instruments could be grouped as follows:

1. Idiophones (80 entries): cymbals, triangle, gongs, castanets, bells, xylophone, glockenspiel, etc.

2. Membranophones (43 entries plus 20 suffix entries): drums, where a membrane or skin is stretched across a resonating cavity.

3. Chordophones (79 entries): instruments producing sound by means of vibration of one or more strings stretched between two fixed points (plucked chordophones - guitar, lute, harp, etc; bowed chordophones - violin, cello, etc.).

4. Aerophones (122 entries): blowing instruments using vibration of the air (trumpets, clarinets, flutes, bagpipes, whistles, etc.).

Using the above table as a guide, the guitar can be clearly defined as a *chordophone*. But now we have to go further and decide what kind of chordophone. Hornbostel and Sachs classified two predominant types of chordophones, the first of these being designated as 'a simple chordophone,' where the following mechanism occurs:

i) strings vibrate either across a structure which carries the string (a 'string bearer') or
ii) a 'string bearer' with a resonator which could be detached without destroying the sound-producing apparatus.[3]

In the 'simple chordophone,' a string tensed across a bow (used for shooting arrows), or bow-like structure, is vibrated to produce an audible twanging sound. When a gourd, box, or shell is attached to the bow, the sound is amplified. (Removal of the gourd or box would not, however, destroy the original sound producing agent.) Many instruments world-wide work on this principle and this kind of chordophone is regarded as the ancestor of all plucked instruments.

'Simple chordophones,' with and without resonators include such instruments as the *ganza* (Lower Guinea), the *hade* and the *thomo* (South Africa), the *vina* (India), the *chakhe* (South-east Asia), the *qin* (China), the *koto* (Japan), the *kani* (Liberia), etc.

Then there are 'composite chordophones.' In this category string bearer and resonator are organically united and cannot be separated without destroying the instrument.[4] These include instruments of great diversity in shape and sound:

Lutes: the plane of the string runs parallel with the soundtable.

Bowl lyres: a natural or carved-out bowl serves as the resonator.

Box lyres: a built-up wooden box serves as the resonator (*kithara,* the most important string instrument of Greco-Roman antiquity, a lyre type

11

with seven or more strings. The word, *kithara,* is etymologically close to *guitar,* signifying for some musicologists at the very least a historical connection between the two instrumental types.)

Spike lutes: the handle of the instrument passes diametrically through the resonator.

Spike bowl lutes: the resonator consists of a natural or carved-out bowl, found in Iran, India, Indonesia.

Spike box lutes or spike guitars: the resonator is built from wood (e.g. the *rabab,* found in Egypt).

Necked lutes: the handle is attached to or carved from the resonator, like a neck.

Necked bowl lutes: (mandolin, theorbo, balalaika).

Necked box lutes or necked guitars: (violin, viol, guitar).

(N.B. A lute where the body is built up in the shape of a bowl is classified as a bowl lute).[3]

This list indicates what a guitar might be and how it differs from similar chordophones. In particular it is defined quite separately from its cousin, the lute. The most recognizable feature of Arabic and European lutes is the bowl shaped (or half-egg shaped) resonator. The guitar, like the lute, is made of wood but possesses a more box-shaped resonator.[5] The distinctive shape of the guitar's resonator, often with incurved waist and flat back, is generally characteristic of the instrument.

Throughout history the strings of guitars and lutes have been played with either a plectrum or fingers, in contrast to the violin family, where strings are played with a bow. As with lutes, guitars usually have a circular soundhole in the center of the table, while the violin family have *f* shaped holes.[6] It is also customary in lute construction, that the instrument should be as light as possible, while the guitar is heavier, in line with appropriate structural principles.

There will always be examples of individual instruments departing from the norm for one reason or another. But here predominantly fashionable and popular forms will be explored rather than exceptions. As we go through the instrument's history in the rest of the book, some reference to guideline definitions touched on in this chapter will be relevant as the overall shapes and tunings of types of guitar alter and develop over the centuries.

Thus the history of lute/guitar type plucked chordophones goes back hundreds of years. Among ancestors of the established instrument forms known today can be included lyres and harps (mentioned in the Old Testament), the long-necked lutes of Mesopotamia, various kinds of stringed instruments depicted in both ancient Babylonian and Egyptian art, and the Hittite stone carvings of three thousand years ago found at Alaca Höyük, in Turkey.

Throughout the Middle Ages, an extravangance of stringed instruments, plucked and bowed, of varied shapes and sizes, were popular household items. The troubadours and jongleurs, wandering minstrels, singing heroic or romantic songs in the twelfth and thirteenth centuries, used them as a means of accompaniment.

The guitar is specifically mentioned in many works of medieval literature. The French poets of *Roman de la Rose* (c. 1280), refer to *gigues e rubebes...quitarres e leüz* (fiddles and rababs, guitars and lutes). Juan Ruiz, Archpriest of Hita, in his poem *Libro de buen amor* (c. 1330) distinguishes between *la guitarra morisca* and *la guitarra latina,* (the Moorish guitar and the Latin guitar), and also cites *el corpudo laúd* (the corpulent lute).[7] Chaucer in *The Pardoner's Tale* writes about the wild young folk, 'with harpes, lutes and gyternes' who visited taverns, and played at

13

dice both day and night.[8]

The exact type of guitar-like instrument referred to in these examples is not always known and issues of precise identification are much discussed by musicologists. Fortunately a clearer picture of instrumental types is possible from the early 16th century onwards when printed methods and books of compositions became available.

Footnotes to the Introduction

1. E.M. Hornbostel, 'The Ethnology of African Sound Instruments', *Africa,* vi, London, 1933, p. 129, quoted in *The New Grove Dictionary of Music and Musicians,* Vol. 9 (Macmillan: London, 1980), p. 237.

2. E.M. Hornbostel and C. Sachs: 'Systematik der Musikinstrumente', *Zeitschrift für Ethnologie,* xlvi (1914), pp. 553-590, quoted in *The New Grove Dictionary of Music and Musicians,* Vol. 9, op. cit., p. 238.

3. Howard Mayer Brown: *The New Grove Dictionary of Musical Instruments,* Vol. 1 (London: Macmillan,1984), pp. 364-365.

4. The composite chordophone category includes the many kinds of harp, (the strings lie at right angles to the sound table), and, by extension, keyboards. Composite chordophones themselves can be sounded by hammers or beaters, with bare fingers, with a plectrum, by bowing, by a keyboard, or by a mechanical drive.

5. Harvey Turnbull, 'The Origin of the Long-necked Lute', *The Galpin Society Journal,* XXV, 1972, pp. 58-66. The ancient long-necked lutes of Mesopotamia may also have had small box resonators, as opposed to a bowl shape.

6. The question of sound holes is complex. Some acoustic jazz guitars are made with *f* shaped holes, and the vihuela itself had several sound holes.

7. Laurence Wright, 'The Medieval Gittern and Citole: A case of mistaken identity,' *The Galpin Society Journal,* XXX, May, 1977, pp. 37-42.

8. Ibid., p. 15.

PART I: THE RENAISSANCE

1. Italy and the Renaissance

Developments in music are best appreciated with some awareness of the cultural background from which they emerged. The exciting potential of the Renaissance (c.1420-c.1600), is well summarized here by a historian:

> *For the Western world was suddenly intoxicated with the new wine of the Renaissance, the golden vision of the Indies and the Americas, the new voyages, the opening suddenly apart of the whole globe like a flower in the sun, the recovered intimate contact with the pagan Greek and Roman civilizations which had already been well under way and which was hastened by the Turkish capture of Constantinople in 1453, the culture pouring from the printing presses, the departure and return of adventurers, the thrill of conflict and conquest...*

15

...the princes, the nobility, and the wealthy middle-class... move amid and are part of a pageantry of gay, precious, decorative dress, deliberately fussy, silks and velvets and furs and lawns, puffings and slashings, costly fabrics encrusted with gold and jewels; hangings of noble tapestry, elaborate domestic utensils of massy gold and silver, the handiwork of artist-craftsmen like Cellini, heavy furniture of fine wood; palaces like those sonnets in stone and glass which stand along the Loire, or like Hampton Court; parks stocked with deer and gardens and terraces laid out with careful science; everywhere perfumes and a spacious air, and a high culture, and the music of lutes... [1]

If these are the colorful characteristics of the Renaissance, how can its achievements be defined?

The movement generally known as the Renaissance was one of the most significant in European history because it effected a change in man's attitude towards the problem of human existence. The word, which was not used to describe the movement until 1835, implies re-birth and renewal... the Renaissance came ultimately to mean... no less than a new venture in living which helped to shape the modern world...

Broadly speaking, it represented a change of outlook as a result of which men began to view the old material of literature and art in a new way, thus arriving at new mental concepts in literature, art, religion and science... The Renaissance generated a rich culture which re-orientated man's style of living...

With this new attitude to life there went a sense of optimism... There was an air of excitement arising from the geographical discoveries which gave additional significance to discoveries in the world of scholarship... The exploration of the mind as of new seas and strange lands demanded an enquiring spirit... This feeling of enthusiasm and of genuine delight at the new discoveries was a characteristic of the Italian Renaissance and in a sense of the whole movement. [2]

In such developments, typical of an era when boundaries and horizons, geographical, political, economic and artistic, were being expanded, music was a vital aspect. Because of the remarkable evolution of printing technology over the second half of the previous century, the 16th century witnessed the publication of a huge treasury of printed music. Thus it is nowadays possible to get to know the lute and guitar music from this period, much of which is truly representative of the Renaissance ideals of discovery, inventiveness, and the expression of profound emotion and performing virtuosity.

It is generally acknowledged that Italy was the cradle of the Renaissance. At this time Italy was not a unified country as it is now but a series of individual states, some under foreign domination:

> *Italy at this moment is a mosaic of self-contained states and republics, small and large, of which the great Republic of Venice, in its decline still aristocratic, wealthy, commercial, art-loving, and powerful, and the constantly disputed Duchy of Milan are the chief. Across the center, a narrow strip containing Rome and running diagonally from the Adriatic to the Tyrrhenian Sea, are the Papal States... Naples, Sicily and Sardinia belong to the Spanish Crown, and therefore after Charles's election, to the Empire. Florence is now a republic, now ruled by the Medici. Mantua is held by the Gonzagas, Ferrara by the House of Este. Venice is strong and independent enough to ally herself with whichever power she chooses - generally France. The real center of policy in Italy is the Duchy of Milan.[3]*

Within the Italian states many great painters, sculptors, and architects flourished, nurtured by traditions stretching back to the time of the ancient Romans. Distinguished artists enjoyed the patronage of rich and cultured princes and dukes, as well as the support of a number of Popes, themselves political leaders. Music was vital to this artistic environment:

> *To judge from the surviving sources, instrumental music was cultivated more richly and more deeply in Italy than in any other country of western Europe during the 16th century.[4]*

2. The Printing of Instrumental Music

As the printing of instrumental music became well advanced, specific techniques were developed for lute music, preparing the way for further possibilities in fretted instrument methods, compositions and styles.

In 1505, Marco Dall'Aquila received a ten-year privilege from the Signoria of Venice to print lute books, though no volumes of this kind are known to have been produced by him.[5] In 1507, Francesco Spinacino's *Intabulatura de Lauto*, Books One and Two, achieved the distinction of being the first printed collection devoted entirely to instrumental music. (His compositions at this time were for solo lute, except for a few pieces for two lutes.)

Spinacino's books were published by Ottaviano Petrucci (1466-1539) who received permission from the Council of the Republic of Venice to print music by the new method over the next twenty years. In 1513, Petrucci took up a fifteen year privilege from Pope Leo X to print within the Papal States (though he returned to Venice in 1536 for the last three years of his life). Petrucci stands at the head of the tradition for the thousands of music publishers who followed his example of excellence over the centuries as printed instrumental music of every kind developed throughout Europe.[6]

From 1507 until the end of the 18th century, works for lute and guitar were written in a system known as 'tablature,' quite different from modern musical notation. Tablature often looks ornate and complicated on the page, but for instrumentalists it is a very practical and straightforward method of transforming symbols into sound.

With tablature, novices did not need to learn all the complexities of reading notation but could start playing from the page from the very first lesson. The system can be rapidly taught and easily absorbed. Tablature is a direct visual indication of where notes are actually played on the instrument. In this way the pupil need only be concerned with the technical approach to performing the music, without immediate visual reference to concepts of pitch and harmony (as is necessary with reading modern notation).

Varieties of tablature were many, adapted according to historical and geographical contexts and specific styles of tablature were used for Renaissance lute, Baroque lute, vihuela, four-course guitar, Baroque guitar, cittern, colascione, etc.

Tablature for fretted instruments works as follows:

1. Horizontal lines, each representing a course (single or double strung) of a particular instrument are drawn on the page in a diagram of the fingerboard.

2. Numbers (or alternatively, letters) are placed to show where the fingers of the left hand should play. (Tablature that uses numbers is known as Italian and the use of letters is designated as French.)

3. The numbers/letters are positioned on a diagram of the strings and the time values of the notes are indicated at the top of the diagram. Each number gives the fret at which the note is stopped by the left hand, open strings being shown by the figure *o*.

An example of a *Pavana* by Luis Milán in tablature and notation:

Tablature undoubtedly possesses advantages for players of fretted instruments. A British musicologist praised lute tablature for its fidelity to musical requirements, comparing it favorably with the less reliable part-books and choir-books:

> *The notations used for lute tablatures were far more precise than staff notation in this respect, since each intersection of string and chromatic fret on the neck of a lute was represented by a separate and distinct symbol; lute-transcriptions of vocal music will thus supply many of the accidentals that were lacking from the vocal texts, and no scholar dare ignore the evidence they provide. But even these transcriptions have to be used with great care. It is as easy to make mistakes in writing or printing lute-tablatures as in any other kind of musical notation.*[7]

3. The Music of the Spanish Vihuela

The Spanish masters of the vihuela, the *vihuelistas,* composed for the *vihuela de mano,* plucked with the fingers (distinct from the *vihuela de púa,* played with a plectrum, and the *vihuela de arco,* played with a bow). The extant literature of the vihuela is a compact collection of work unlike the more extensive selection of lute books printed in various countries over a longer period of time.

The vihuela tradition is represented by the following texts:

Luis Milán: *Libro de Música de vihuela de mano intitulado El Maestro* (Valencia, 1535/1536). Italian lute tablature. Pieces for voice and vihuela, and solo vihuela.

Luis de Narváez: *Los seys libros del Delphin de música* (Valladolid, 1538). Italian lute tablature. Pieces for voice and vihuela, and solo vihuela.

Alonso Mudarra: *Tres libros de música en cifra para vihuela* (Seville, 1546). Italian lute tablature, harp (or organ) tablature and mensural notation. Solo vihuela, solo four-course guitar, voice and vihuela, and solo harp or organ.

Enríquez de Valderrábano: *Libro de música de vihuela intitulado Silva de Sirenas* (Valladolid, 1547). Italian lute tablature and mensural notation. Solo vihuela, voice and vihuela, two vihuelas.

Diego Pisador: *Libro de música de vihuela* (Salamanca, 1552). Italian lute tablature and mensural notation. Solo vihuela, voice and vihuela.

Miguel de Fuenllana: *Libro de música para vihuela intitulado Orphenica lyra* (Valladolid, 1554). Italian lute and guitar tablature and mensural notation. Voice and vihuela, five-course vihuela, six-course vihuela, four-course guitar.

Esteban Daza: *Libro de música en cifras para vihuela intitulado El Parnasso* (Valladolid, 1576) Italian lute tablature. Solo vihuela, voice and vihuela.[8]

Six-course vihuela music was usually written for an instrument tuned according to these intervals:[9]

21

Though a reasonable amount is known about the music played by the vihuela composers, precise details of the instruments on which they performed remain obscure. Whereas various excellent 16th century lutes are extant all but two of the vihuelas from that time have been lost.

A surviving vihuela is in the Musée Jacquemart-André, Paris:

This pine topped instrument has no less than five distinctive sound holes, and is beautifully ornamented with marquetry of dark and light wood on sides, back, fingerboard and neck.

Unfortunately the bridge is missing, making it difficult to estimate the true original string length. The instrument was presumably not representative of a typical vihuela. Its comparatively large size suggests that it could have been a bass instrument, suitable for use in ensemble work, perhaps in an accompanying role.

Another vihuela is in Quito, Ecuador, in the church of the *Compañía de Jesús,* exhibited as a relic among the belongings of Saint Mariana de Jesus (1618-1645). It was probably made about 1625 and after the death of Mariana was kept by the nuns in convents until 1911-12, when it was placed in the church.[10] Comparative measurements of the two instruments are as follows:[11]

	Quito	Paris
Overall length	101.5	111.3
Length of Soundbox	50.5	58.8
Length of Neck	31.5	33.8
Length of Pegbox	19.0	18.0

It is possible that the vihuela took after the lute in respect of lightness of construction. But its guitar-like waisted structure, quite distinct from the round bowl of the lute, would endow the vihuela with unique tonal characteristics.

4. Luis Milán and the Vihuela

Luis Milán's *El Maestro* represents one of the first examples of an instructional method for a fretted instrument. Many of the problems dealt with in his text can be found, in one form or another in guitar methods ever since.

A significant question for all string players concerns tuning the instrument. Tuning difficulties can trouble students of the guitar even now when nylon strings have replaced the traditional use of gut. For the vihuela novice the spectacle of six courses strung with a rather unstable material must have seemed daunting. Even to tune one course so that two strings of equal pitch were exactly correct (and remained in tune), would have been no easy task at first.

However, methods have a way of making such matters sound easy enough to deal with. Milán's advice was to tune the first string *tan alto quanto lo pueda suffir* (as high as possible). The other strings were then tuned to the top string. Milán also offers advice on the intricacies of *compás* (a word still used by flamenco players to signify rhythm), and *mesura,* the individual note values. For beginners, Milán selected simple rhythmic patterns with great care, relying on repeated note-values to convey to the student the essential principles to follow.

Milán does not attempt to describe the actual hand positions. He seems to have found it unnecessary to give detailed instructions about holding the vihuela and the actual playing and fretting of the notes.

However, *El Maestro* caters particularly for novices in other ways:

> *This book entitled* El Maestro *is divided into two books. The first book is for beginners and therefore contains easy music and is appropriate to the hands of a beginner.*[12]

Vihuela tablature, like all early guitar and lute music, shows the exact fingerings used by the composer/performer, and makes copious use of open strings. There is not a lot of playing in higher positions as this kind of instrument tends to lose resonance further up the fingerboard. From Milán's book it appears that nine or ten frets span the usual limits of the vihuela's fingerboard.

A book on Milán by an eminent musicologist of the 1920's offers useful tips on stylistic elements of 16th century instrumental music and its constant imitation of vocal counterpoint:

> *Luis Milán and the earlier lutenists thought entirely in terms of counterpoint, and not in terms of harmony. They regarded music as made by a number of voices moving horizontally; they did not think of it vertically as a succession of chords. Viols and wind-instruments could take the place*

of voices (as indeed they frequently did) and make music in the same
way; they could play all the notes sung by the voices, and hold them for
as long as the voices themselves...

This was one of the beginnings of the instrumental style in music, as distinct
from vocal style, and in this differentiation the lute, vihuela, *and guitar*
led the way. They could not even play all the notes sung by voices, much
less sustain them, and thus, when a composition for voices was transferred
to the lute, it was not reproduced but only suggested...[13]

The contrapuntal nature of 16th century fretted instrumental music is central to its appeal and, in vihuela music, it is enhanced by the delightful textural contrasts between *consonancias* (chordal passages) and *redobles* (scale passages).

5. The Four-Course Guitar

Co-existing throughout the 16th century along with the lute and the vihuela, was the four-course guitar, known by a variety of names depending on locality:[14]

Spain: *guitarra*
Italy: *chitarra da sette corde* or *chitarrino*
France: *guiterre* or *guiterne*
England: *gittern*

This instrument is described in Bermudo's *Declaración de Instrumentos Musicales* (Osuna, 1555), a lengthy treatise in five parts dealing with plainsong, polyphony, performance on keyboard, plucked string instruments, and the art of composition. Bermudo observed the close family relationship between vihuela and guitar, the latter being smaller with fewer strings, (usually four courses rather than six).

Unfortunately no 16th century four-course guitar has survived. But there is a later four-course guitar, dated 1646, by Giovanni Smit of Milan in the Kunsthistorisches Museum, Vienna:

> *Overall length: 56.5 cm, Scale length: 37 cm, Body length: 26 cm, Body width: upper bout 12.1 cm, waist 11.3 cm, lower bout 14.2 cm, Body depth: depth of sides 5.5 cm.*[15]

Some scholars have suggested that the oldest surviving five-course guitar, by Belchior Dias of Lisbon, dated 1581, now in the Royal College of Music, London, was altered from a four-course guitar.[16] Its measurements are larger than the Giovanni Smit model:

> *Overall length: 76.5 cm, String length: 55.4 cm, Body length: 36.6 cm, Body width: upper bout 16.5 cm, waist 14.5 cm, lower bout 20 cm, Body depth: depth of sides: at upper bout 4 cm, waist 6.5 cm, lower bout 5 cm.*[17]

The first printed examples of music for four-course guitar in Spain can be found in Alonso Mudarra's vihuela book, *Tres libros de música en cifra para vihuela* (Seville, 1546), and Miguel de Fuenllana's *Orphenica Lyra*, Book Six (1554).

In Italy, the tenth book of Melchiore de Barberiis's *Opera Intitolata Contina* (1549), offers four fantasias for the guitar which he calls *chitara da sette corde* (guitar with seven strings), referring to the seven strings of the four courses, (the top string being single).[18]

The four-course guitar flourished most of all in France, where a number of books of compositions for it were published. The instrument may have been especially popular as King Henri II (1519-1559, ascended the throne,1547), was in Spain with his elder brother from 1526 until 1530 as hostage for his father and presumably enjoyed the guitar music he heard there. Thus a wide range of four-course guitar books appeared between 1551 and 1570:

1551: Simon Gorlier: *Le Troysieme livre contenant plusieurs duos et trios, mis en tabulature de Guiterne, par Simon Gorlier, excellent joueur* (Robert Granjon & Michel Fezandat, Paris). French guitar tablature.

1552: Guillaume Morlaye: *Le Premier livre de chansons, gaillardes, pavannes* (Paris). French guitar tablature.

1552: Guillaume Morlaye: *Quatriesme livre contenant plusieurs fantasies* (Paris). French guitar tablature and some compositions in French cittern tablature.

1553: Gregoire Brayssing: *Quart livre de tabulature de guiterre* (Paris). French guitar tablature, all pieces for solo guitar.

1553: Guillaume Morlaye: *Le second livre de chansons, gaillardes, paduanes* (Paris). French guitar tablature, all pieces for solo guitar.

1554: Adrian le Roy:*Cinqiesme livre de guiterre* (Adrian le Roy & Robert Ballard, Paris). Superius in mensural notation, accompaniment in French guitar tablature, all compositions are for solo voice and guitar.

1556: Adrian le Roy:*Second livre de guiterre* (Adrian le Roy & Robert Ballard, Paris). Superius in mensural notation, accompaniment in French guitar tablature, all compositions are for solo voice and guitar.

1570: Pierre Phalèse and Jean Bellère, publishers: *Selectissima elegantis* (Louvain). French guitar tablature, all pieces for solo guitar.[19]

Footnotes to The Renaissance

1. D.B. Wyndham Lewis, *Emperor of the West, A Study of the Emperor Charles the Fifth* (London: Eyre and Spottiswoode, 1932), pp. 12-13.

2. V.H.H. Green, *Renaissance & Reformation, A Survey of European History between 1450 & 1660* (London: Edward Arnold, 1974), pp. 29-34.

3. Wyndham Lewis, op. cit., p. 48.

4. Howard Mayer Brown, *Music in the Renaissance* (Englewood Cliffs, New Jersey: Prentice-Hall Inc., 1976), p. 258.

5. Howard Mayer Brown, *Instrumental Music Printed before 1600, A Bibliography* (Cambridge, Mass: Harvard University Press, 1965), p. 11.

6. Martin Pickles, *The New Grove Dictionary of Music and Musicians*, Vol. 14 (London: Macmillan, 1980), pp. 595-597.

7. Thurston Dart, *The Interpretation of Music* (London:Hutchinson, 1954), p. 137.

8. For lists of music for each composer see Howard Mayer Brown, *Instrumental Music Printed before 1600, A Bibliography*, op. cit., pp. 47-50, 57-59, 87-89, 99-104, 139-142, 153-159, 281-283.

9. For a discussion of vihuela tunings see Diana Poulton, *The New Grove Dictionary of Musical Instruments*, Vol.3 (London: Macmillan, 1984), pp. 724-725.

10. Egberto Bermudez, 'The Vihuela: The Paris and Quito Instruments', in *La Guitarra Española* (New York: The Metropolitan Museum of Art, 1992,) pp. 25-47. Antonio Corona-Alcalde, 'The Viola da mano and the Vihuela, Evidence and Suggestions about their Construction,' *The Lute Society Journal*, 1984, p. 12.

11. Bermudez, op. cit., p.47.

12. Leo Schrade, ed., *Libro de Música de Vihuela de Mano Intitulado El Maestro, Luys Milán* (Hildesheim: Georg Olms, Wiesbaden: Breitkopf & Härtel, 1976), p. xxviii.

13. J.B. Trend, *Luis Milán and the Vihuelistas* (Oxford University Press, 1925), pp. 31-32.

14. James Tyler, *The Early Guitar* (Oxford University Press, 1980), p. 25.

15. Tom and Mary Anne Evans, *Guitars, From the Renaissance to Rock* (New York & London: Paddington Press, 1977), p. 22.

16. Gerardo Arriaga, 'The Renaissance Guitar', *La Guitarra Española*, op. cit., pp. 66-67: 'This theory is supported by the small size of the instrument, its narrow neck, the clear signs of restoration and conversion, and its age.'

17. Evans, op. cit., p. 27.

18. Tyler, op. cit., p. 26, suggests that the top string was single because of the difficulty of finding 'treble strings of gut with equal thickness throughout their length, a requirement for good intonation. The problem of finding two matching strings was even greater, hence a single first course was probably a matter of simple practicality.'

19. Mayer Brown, op. cit., pp. 127, 138, 148, 159-160, 172, 248.

PART II: THE BAROQUE

6. The Five-Course Baroque Guitar

Definitions of the term 'Baroque' have been attempted in a number of encyclopedias and by many musicologists:

The Baroque ...covers roughly the 17th century and the first half of the 18th century. Signs of the stylistic change became noticeable as early as the late 16th century, and for some time Renaissance and Baroque traits ran side by side...[1]

Another musicologist summed up the Baroque in terms of 'what everybody knows':

'What everybody knows' can probably be summarized as follows: The Baroque period ran approximately from 1600 to 1750. Music written during this period shared certain characteristics: it was largely contrapuntal and became increasingly harmonic; it relied heavily on ornamentation... 'What everybody knows' does not include the fact that strong Baroque influences began around 1575 and persisted to around 1800. Nor does it include the fact that ornamentation could either be written out in full, as in many of the keyboard works of Bach; or jotted down in a sort of musical shorthand... or left out entirely with the understanding that the performer would put in his own.[2]

Thus Baroque manuscripts, tablatures and printed music, leave considerable responsibility in the hands of the performer, not all the data for the interpretation of such music being indicated on the score. This is particularly relevant to the guitar, which steadily developed its own characteristic features and an extensive literature.

A certain mystery surrounds the emergence of the five-course Baroque guitar. Towards the end of the 16th century this species of instrument became fashionable in several European countries, retaining its popularity for the best part of two centuries. In Spain the belief arose that the fifth string of the guitar had been originated by Vicente Martínez de Espinel (1550-1624), poet, novelist and musician, who was also credited with the invention of a special kind of poem:

> *He was known to his contemporaries mainly by his alleged invention of the* décima *(known after him as the* 'espinela'*) and for adding the fifth string to the guitar.*[3]

In Lope de Vega's play *La Dorotea* (1632), one of the characters comments:

> *May Heaven forgive that Espinel! He has brought us those new verses,* décimas *or* espinelas, *and the five strings of the guitar, so that now everyone forgets the old noble instruments as well as the old dances, what with these wild gesticulations and lascivious movements of the chaconne, which are so offensive to the virtue, the chastity and the seemly silence of the ladies!* [4]

But there were also five-course instruments in the 16th century. Miguel de Fuenllana's *Libro de Música para Vihuela* of 1554 contains pieces for a 'vihuela de cinco órdenes' (vihuela with five courses) including six *fantasias.*

Bermudo's *Declaración de instrumentos musicales* gives further information on the 'guitarra de cinco órdenes.'

> *...if you want to make the vihuela into a guitar in the new style take off the first and sixth, and the four strings that are left are those of the guitar. And if you wish to make the guitar into a vihuela, put on the sixth and the first.* [5]

The addition of another course to a four-course guitar was sufficient to bring about a change in its expressive powers. Moreover, it can be presumed that when a guitarist acquired a five-course instrument, it was not according to human nature to be content with the limitations of only having a four-course. On the five-course everything could be done possible on the four-course, but other things could be attempted musically which could not be contemplated on the smaller instrument.

Even with five courses the guitar was modest in its number of strings compared with the vihuela's six courses and the six, seven or eight courses of varied Renaissance lutes (the added bass courses being known as 'diapasons').

The guitar's stringing thus developed slowly and once the four-course guitar went out of fashion, five-course instruments remained at the heart of guitaristic activities for several generations.

7. Joan Carles Amat and the Five-Course Guitar

Joan Carles Amat's *Guitarra española de cinco órdenes,* (publ. 1596) is one of the most useful printed sources of early five-course methods.[6] The first copies of this book were lost, but later editions appeared throughout the next two centuries.

Amat's tuning follows in its intervals the top five strings of the modern classic guitar, though it enjoyed a specific tonal quality from the split octave tuning of the lowest two strings:

Amat's book goes into some detail concerning the playing of chords in *rasgado* (strumming) style. After the delicate polyphony of the vihuela composer/performers, came a different kind of playing which would ultimately be characteristic of certain Baroque guitarists. The contrast between strummed chords for rhythmic accompaniment and the playing of extended melodic lines is a constant factor of guitar history. Less accomplished guitarists at any time do little more than strum, while distinguished artists of the instrument throughout the ages weave intricate melodic patterns with fully supportive harmonic or polyphonic techniques, though strummed chordal textures may at times be tastefully incorporated.[7]

Amat gave fingerings for 'playing *rasgado* all the natural chords' (these being three note chords with root, third and fifth).[6] Indicating twenty-four different chords, twelve major and twelve minor, Amat numbers each one from 1 to 12, denoting major chords by the letter *n* after the figure, and minor chords by *b*.

Amat's book shows clearly which fingers should be used to play the various chords.

This book can therefore be considered the worthy ancestor of the host of tutors published over the centuries in order to instruct guitarists in chord methodology and chord shapes in terms of the fingerboard.

8. Opposition to the Guitar

As the five-course guitar became more popular, it aroused opposition in various quarters. The Inquisitor Sebastián de Covarrubias complained about the shift in fashion from the complexity of the vihuela to the strumming of the guitar:

> *...since guitars were invented, those who devote themselves to a study of the vihuela are small in number. It has been a great loss, as all kinds of plucked music could be played on it: but now the guitar is no more than a cowbell, so easy to play, especially* rasgueado, *there is not a stable lad who is not a musician on the guitar.*[8]

Praetorius in his *Syntagma Musicum* (c.1614), wrote scornfully about 'the charlatans and saltimbanques' who use the guitar for strumming, 'to which they sing villanelles and other foolish folk songs.'[9]

9. Luis de Briceño's Guitar Method

Luis de Briceño's *Método muy facilíssimo para aprender a tañer la Guitarra a lo Español* (Very Easy Method to Learn to Play the Guitar in the Spanish Style) (Paris, 1626) was the only Spanish guitar book to appear in the early 17th century. It includes accompanied dance songs *(villano, sarabanda, folias, chacona,)* as well as some instrumental pieces *(pasacalle, gallarda romanesca, sarabanda francesa,* and *españoleta).*[10] Briceño praised the guitar as 'the most suitable instrument for our time one could imagine... It has none of the inconveniences to which the lute is subject... It is always fresh as a rose. If it gets out of tune easily, it is just as easy to tune it again... the guitar, whether well played or badly played... is pleasant to hear and listen to.'[11]

10. The Five-Course Guitar and Alfabeto

The five-course guitar began its most rapid development in the early 17th century, a number of method books being published over the years, mainly in Italy.

Girolamo Montesardo's book, *Nuova inventione d'intavolatura per sonare li balletti sopra la chitarra spagniuola senza numeri e note* (New Method of Learning to Play Dances on the Spanish Guitar without Numbers and Notes), was published in Florence in 1606. This employed the significant term *alfabeto.*[12]

With this system, selected chords were allocated letters of the alphabet for easy reference by any wishing to learn how to play. (Amat, as we have seen, had used numbers to show which chord was to be played.) *Alfabeto* was to become the preferred method for most writers from now on for the designation of chords. Montesardo's use of *alfabeto* was continued and refined in various publications by other guitarists over the next few years.

One of these was Benedetto Sanseverino, musician at S. Ambrosio Maggiore, Milan, who in 1620 published his *Intavolatura facile... per la chitarra alla spagnuola.* Sanseverino uses Montesardo's basic *alfabeto,* indicating such chords by capital letters but moving on to include chord transposition:

He also introduces a new series of chords, indicated by small letters and produced by shifting position of the entire hand. Thus, a chord designated by a small letter is produced by first positioning the hands on the proper frets to produce the chord of the corresponding capital letter. The fingers are then shifted on all the strings two frets further, thus producing a chord sounding one whole step higher than that on the capital letter...[13]

Sanseverino makes a further spectacular advance by including a time signature, bar lines and note values for his *alfabeto*.

Another who followed in the footsteps of Montesardo, was Giovanni Ambrosio Colonna, an Italian guitarist and printer, possibly from Milan. In his *Intavolatura di chitarra alla spagnuola* (1620), he included accompaniments to songs and dances in strummed style, informing the reader how to play correctly with advice on appropriate tempos for the pieces.

In his third book, published in 1623, *Intavolatura di chitarra alla spagnuola,* Colonna expands the concept of *alfabeto* to incorporate sophisticated transposition:

> *Colonna continues the table of chords established by Montesardo. Sanseverino added a shift of position to obtain a new chord a whole step higher in pitch than each capital letter. Colonna expands this idea to include an entire series of chords proceeding from each letter. A letter G with a 2 above it means that the hand is placed on the frets ready to play the chord on the letter G, and then shifts the position on each string two frets.*[14]

Unfortunately *alfabeto* in its more basic applications could lead to a musical habit of which less competent guitarists are accused even nowadays - a preference to concentrate on strumming simple chords rather than a cultivation of the difficult art of playing plucked melodic lines and counterpoint. As always the guitar was torn between two aspects of its technique, the *rasgueado* strumming style, suitable for song accompaniment and relatively easy to learn, and the playing of interweaving lines (known as *pizzicate* or *punteado*), which demanded more sophisticated musical skills.

Popular folk styles emphasized the virtues of simplicity and rhythmic vigor, while court guitarists generally preferred a more complex art on a level equal to contemporary keyboard and ensemble music. The ideal guitarist would combine dance and song accompaniment styles (involving strumming) with intricate part-writing and articulated melodic lines.

Much of the prejudice against the guitar came from lutenists whose traditions throughout the 16th century established a remarkable standard of expressive polyphony. They resented the popularity of the guitar which seemed to strip the music down to an unseemly one-dimensional simplicity, and, moreover, could challenge their own esteem. However, some of the finest guitarists of the age were also lutenists and thus were well aware of what was needed in terms of instrumental virtuosity.[15]

The guitarists of the 17th century were to develop their art to its ultimate conclusions. This eventually brought about the happy integration of *battute* or *rasgueado* (strummed) and *punteado* or *pizzicate* (plucked) techniques side by side in satisfyingly contrasting timbres.

11. Developments by Foscarini and Others

A decisive step forward in this direction was achieved by Giovanni Paolo Foscarini (*fl.* before 1621-1649), guitarist and lutenist, who, at various times, served at the courts of Brussels, Rome, Paris and Venice:

In the 1630's, there was a fundamental innovation in the art of guitar playing, thanks to the Italian Giovanni Paolo Foscarini: the mixing of strummed and plucked styles. Foscarini played theorbo and lute, composed, and was a musical theorist: naturally he played the guitar, and he introduced this mixed style into his strumming books as a novelty, in imitation of lute music, probably without suspecting that his invention was to become the fundamental characteristic of guitar music. From then on, solo guitar books can be divided into three groups: the great majority in mixed style, some in an exclusively plucked style, extremely rare and of exceptional musical quality...and finally, those given over solely to the strummed style.[16]

The same authors point out that, following the three playing styles, more than a hundred Italian, French and Spanish volumes, were printed between 1600 and 1750. However, publications offering strummed guitar music 'gradually became less and less interesting, heavily plagiarized and filled with clichés and anachronisms.'[16]

Foscarini's third publication, (c.1630), *Il primo, secondo e terzo libro dell chitarra spagnuola* combined *alfabeto* with the intricacies of Baroque guitar tablature:

> *...Foscarini was the first 17th century composer to write out combinations of the earlier strumming, or* rasguedo, *style of guitar playing and single-note plucking as used in playing the lute, though he himself observed that he included such pieces in his book 'more for the embellishment of the work than for other reasons, since I know well that they are more suited to the lute than the guitar.'*

> *Even with the strummed music he defined a melody, using the top string or the top note of an inverted chord...*[17]

Foscarini's influence was extensive and he would be duly acknowledged by Gaspar Sanz in his *Prologue* (1674), along with Amat, Kapsberger, Pellegrini, Fardino, Granata, and Corbetta, as one of the great Maestros.

Another Italian, Pietro Millioni (dates unknown), also wrote an influential book. With his co-author, Lodovico Monte, he published *Vero e facil modo... la chitarra spagnola* (Rome, 1637), which would appear in almost a dozen reprintings over the next hundred years. Millioni was primarily interested in the strummed style of playing, and gave instruction in the proper right-hand method of striking the strings. But he succeeded in developing the art of *alfabeto* to include dissonant chords *(lettere tagliate)* and some advanced fingering for common chords.[18]

A radical change occurred in 1640:

The year of 1640 marked a great change in guitar music. The change came about when guitarists fused the old strummed style with the punteado *style and its notation in lute tablature... The most attractive solo guitar music in Italy from 1640 to the end of the century combined the old* alfabeto *with lute tablature. The resulting notation may be appropriately called mixed tablature. It proved to be the ideal medium for adding the innovations and techniques of lute players to the previous tradition of guitar music. The repertoire became more difficult to play as guitarists strove for aesthetic improvements; it became music to be performed by expert professionals and not by dabbling amateurs.[19]*

Thus in 1640 a number of guitar books appeared in Italy:

Giovanni Paolo Foscarini: *Li 5 libri della chitarra alla spagnuola...* (Rome);

Inventione di toccate sopra la chitarra spagnuola ... (Rome).

Angelo Michele Bartolotti: *Libro primo di chitarra spagnola...*(Florence).

Antonio Carbonchi: *Sonate di chitarra spagnuola con intavolatura francese...*(Florence).

Nicolao Doizi de Velasco: *Nuevo modo...de la guitarra...* (Naples).[20]

Stefano Pesori: *Lo scrigno armonico...* (Mantua).[21]

Bartolotti (c.1615-c.1682) (also a player of theorbo), is considered, in terms of the guitar, as 'one of the very first to emancipate this instrument, which had hitherto been confined to a set of hackneyed formulas strummed over and over again by amateurs of little culture.'[22]

His first book, dedicated to the Duke of Salviati, dated August, 1640, includes 24 *passacaglie* and 6 suites, (mainly *allemanda, 2 correnti,* and *sarabanda).* A second, more sophisticated book (c.1655), dedicated to Queen Christina of Sweden, has seven assortments of pieces in specific keys, each tonality offering two or more suites.[23]

Carbonchi (dates unknown), used French tablature in his first book to make his publications 'more widely understood in the ultramontane countries and in other nations.'[24] This contained both plucked and strummed styles but a second publication, *Le dodici chitarre spostate* (Florence, 1643), relied entirely on strummed techniques.[25]

Doizi de Velasco (c.1590-c.1659), a Portuguese guitarist, lived in Spain and Italy, becoming one of Philip IV's chamber musicians in 1641. He praised the guitar as 'a perfect and most abundant instrument' and also for its capability of being played equally well in twelve different keys.[26]

Stefano Pesori (dates unknown, d. post c.1650), published several books employing both strummed and plucked styles, including *battute* accompaniments to songs and dances:

He was a popular musician and in his last known work, listed over 140 students, past and present, including Venetian nobility, professional people and cognoscenti... His books are most attractive and are of considerable historical interest beyond the music they contain, having beautifully decorated margins, many illustrations and two portraits of the composer, as well as descriptive titles, puns, sonnets and proverbs.[27]

12. Francesco Corbetta

Early Baroque guitarists are generally more familiar to scholars than to the public. But one of the masters better known (at least among modern guitarists), is Francesco Corbetta. His genius advanced the instrument in its range of imaginative compositions and in the skilful notation of various guitar techniques.

Corbetta, born in Pavia, northern Italy in 1615, published his first book, *De gli scherzi armonici trovati... sopra la chitarra spagnuola,* (Bologna, 1639), at the age of twenty-four. Already he had wealthy patrons, his first book making special mention of Count Pepoli and offering compositions in the Count's honor. The collection contains *passacagli, chiaccona, folía, spagnoletta, ruggiero, pavaniglia, passamezzo, corrente, gagliarda, mantovana, alemana, aria di Fiorenza, bergamasco, sarabanda, balletto,* etc.

Here the strummed style elegantly juxtaposes with expressive plucked lines. The book included an *alfabeto* method indicating chords by letters in a similar manner to that of Montesardo.[28]

Over the next few years, Corbetta's influence became international. In 1643, his second book, *Varii capricci per la ghitarra spagnola,* dedicated to Carlo V, Duke of Mantua and Monferrato, was published in Milan. About this time Corbetta went to Spain, where he may have worked on a third book of music (now lost).[29] From Spain, Corbetta moved to the French court. Recommended by the Duke of Mantua, and summoned by Cardinal Mazarin, the successor to Richelieu, Corbetta became guitar tutor to the Dauphin, on whose progress a contemporary historian commented:

> I believe it is proof of the greatness of His Majesty that they say he equalled, after eighteen months, his guitar master whom Cardinal Mazarin had brought from Italy expressly to teach him to play this instrument, much in vogue at the time.[30]

The guitar's popularity, greatly increased by royal participation, was not welcomed by everybody. Pierre Trichet, in *Le Traité des Instruments de Musique* (c.1640), argued fiercely on behalf of the lute:

> The guiterre or guiterne is a musical instrument widely used by the French and Italians, but still more among the Spanish, who were the first to make it fashionable, and who know how to play it more madly than any other nation, using it particularly for singing and for playing their sarabands, galliardes, espagnolettes, passemezes, passacaglias, pavanes, allemandes and romanesques with a thousand gestures and body movements which are so grotesque and ridiculous that their playing is bizarre and confused... Who is not aware that the lute is what is proper and suitable for the French, and the most delightful of all musical instruments? Still there are some of our nation who leave everything behind in order to take up and study the guitar. Isn't this because it is much easier to perfect oneself in this than in lute-playing, which requires long and arduous study before one can acquire the necessary skill and disposition? Or is it because it has a certain something which is feminine and pleasing to women, flattering their hearts and making them inclined to voluptuousness.[31]

Despite such attacks, Corbetta's career continued at the highest level. In 1648, his fourth book, *Varii scherzi di sonate per la chitara spagnola, Libro Quarto*, dedicated to the Archduke of Austria, was published in Brussels. In 1652 Corbetta became court guitarist at Hanover, returning to the French court the following year.

After the restoration of Charles II in 1660, Corbetta moved to England where he spent several years. His next book, *La Guitarre Royalle, dediée au Roy de la Grande Bretagne* (dedicated to Charles I), appeared in 1671, printed in Paris by permission of Louis XIV.

Corbetta's last publication, entitled *La Guitarre Royalle* (1674), was dedicated to Louis XIV, the Sun King. This included a number of strummed pieces and compositions evoking the fanfares and trumpets of battle, designed to appeal directly to the king himself. His desire to please the monarch is explicitly stated in the Preface:

> *I intended to restrict myself to the manner that would best please His Majesty...*[32]

Corbetta died at the age of sixty-six in Paris in 1681. A poem written by one of his students, Rémy Médard, expresses the profound respect and affection inspired by the man and his guitar:

Epitaphe De Francisque Corbet

Cy gist l'Amphion de nos jours,
Francisque, cet homme si rare,
Qui fit parler à sa guitarre
Le vray langage des amours.

Il gagna par son hamonie
Les coeurs des Princes & des Roys,
Et plusieurs ont cru qu'un génie
Prenoit le soin de conduire ses doigts.

Passant, si tu n'as pas entendu ces merveilles,
Apprens qu'il ne devoit jamais finir son sort,
Et qu'il auroit charmé la Mort;
Mais, hélas! par malheur, elle n'a point d'oreilles.

(Here lies the Amphion of our time, Francesco, that exceptional man, who made the guitar speak the true language of love. By his harmony he won the hearts of princes and kings, and some believed that a spirit took care to guide his fingers. As you pass by, if you have not heard these miracles, understand that he would never have met his fate and would have charmed Death itself. But, alas, unfortunately, Death has no ears.)[33]

13. Giovanni Battista Granata

Corbetta's influence continued in Italy through his pupil, Giovanni Battista Granata, guitarist and surgeon, who with the following books, published between 1646 and 1684, established his reputation as the most prolific author of the Italian Baroque guitar tradition:

1646:   *Capricci armonici sopra la chitarriglia spagnuola.* (Bologna)

c.1650:   *Nuove suonate di chitarriglia spagnuola piccicate, e battute... opera seconda.*

1651:   *Nuova scielta di capricci armonici e suonate musicali in vari tuoni, opera terza.*

1659:   *Soavi concenti di sonate musicali per chitarra spagnuola, opera quarta.* (Bologna)

1674:   *Nuovi capricci armonici musicali (in vari tuoni per la chitarra spagnuola, violino e viola concertati et altre sonate per la chitarra sola), op. quinta.* (Bologna)

1680:   *Nuovi soavi concenti (in vari tuoni per la chitarra spagnuola, violino e viola concertati et altre sonate per la chitarra sola), op. sesta.* (Bologna)

1684:   *Armoniosi toni di varie suonate musicali, op. 7.* (Bologna)[34]

In his first two books Granata explored concepts which had appeared in the publications of Foscarini and Corbetta, such as *alfabeto* chord diagrams and dances in the style of the older *rasgueado* or *battute* (strummed) type of playing. From 1651 onwards he developed more complex *pizzicate* styles. His book of 1659 has been described as 'the largest, most comprehensive work on the guitar up to that time'.[35]

In the Preface of *La Guitarre Royalle* of1671, Corbetta accused Granata of stealing some of his compositions and having them printed in Venice. Such practices were not unknown in music and literature in an age when the laws of copyright did not exist.

Granata's sixth book (1680), intended entirely for masters of the guitar, offers music of some difficulty, with particular passages extending inventively above the tenth fret. Despite such progressive virtuosity, Granata's music has been neglected by modern concert guitarists.

14. Robert de Visée

The music of Robert de Visée has a wide appeal to both students and recitalists nowadays. The revival of interest began with Emilio Pujol's transcription (Eschig,1928) of de Visée's *Suite in D minor*, continuing with a popular arrangement by Karl Scheit (Universal Edition, 1944).[36]

Robert de Visée's life is less well documented than Corbetta's. Scholars usually presume he was born between 1650 and 1660, and died about 1732.[37] It seems likely that de Visée studied with Corbetta, and in 1682 he published a homage to the master, *Tombeau de Mr. Francisque.*

De Visée is first mentioned as a theorbo player in a letter (1680), to Mademoiselle Regnault de Solier written by Jean le Gallois (royal librarian and a member of the French Academy), who comments on the three guitar masters in Paris that year, Monsieur de Valroy, Corbetta and de Visée.

De Visée's first book of 1682 tells us that it was customary for the king to ask him to entertain the Dauphin. In similar vein, the diary of the Comte de Dangeau (1686), remarks that de Visée frequently played the guitar in the evenings at the bedside of Louis XIV. In 1709 de Visée was appointed as singer in the royal chamber, and in 1719 he became the official guitar tutor to Louis XV, then nine years old.[38] Robert de Visée is listed among those employed by the royal family from 1680 until 1732. In 1733 only François de Visée, his son, is included, a possible indication that his father had died in the previous year.

Robert de Visée's publications comprise a number of suites. These are not organically evolving suites in the style of Bach, but a fairly informal collection of dances grouped around the same key, presumably to be played by the performer in a convenient sequence as circumstances required. In his *Livre de pièces pour la guittarre* (1686) de Visée comments in his introduction:

So many people have applied themselves to the guitar and offered their pieces to the public that I do not know if by putting mine into print I am able to present something new to the liking of those interested. However I have worked only with this in mind, and in order to succeed I have applied myself to the melody to make my compositions natural as much as possible, knowing only too well that I could not claim to excel on the structural side of composition.

I have endeavored to conform, as far as my inadequacy will allow, to the tastes of skilled players, by giving my compositions the same style as those of the inimitable Monsieur de Lully. Because I have followed his example, even if from afar, I am persuaded that I have had the good fortune to have my pieces favorably received by His Majesty and all his court.[39]

The performance of de Visée's music on the modern classic guitar has necessarily involved a number of transcriptions which sound quite different from authentic performance on the Baroque guitar working from the original tablature. Some editors have expressed concern:

> *This* Suite in D minor *by Robert de Visée, from its first hearing in the concert world which goes back to the 19th century, has suffered an incredible series of vicissitudes. Scanning the editions which have been printed recently, even very recently, one cannot but be appalled by the astonishing transformation that the text has undergone, moving further and further away from the original which is an object lesson in musical clarity and unusually careful printing.[40]*

Prélude from de Visée's *Suite in D minor* in tablature, with a version in notation:

De Visée was undoubtedly the greatest French guitarist of the 17th century. His music has been described as 'a viable continuation of past achievements and a logical step in a new direction,' as he 'took much from the style of Corbetta without ever duplicating any of his pieces.'[41] In particular, whatever the problems of arranging his works for the modern guitar, de Visée's music has continued to provide pleasure and an awareness of the glories of the guitar in this era.[42]

15. Gaspar Sanz

That Gaspar Sanz's music is now widely appreciated by the public owes much to Rodrigo's Concerto, *Fantasía para un gentilhombre*, composed around themes from Sanz's publication of 1674.

Of the relationship between Sanz and this Concerto, Joaquín Rodrigo commented:

> *All of its thematic material, except for certain brief episodes in the last movement, is derived, as is no small part of the harmonic texture, from the work of Gaspar Sanz, who was employed by Philip IV of Spain and more especially by his son, John of Austria. Musical taste had greatly changed in the years that passed between the reigns of Philip II and Philip IV. Unlike poetry, music had too faithfully followed the pull of the people, and had been extensively popularized. To the noble grace of pavanes and galliards there succeeded the lighter style of* marizapalos, villanos, españoletas, canarios, *and so on, which were more appropriate to the hurly-burly of the popular theater than to palace balls. The dances which Gaspar Sanz wrote on these and other tunes...faithfully reflect these tastes and manners, and are, for the most part, short, simple and light.*[43]

As with de Visée, little is known for sure about Sanz's life. It is thought that he attended the University of Salamanca, being awarded a Bachelor of Theology degree, and later studied music in Italy.

But any consideration of his music centers around the publication of *Instrucción de música sobre la guitarra española* (Zaragoza, 1674). With this book, one of the most fascinating guitar texts of its time, Sanz secured a central historical significance in the five-course tradition.

Sanz's work consists of three progressive units. Instruction is first given in stringing, fretting, and tuning, with explanations of strummed and plucked techniques of performance. The music contained in the publication, some ninety pieces in all, often takes its strength from the folk elements of Spanish dance, his *españoletas, folias, marizapalos,* and *canarios,* being juxtaposed with *pavanas, gallardas, passacalles, corrientes* and *gigas* from French and Italian traditions.

Canarios by Gaspar Sanz, in tablature and notation:

16. Lucas Ruiz de Ribayaz

A method following in the footsteps of Gaspar Sanz was *Luz y norte musical* (1677) by Lucas Ruiz de Ribayaz, a Spanish priest, guitarist and harpist, with the intention of enabling the student to learn guitar (and harp), without a teacher. The book includes theoretical chapters on musicianship and an appendix, *Ecos del libro,* where the author offers (as well as harp pieces and his own compositions) a number of the dances of Sanz. The latter, in their modified form, aroused the irritation of one scholar:

> *Together with some of his own pieces in the collection, found at the end of the book, Ribayaz presents us with a selection of Gaspar Sanz's pieces, which have been altered for use on a guitar with* bourdons *on the fourth and fifth courses.*

> *He leaves out all the sections of Sanz's pieces which use the special idioms requiring the re-entrant tuning, and thus has the dubious distinction of being the forerunner of modern editors who similarly distort Sanz's music today.[44]*

Though his music may not always be entirely original, he remains of significance in guitar history for having introduced some European guitar music to the New World during a trip to 'remote and overseas provinces.'[45]

17. Ludovico Roncalli

Apart from the eminence of Francesco Corbetta the best known Italian guitarist of the late 17th century was Conte Ludovico Roncalli, whose *Capricci Armonici sopra la Chitarra Spagnola* was published in Bergamo in 1692. The nine suites in his book unite melodic *punteado* styles and the *rasgueado*, indicated by Roncalli's use of *alfabeto* in conjunction with Italian guitar tablature.

Each of Roncalli's suites begins with *preludio* and *alemanda*, followed by a mixture of other dances:[46]

Suite No. 1 in G: *Preludio, Alemanda, Corrente, Sarabanda, Gavotta, Gigua.*
Suite No. 2 in E minor: *Preludio, Alemanda, Gavotta, Sarabanda, Gigua.*
Suite No. 3 in B minor: *Preludio, Alemanda, Corrente, Sarabanda, Minuet.*
Suite No. 4 in D: *Preludio, Alemanda, Corrente, Sarabanda, Minuet, Gigua.*
Suite No. 5 in A minor: *Preludio, Alemanda, Corrente, Sarabanda, Gigua, Passacaglii.*
Suite No. 6 in F: *Preludio, Alemanda, Corrente, Sarabanda, Minuet, Gavotta, Gigua.*
Suite No. 7 in D minor: *Preludio, Alemanda I & II, Corrente, Sarabanda, Minuet, Gigua.*
Suite No. 8 in C: *Preludio, Alemanda, Corrente, Minuet, Gavotta, Gigua.*
Suite No. 9 in G minor: *Preludio, Alemanda, Corrente, Minuet, Gavotta, Passacaglii.*

18. Francisco Guerau

Poema Harmónico (Madrid, 1694), by Francisco Guerau, priest and musician at the court of Charles II of Spain, was the last Baroque guitar publication to appear in Spain during the 17th century. His compositions, including *passacalles, jácaras, mariona, pavana, gallarda, folías, villano* and *canario,* are played in *punteado* style, rather than the usual *rasgueado.* As the author explains, the contents of the book are 'more for those who have some experience and ability than for those who lack practice.'[47]

He advocates that in the sitting position, the instrument must not be held with the left hand, but is supported by 'placing the right arm over it' to enable the left hand to 'remain free to run lightly up and down the whole range of the guitar'. Scale passages are to be played with alternating index and middle fingers 'for if you play many notes with only one finger it cannot be either light or clean.'[48]

On an important stylistic matter, Guerau comments on 'the most beautiful and harmonious thing of all' for anyone who wishes to play with excellence - 'a continuous series of trills, mordents, slurs and arpeggios,' which he regards as 'the soul of music.' Those who cannot achieve this continuity of trills are exhorted not to 'despair, nor be discouraged' but to play the music 'even without the ornaments, for they are not an inviolable law.'[49]

19. The Guitar in the Early 18th Century

Even allowing for a recent resurgence of interest in the music of Santiago de Murcia, the first half of the 18th century could never be considered with hindsight as one of the finest eras of guitar playing. The giants of this period such as J.S. Bach (1685-1750), G.F. Handel (1685-1759), Antonio Vivaldi (1678-1741), and Jean-Philippe Rameau (1683-1764), represent the musical greatness of their time. But their works show no apparent awareness of the guitar's presence in their society. (In contrast, both Bach and Vivaldi wrote for the lute in one context or another, and the former was certainly acquainted with Sylvius Leopold Weiss (1686-1750), the supreme lutenist of the 18th century.)

The great composer of this period closest to the guitar was undoubtedly Domenico Scarlatti (1685-1757):

> As far as we know, Scarlatti never played the guitar, but surely no composer ever fell more deeply under its spell. In the Spanish dance pieces its strumming open strings form many an internal pedal point and its arpeggiated figurations evoke a kind of intoxicating monotony.
>
> Some of Scarlatti's wildest dissonances seem to imitate the sound of the hand striking the belly of the guitar, or the savage chords that at times almost threaten to rip the strings from the instrument. The very harmonic structure of many such passages that imitate the guitar seems to be determined by the guitar's open strings and by its propensities for modal Spanish folk music...[50]

If the guitar was relegated to being, at best, an influence on some of the finest keyboard sonatas of the late Baroque, a further reference point was in the visual arts. The artist, Antoine Watteau (1684-1721), as a painter of *fêtes galantes,* adored the instrument, depicting it as an essential component in a world of make-believe and idealized nature:

> What exactly is a fête galante? ...it is the new form that Watteau gave to mankind's abiding dream of a golden age, a refuge of happiness where time will pass in a perpetual carnival.
>
> Couples stroll and talk together; in the Gamme d' Amour (Gamut of Love) they sing or play the guitar; they dance; and above all, they just idle. Watteau has caught all the attitudes of relaxation, graceful detachment and nonchalance; the dresses with their folds broken over a knee or spread upon the ground; the poses that indicate whispered secrets, fond confessions, groundless anticipations and aimless departures.[51]

Thus the guitar became romantically associated with Utopian ideals, languor and romance, an escape from the ordinary world. These qualities are a part of a certain kind of poetry, and the guitar often belongs to that area of the imagination in much of its history and repertory.

Throughout the 18th century there were several editions of earlier works (including Amat's *Guitarra española*, and Millioni and Monte's publication of 1637, still being reprinted in 1737). These texts continued the five-course guitar tradition and perpetuated the instrument's popularity.

Another significant guitarist was François Campion (1686-1748), a French musician of English extraction and possibly a descendant of Thomas Campion (1567-1620), who was one of the great English lute-song composers. François Campion taught both guitar and lute at the Académie Royale de Musique in Paris (1703-1719), with a visit to England in 1731 or 1732. Strong claims have been made on his behalf:

> *There is no doubt that his powerful artistic personality dominated the world of the guitar in the first third of the 18th century. He exploited the resources of the instrument to their utmost limit; in addition to very complex writing he used no fewer than eight different chords and seems to have been the only composer to write fugues for the guitar.*[52]

Another scholar has remarked how Campion 'carried on the breakaway from the *rasgueado* style in his *Nouvelles Découvertes sur la Guitarre* (1705), notable for its plucked fugal style.'[53]

20. Santiago de Murcia

There was little reliable information about Santiago de Murcia (c.1682-c.1745) until the publication by Craig H. Russell of an extensive treasury of the composer's work known as *Códice Saldívar No. 4.*[54]

Russell concluded that Murcia was probably born in Madrid about 1682, the son of Gabriel de Murcia, the royal instrument maker. Santiago may have studied with Francisco Guerau and later travelled to Naples with

Philip V (where he met Arcangelo Corelli and Alessandro Scarlatti). Some time after 1717 it is likely that Murcia visited Mexico where collections of his music have quite recently been located.

Santiago de Murcia's *Resumen de Acompañar la Parte con la Guitarra* (Madrid, 1714), shows a clear Italian influence, partly perhaps to impress Philip V's Italian wife,[55] and because all eminent players appreciated the great tradition of Italian guitarists.

Murcia's manuscript collection of 1732, *Passacalles y obras de guitarra por todos los tonos naturales y acidentales* includes 24 *passacalles,* and 11 *obras* (suites). The suites are characteristically built round a structure of *Prelude, Allemanda, Correnta, Zarabanda,* and *Giga,* with additional pieces such as *Tocata, Bourrée, Gavota, Rondo,* etc., included according to the composer's fancy.[56]

Passacalles y obras is of historical significance as the last major source to include only tablature. (Minguet y Irol's *Advertencias* (1752) contains pieces in tablature and mensural notation thus initiating a move away from the precedents since the early 16th century of printed music for guitar and lute.)[57]

21. The End of the Five-Course Tradition

Between 1752 and 1774 Pablo Minguet y Yrol (*fl.* Madrid, 1733-1775), published *Reglas, y advertencias generales que enseñan el modo de tañer todos los instrumentos mejores, y mas usuales* ('Rules and general advice which show how to play all the finest and most usual instruments'). This series of pamphlets was for amateurs wishing to learn about instruments such as the guitar, bandurria, violin, flute, clavichord, harp, etc. In the aspects relevant to guitar playing, Minguet borrowed material from Murcia, Sanz and Amat.[58] Because of this plagiarism one scholar has acknowledged Minguet's place in guitar history:

> *An astute businessman, Minguet rarely risked publishing anything new and untried in the marketplace - instead he pasted together excerpted condensations of the current best-sellers. In nearly every case he discretely deletes the true author's name from the plagiarized version.*
>
> *He did not trouble himself with citing his sources unless the prestige of the attribution might increase sales. Significantly then, Minguet makes a special point to mention Murcia and Sanz by name... Murcia's name must have been familiar and well-respected as late as 1752 to warrant Minguet's unusual care in identifying his source.*
>
> *The page preceding Murcia's scales is noteworthy in that its six short dances are the last known instance of tablature notation in Spain.[59]*

22. A Digression Concerning the Baroque Lute

Though achieving a remarkably high level of composition and performance, the lute now faced a decline in popularity. Throughout the lifetime of J.S. Bach (1685-1750), many lutenists continued their profession as court musicians, frequently travelling to centers of musical excellence to demonstrate their prowess. Players such as Losy von Losingthal (c.1645-1721), Ferdinand Hinterleithner (1659-1710), David Kellner (c.1670-1748), Wolff Jakob Lauffensteiner (1675-1754), Adam Falckenhagen (1697-1761), Ernst Gottlieb Baron (1696-1760), the lute's chronicler and fervent advocate, and the great Sylvius Leopold Weiss (1686-1750), kept the lute's prestige alive in the high Baroque period.

The 18th century witnessed the culmination of hundreds of years of lute tradition. From its ancient roots, the lute had developed to a special peak in the 16th century when the printing press first enabled many fine collections of music to reach a wide audience. The English lutenists,

54

including John Dowland, Francis Cutting, John Johnson, Thomas Robinson and Robert Dowland, continued the forward march of the lute's repertoire to immense heights of virtuosity and finesse.

In the 17th century, lutenists were interested in advancing the bass resources of the instrument. Various types of lute proliferated, including archlutes, theorbos and chitarrones. Sometimes lutes were built with a massive string length, extra bass strings being attached to a separate pegbox on the neck of the lute.

By the 18th century the lute had become complex in technique and the care needed to keep it maintained. The instrument competed at a disadvantage with keyboards, easier for novices to learn and endowed with a distinguished repertory. The critics directed their attacks at the lute's impracticality. Ernst Gottlieb Baron, the lute's most persuasive apologist, in his *Study of the Lute* (1727), quoted the complaints of his opponent, Johann Mattheson (1681-1764):

> *We pay twice for the best lute piece, for we have to hear the eternal tuning that goes with it. If a lutenist lives to be eighty years old, surely he has spent sixty years tuning. The worst of it is that among a hundred (especially non-professionals) scarcely two are capable of tuning accurately. In addition, there is trouble with bad or spliced strings, especially the chanterelle, and trouble with frets and tuning pegs, so that I have heard that it costs as much in Paris to keep a lute as it does a horse.*[60]

Mattheson also attacked the sound of the lute:

> *The insinuating sound of this deceitful instrument always promises more than it delivers, and before we know where its strength and weakness lies, we think that nothing more charming may be heard on earth, as I myself was deceived by this siren. But once we see through these pitiful artifices, all the lute's virtue vanishes immediately.*[61]

Baron defends the lute, accusing Mattheson of misrepresentation:

The annoying and wearisome tuning is not at all as Herr Mattheson has represented it. A master must be able to tune his instrument instantly while playing, so that it is scarcely heard, even when a peg has slipped... That there are from time to time amateurs who cannot handle it very well is a flaw in their own nature, and this cannot detract from the instrument in the slightest, since there are few of these people.[62]

From a historical perspective, Mattheson seems to have won the argument. It was certainly true that the lute was now less attractive to amateurs as it required a high level of professional skill, and was difficult to keep in tune. But the bigger challenge to the lute was the popularity of the keyboard. Baron, however, attempted a valiant rearguard defense:

The lutenist can strike a chord very strongly and allow the tone to die away imperceptibly while arpeggiating... Further, the lute can very conveniently be carried along on trips. The player can even walk back and forth in a room with it, playing the loveliest passages and harmonies, which can be done neither with the clavichord nor the harpsichord.[63]

A further blow to the lute's ultimate survival was the lute-harpsichord, a keyboard played like a normal harpsichord but sounding like a lute. No lute-harpsichord has survived but Johann Friedrich Agricola, writing in 1768, describes what he saw:

The author of these notes remembers, about the year 1740, in Leipzig, having seen and heard a lute-harpsichord (Lautenclavicymbal) *suggested by Mr. Johann Sebastian Bach and executed by Mr. Zacharias Hildebrand, which was of smaller size than the ordinary harpsichord, but in all other respects was like any other harpsichord. It had two sets of gut strings, and a so-called little octave of brass strings. It is true that in its regular setting (that is when only one stop was drawn) it sounded more like the theorbo than like the lute. But when the stop which on harpsichords is called the lute stop... was drawn with the cornet stop, it was almost possible to deceive even professional lute players.[64]*

Thus throughout the second half of the 18th century the lute's gradual demise anticipated radical developments in the guitar.

Footnotes to The Baroque

1. Manfred F. Bukofzer, *Music in the Baroque Era* (London: J.M. Dent, 1947), p. 2.

2. Victor Rangel-Ribeiro, *Baroque Music, A Practical Guide for the Performer* (New York: Schirmer, 1981), pp. 1-2.

3. Philip Ward, ed., *The Oxford Companion to Spanish Literature* (Oxford University Press, 1978), p. 191. The *décima* was a poem with stanzas of ten octosyllables with the rhyme scheme abba:ac:cddc.

4. Quoted in Frederic V. Grunfeld, *The Art and Times of the Guitar, An Illustrated History of Guitars and Guitarists* (New York: Macmillan, 1969), p. 102, trans. Grunfeld.

5. Rudesindo F. Soutelo, ed., *Bermudo, Declaración de instrumentos musicales*, Bk IV, Chapter LXV, fol. XCVII (Madrid: Arte Tripharia, 1982).

6. Monica Hall, ed., Facsimile edition, *Joan Carles Amat's Guitarra española* (Monaco: Editions Chanterelle, 1980).

7. Flamenco guitarists have refined the art of *rasgueado* to the ultimate limits but use it juxtaposed with techniques such as tremolo, arpeggio, and rapid scale passages. Jazz players develop improvised melodic lines but also provide strummed chordal accompaniments for their improvising group. Segovia, at the extreme end of the spectrum, never offered more than a token strum, and proclaimed the virtues of instrumental polyphony.

8. Quoted in Grunfeld, op. cit., pp. 105-106. Harvey Turnbull, *The Guitar from the Renaissance to the Present Day* (London: Batsford, 1974), p. 41. Don Sebastián de Covarrubias Orozco, *Tesoro de la Lengua Castellana, o Española*, 1611, entry 'vihuela'.

9. Grunfeld, op. cit., pp. 2-5.

10. Richard T. Pinnell, *Francesco Corbetta and the Baroque Guitar*, Vol. 1 (Ann Arbor, Michigan: UMI Research Press, 1980), pp. 43-45.

11. Grunfeld, op. cit., p. 109.

12. Richard Hudson, *Passacaglio and Ciaccona, From Guitar Music to Italian Keyboard Variations in the 17th Century* (Ann Arbor, Michigan:UMI Research Press, 1981), p. 19.

13. Ibid., pp. 25-26.

14. Ibid., p.35.

15. Stylistic struggles continue. Segovia disliked flamenco. Both classic and jazz guitarists often express strong reservations about rock music. There is constant conflict between opposing camps and values represented by each style.

16. Christina Bordas-Gerardo Arriaga, 'The Guitar from the Baroque Period to the 1950's', *La Guitarra Española/The Spanish Guitar* (New York: Metropolitan Museum of Art, 1991-1992), p. 83.

17. Notes by Harvey Hope for his recording, *Italian Baroque Guitar,* Response Records RES 804, 1980.

18. Robert Strizich, *The New Grove Dictionary of Music and Musicians,* Vol. 12 (London: Macmillan, 1980), p. 310. Hudson, op. cit., pp. 43-50.

19. Pinnell, op. cit., pp. 87-88.

20. James Tyler, *The Early Guitar* (Oxford University Press, 1980), p. 128.

21. Pinnell, op. cit., footnote 24, p. 90,

22. Claude Chauvel, *Angelo Michele Bartolotti, Libro primo et secondo di chitarra spagnola* (Geneva: Minkoff Reprint, 1984), *Introduction.*

23. Recordings of Bartolotti's music are Lex Eisenhardt, *Baroque Guitar (Suites in D minor, D major, G minor, E minor),* Etcetera Records KTC 1174, recorded October 1993, issued 1994; Harvey Hope, *Italian Baroque Guitar (Prelude, Caprice, Sarabanda, Gigue),* Response Records RES 804, 1980; Yves Storm *(Follias),* EMI 1A 065 165179, date unknown.

24. Robert Strizich, *The New Grove Dictionary of Music and Musicians,* Vol. 3, op. cit., pp. 771-772.

25. Pinell, op. cit., pp. 70-71.

26. Robert Stevenson, *The New Grove Dictionary of Music and Musicians,* Vol. 5, op. cit., p. 525. Pinell, op. cit., pp. 73-74.

27. Notes by Harvey Hope for his recording of pieces by Pesori *(Saltarello, Gallo di Donna Checca, La Speranza mi va Consolando,* and *La Piva Arietta Bizarra),* on *Italian Baroque Guitar,* Response Records RES 804, 1980.

28. One chord is shown by the symbol of a cross, the rest by letters of the alphabet from A to Z. 'Composers publishing for the guitar between 1620 and 1637 all used the alfabeto.' Pinnell, op. cit., pp. 31-33.

29. Ibid., p. 86.

30. Ibid., p. 95; and Jakob Lindberg, liner notes for *Francesco Corbetta-Guitar Music,* BIS CD - 799, 1997, p. 5.

31. Quoted in Pinell, op. cit., p. 94, from François Lesure, 'Le Traité des Instruments de Pierre Trichet', *Annales Musicologiques,* Vol. iv, 1956, pp. 216-217.

32. Ibid., p. 180.

33. Ibid., quoted p.186. (Trans. GW.)

34. Tyler, op. cit., pp. 128-132.

35. Pinnell, op. cit., p. 106.

36. Recordings of Robert de Visée's *Suite in D minor* have been made by Segovia, Diaz, Bream, Almeida, Bonell, Hope, North, Provost, Ragossnig, C. Romero, Ybarra, etc.

37. Gerardo Arriaga, liner notes for José Miguel Moreno, *Pièces de Théorbe-Robert de Visée,* Glossa GCD 920104, 1996, pp. 24-25. In *The New Grove Dictionary of Music and Musicians,* Vol. 20, op. cit., p. 14, Robert Strizich gives de Visée's dates as born in the second half of the 17th century, died early in the 18th century.

38. Robert W. Strizich, *Robert de Visée, Oeuvres Complètes pour Guitare* (Paris:Heugel, 1969), p. iv.

39. Alvaro Company and Vincenzo Saldarelli, eds., *Robert de Visée, Suite in Sol minore* (Milan: Edizioni Suvini Zerboni, 1975), *Advis.*

40. Paulo Paolini, *Robert de Visée, Suite in D minor* (Milan: Ricordi, 1973), Preface.

41. Pinnell, op. cit., pp. 197 -198.

42. Julian Bream performed de Visée's *Suite No. 6 in C minor* in recitals in various years including 1999 and 2000.

43. Joaquín Rodrigo, quoted in notes from *Segovia - Golden Jubilee Vol. 1,* Brunswick Mono AXTL1088, 1959.

44. Tyler, op. cit., p. 51.

45. R. Strizich, 'A Spanish Guitar Tutor: Ruiz de Ribayaz's *Luz y norte musical* (1677)', *Journal of the Lute Society of America,* VII, 1974, pp. 51-81.

46. Bruno Henze, ed., *Ludovico Roncalli, Neun Suiten* (Leipzig: Hofmeister, 1955).

47. Brian Jeffery, ed., Facsimile edition, *Francisco Guerau, Poema Harmónico* (London: Tecla www.tecla.com, 1977), p. 84.

48. Ibid., p. 85.

49. Ibid., p. 85.

50. Ralph Kirkpatrick, *Domenico Scarlatti* (Princeton University Press, 1953), p. 205.

51. Luc Benoist, *Handbook of Western Painting* (London: Thames and Hudson, 1961), p. 195.

52. Guy Bourligueux, *The New Grove Dictionary of Music and Musicians,* Vol. 3, op. cit., p. 656.

53. Turnbull, op. cit., p. 52.

54. Craig H. Russell, ed., *Santiago de Murcia's "Códice Saldívar No. 4",* A Treasury of Secular Guitar Music from Baroque Mexico, Vols 1 & 2 (Urbana & Chicago: University of Illinois Press, 1995).

55. Neil D. Pennington, *The Spanish Baroque Guitar, with a Transcription of De Murcia's Passacalles y Obras,* Vol. 1 (Ann Arbor, Michigan: UMI Research Press, 1981), p. 11.

56. Ibid., Vol. II, contains transcriptions of all the suites.

57. Ibid., Vol. I, p. 42.

58. Ibid., Vol. I, p. 102.

59. Russell, op. cit., Vol. 1, p. 2.

60. Ernst Gottlieb Baron, *Study of the Lute,* trans. Douglas Alton Smith (California: Instrumenta Antiqua Publications, 1976), pp. 95-96.

61. Ibid., p. 94. This criticism is often levelled against guitar music - that the instrument promises well but the quality of music written for it is disappointing.

62. Ibid., pp. 96-97.

63. Ibid., p. 107.

64. Johann Friedrich Agricola in Jacob Adlung's *Musica mechanica organoedi* (1768). Quoted in Hans T. David & Arthur Mendel, *The Bach Reader, A Life of Johann Sebastian Bach in Letters and Documents* (New York: Norton, 1966), p. 259.

PART III: THE CLASSIC GUITAR

23. The Six String Classic Guitar

From the middle of the 18th century another type of guitar, now often termed the 'classical' or 'classic' guitar became popular. The double strings of the courses lost favor and six single strings eventually represented for many players their preferred type of instrument.

Over recent years, scholars have searched for evidence of when and how the guitar developed from five-course Baroque to what became the six string classic guitar. This quest explores the world's museums to discover genuine six string instruments (preferably containing evidence of maker and date) which are not altered versions of five-course guitars. A second line of enquiry is directed towards the published guitar books of the later 18th century.

One interesting aspect concerns the changing physical structure of the guitar during the last decades of the 18th century:

The weakening of the power of the craft guilds over the artisans, already apparent in the closing decades of the 18th century, allowed for a freer practice in the production of all types of products, including musical instruments. Craftsmen could now produce without the rigorous and sometimes costly examinations and the constraining supervision of the masters of the craft - guilds who dictated the conditions for the manufacture and marketing of the products.

The social changes that were taking place in 18th century Spain were also reflected in the construction of guitars... Perhaps the most innovative element in the Spanish guitar of that period was the introduction of the fan-strutting system, reinforcing the lower bout of the soundboard in order to produce a more resonant instrument. This innovatory idea can be traced back to Sevilla and to the work of Francisco Sanguino, a master craftsman whose work stands out amongst his contemporaries.[1]

The decline of the guilds is highlighted here as a reason for change in a number of areas in Spanish life. The introduction of fan-strutting (the inclusion of a number of supporting strips glued on the inside of the front of the guitar), strengthened the delicate table or *tapa* of the instrument and improved the sound. But the ultimate developments in fan-strutting design would come in the 19th century with the great luthier, Torres.

Another scholar emphasizes the complexity of the guitar's metamorphosis from five-course to six string between 1740 and 1790 and the significance of the work of Sanguino:

In reality, the Classical period of ca. 1740-90... is a time of transition for the guitar, during which at least four kinds of guitars were in common use, each requiring somewhat different tuning, stringing and playing techniques... The four kinds of guitars that existed in the late 18th century are the five-course, six-course, five-string and six-string varieties...

Some of the earliest examples of a newly developed six-course guitar were made by Francisco Sanguino of Sevilla in the late 1750's. One of these instruments, dated 1759, is housed at the Gemeentemuseum, The Hague, and another is housed at the Museu de la Música in Barcelona. While these guitars may have been isolated examples of a newly emerging instrument, by the early 1770's the six-course guitar had become firmly established in both Spain and Latin America.[2]

The prevalence of the six-course guitar in Iberia is a vital aspect:

The date of the addition of the sixth string to the guitar is uncertain. It is clear, however, that during the last decades of the 18th century in Spain, the phrase "para guitarra de cinco o seis órdenes" was commonly used in printed editions of guitar music. Indeed, the six-course guitar (as opposed to an instrument with six single strings) appears to have flourished only in Spain, since all the extant six-course instruments and all of the published methods for the six-course guitar derive from the Iberian peninsula.[3]

24. A Multiplicity of Guitars, 1750-1815

Here is a selection of existing instruments dated between 1750 and 1815 indicating the variety of guitar types during this period:

c. 1750, five-course guitar: José Massague (Massaguer), Barcelona, (Metropolitan Museum of Art, New York), no fan struts.

c. 1759, seven-course guitar: Francisco Sanguino, Seville, (Gemeentemuseum, The Hague), fan strutting.

1773, six string guitar: François Lupot, Orléans, (Smithsonian Institution, Washington D.C.).

c. 1777, five-course guitar: Joseph de Frías, Seville, (Museo de la Festa, Patronato Nacional del Misterio de Elche, Alicante), fan strutting.

c. 1780's, seven-course guitar: Francisco Sanguino, Seville, (Instrument Museum of the Barcelona Conservatory), fan strutting.

1783, six-course guitar: Josef Benedid, Cádiz, (Museu de la Música, Barcelona), fan strutting.

1784, six-course guitar: Dionisio Guerra, Cádiz, (Ramírez Collection, Madrid), no fan strutting.

1786, five-course guitar: Lorenzo Alonso, Madrid, (Private Collection), no fan strutting.

1790, six string guitar: Antonio Vinaccia, Naples, (Smithsonian Institution, Washington D.C.).

c. 1790's, six-course guitar: Pedro Ferreira Oliveira, Lisbon, (Dolmetsch Collection), no fan strutting.

1792, six string guitar: Gioacchino Trotto, Naples, (Instrument Museum, Leipzig University).

c. 1792, six-course guitar: Joseph Martínez, Málaga, (Collection of Angel Luis Cañete, Málaga), fan strutting.

1792, six-course guitar: Juan Pagés, Cádiz, (Museu de la Música, Barcelona), fan strutting.

1794, six-course guitar: Josef Benedid, Cádiz, (Museo Nacional de Cerámica y de las Artes Suntuarias, *González Martí,* Valencia), fan strutting.

1795, six string guitar: Giovanni Battista Fabricatore, Naples, (Jack and Dorinda Schuman Collection, Cleveland, Ohio), no fan strutting.

1796, six-course guitar: Ignacio de los Santos, Seville, (Instrument Museum of the Barcelona Conservatory), no fan strutting.

1797, six-course guitar, Benito Sánchez de Aguilera, Madrid, (Metropolitan Museum of Art, New York), no fan strutting.

1800, six string guitar: Josef Benedid, Cádiz, (Jack and Dorinda Schuman Collection, Cleveland, Ohio), fan strutting.

1803, six string guitar: Agustín Caro, Granada, (Collection of Angel Luis Cañete, Málaga), fan strutting.

1804, six-course guitar: Manuel Muñoa, Madrid, (Ramírez Collection, Madrid), no fan strutting.

1815, six-course guitar: Joan Matabosch, Barcelona, (Museu de la Música, Barcelona), no fan strutting.[4]

The problem is clearly the co-existence of a number of types. The late 18th century/early 19th century should therefore be regarded as a transitional period when the guitar was popular in varied forms and stringings. Eventually the six string guitar would be identified as the central focus of classic guitar activities:

The various trends taken by the guitar in the preceding centuries can, in retrospect, be viewed as so many roads and byways that led to one destination - the six single string guitar. The 18th century had progressed to this point, but it was not until the 19th that the instrument was to reach the peak of its development. By then, the results of experimentation had been evaluated. Technical improvements that could not be adapted to the instrument were soon forgotten or were incorporated in other instruments unrelated to the guitar.

The acceptance of the six single string guitar became universal in the 19th century, spreading not only to every part of Europe but to the American continent as well.[5]

The progressions by which the guitar became settled in six single strings are too convoluted to chart with certainty. Sor's biographer suggests that even this great player, famous for six string guitar compositions, began on a five-course instrument:

What kind of guitar did Sor play at this time? At home in the 1780's, his father's guitar would almost certainly have had five courses rather than six, and double rather than single strings. The sixth course was added towards the end of the 18th century in Italy and France, and was probably not common in Spain until around 1800 and after. [6]

But by the time of his *Méthode de la Guitare* (c.1828), Sor was informing readers about his guitar makers, now constructing six string guitars:

...the manner of constructing the body of the instrument is almost everywhere understood extremely well, and most Neapolitan, German, and French guitars leave in this respect very little superiority to the Spanish. In the goodness of the body or box, the Neapolitan guitars in general long surpassed, in my opinion, those of France and Germany; but that is not the case at present, and if I wanted an instrument, I would procure it from M. Joseph Martínez of Málaga, or from M. Lacôte, a French maker, the only person who, besides his talents, has proved to me that he possesses the quality of not being inflexible to reasoning...

The guitars to which I have always given the preference are those of Alonzo of Madrid, Pagés and Benedid of Cádiz, Joseph and Manuel Martínez of Málaga, or Rada, successor and scholar of the latter, and those of M. Lacôte of Paris. I do not say that others do not exist; but never having tried them, I cannot decide on that of which I have no knowledge.[7]

Only one instrument by Lorenzo Alonso survives today. He is believed to have had a workshop at 5 Calle del Carmen (1758 -1788), and died in 1796. There are more than fifteen surviving instruments of Juan Pagés (17? - 1821), who came from Ecija and settled in Cádiz around 1770. From Josef Benedid (1760-1836) seven guitars are still extant. Joseph Martínez was examined to become a master guitar maker on 13 December, 1808 and was active until at least 1829.[8]

Apart from Spanish makers mentioned by Sor, René Lacôte (1785-1855) was the most successful Parisian luthier:

René Lacôte (who had workshops first in the Place des Victoires (c.1820), then the rue de Grammont (1832), rue des Martyrs (1845), rue Louvois (1850's), as well as a London outlet in Ebury Street), followed the general Parisian style, but also made several innovations. His early guitars, from the 1820's, were fitted with patent tuning pegs which could be locked in place after the string had been tuned, and couldn't slip. Later, he developed a sophisticated head construction in which geared tuning machines were built into the head and completely concealed, the pegs sticking out from the rear. Both of these inventions appear on guitars by one or two luthiers, who used them under license...

Lacôte's most interesting experiments involved the guitar fingerboard. He popularized the manche coulé, *in which the spaces between the frets were scooped away and the frets set flush with the peaks that were formed. This facilitated the playing of glissando passages, but caused intonation problems. It may have been this experience of the* manche coulé *that prompted Lacôte to experiment with ways of achieving perfect intonation on the guitar.[9]*

Sor also mentions another influential guitar maker:

Experiment has proved it in London, where Mr. J. Panormo made some guitars under my direction...[10]

Much research has been undertaken on Joseph Panormo (1768-1834) and his family over recent years, correcting many former misconceptions. But obscurities remain, not least the details of any collaboration with Sor:

> *It is difficult to appreciate, from these guitars made by Joseph, whether or not the improvements that Sor suggested were all his own ideas or based on those of Spanish makers, whose instruments Sor preferred. However, the result of Joseph's work was a blend of Spanish design and Italian craftsmanship, and these new guitars became the model of the larger, deeper bodied instruments, made by other members of the Panormo family.[11]*

25. Luigi Boccherini

Guitar history between 1750 and 1800 is often considered as a time when the instrument remained outside the musical mainstream. Yet some of the most interesting guitar writing came from Luigi Boccherini (1743-1805), at the heart of the central traditions of European music.

Born in Lucca, Italy, Boccherini established a reputation as a child prodigy of the cello. His remarkable compositional gifts also soon became apparent. After working in various musical centers of Europe, including Vienna and Paris, Boccherini went to Madrid, where in 1770 he was appointed *virtuoso di camera* and composer of music to the king's younger brother, the Infante Don Luis.[12]

Boccherini's sojourn in Spain brought him in touch with guitar through one of his patrons, the Marquis of Benavente-Osuna, a keen amateur guitarist. Throughout his life, Boccherini wrote over 100 string quintets, almost 100 string quartets and over 100 other chamber works. For the Marquis, the composer wrote several quintets (eight such works are extant, though it seems likely that he wrote more), for two violins, guitar, viola and cello and a *Sinfonia concertante in C major, Op. 21,* with obligato guitar arranged from his String Quintet, Op. 10, No. 4.

It is not known what kind of guitar the Marquis of Benavente-Osuna preferred, whether five or six course. Yet Boccherini's guitar writings provide an indication of the instrument's potential charm and its versatility in a chamber music context.[13]

26. Padre Basilio

One of Boccherini's quintets includes a Fandango, and on the manuscript is the note, 'Quintet imitating the fandango played by Padre Basilio on the guitar'. Basilio himself remains an obscure figure, though the 19th century historian, Mariano Soriano Fuertes provides useful information:[14]

> Soriano Fuertes relates that Padre Basilio, Cistercian organist in the convent of Madrid, 'was summoned to the Escorial in order that Their Majesties Carlos IV and María Luisa might hear him play the organ and the guitar, and this was so pleasing that he remained in the court as maestro of Her Majesty the Queen.' Padre Basilio's actual name was Manuel García, and he was the teacher of Dionisio Aguado, Francisco Tostado y Carvajal, and also Godoy. His pieces circulated in manuscript, which is why most of them have been lost, but he may be considered as the initiator of the modern school of guitar and he influenced Fernando Sor, and above all, Aguado. His music must have been very popular to the extent that Boccherini in one of his last quintets wrote that he was imitating the 'fandango played on the guitar by P. Basilio.'[15]

Thus at the court of Carlos IV of Spain, (reigning 1788-1808), the arbiters of taste and fashion in the arts were well disposed towards the guitar.

27. Three Publications

In 1777, Giacomo Merchi's *Traité des Agrèmens de la Musique executés sur la Guitarre,* indicates that five-course guitars were being given single strings:

> I am taking advantage of this foreword to say a word about the way to string the guitar with single strings. It is very easy now to find a great number of true strings. The single strings are very easy to tune and pluck cleanly. They make a pure sound, strong and mellow, and approach that of a harp, especially if one uses thicker strings. [16]

In contrast to this, over twenty years later, Fernando Ferandiere's *Arte de tocar la guitarra española por música* (Madrid, 1799), setting out (in notation, not tablature) some Spanish concepts of the guitar, shows that the double strung courses were still part of the scene. For Ferandiere the guitar must have seventeen frets, and 'six courses, with six bourdons (bass strings) and five strings'. The instrument 'is tuned entirely in fourths, except for the second course, which has a third'.[17] From such nuggets of information can be glimpsed something of the variety of guitar construction at that time.

Also published in Madrid in 1799, Federico Moretti's *Principios para tocar la guitarra de seis órdenes* reveals a sense of ambiguity concerning the movement towards six strings:

> Although I myself use a guitar of six single strings, it has seemed to me more appropriate to adapt these principles for the guitar of six courses, since it is that which is generally played in Spain. For the same reason, I was obliged to publish these same principles in Italian in 1792 adapted for the guitar of five courses, because at that time the guitar of six [courses] was scarcely known in Italy.[18]

Moretti eventually emigrated from Italy to take up a military post at the court of the Spanish King, Carlos IV, where the guitar was already popular.[19] This had a significant inspirational (as well as geographical), effect on the guitar's development:

> *Historically the most important guitarist to leave Italy, and certainly the earliest (pre-1800) in the exodus under discussion, was a certain Federico Moretti. His importance stems from the fact that both Sor and Aguado claim that he was the man who made them aware of the possibility of sustaining two or more parts on the guitar, and of accurately reflecting this fact in the musical notation. Thus Moretti the* Italian *teaches the most influential of the* Spanish *early-19th-century guitarists how to play and write for the* classic guitar. *The unavoidable conclusion is that the six-string guitar, which so many of us today regard as native to Spain, is - as an instrument of art music - of Italian origin, apparently owing only its figure-8 shape to Spain. It acquired its six strings, and its mensural notation, in Italy.[20]*

Moretti can thus be considered as one of the central links between the late 18th century and subsequent developments in the guitar repertoire. His important influence on Fernando Sor (1778-1839), destined to become one of the great maestros of the guitar's history, is explicitly acknowledged in Sor's *Method for the Spanish Guitar:*

> *I heard one of his accompaniments performed by a friend of his, and the progression of the bass, as well as the parts of the harmony which I distinguished, gave me a high idea of his merit. I considered him as the flambeau which was to serve to illuminate the wandering steps of guitarists.[21]*

There was a further significance to the innovations of Moretti in the area of guitar mensural notation methods. The stages by which guitar notation evolved (moving away from the gravitational pull of centuries of tablature and joining the rest of the musical world in using notation) are a vital process in the development of the repertoire. But at first the polyphonic indication of part writing was, as one scholar put it, 'primitive':

> *When guitar music first took that fateful step into mensural notation, it had to be fitted to a system of instrumental notation adequate to its resources. Its range was not as extended as that of the piano, therefore two staves were out of the question. It was accommodated most readily and simply by the same single musical staff used for other string instruments. In fact, what better system than that of - the violin?...*
>
> *In experimenting with the newly acquired mensural notation - from the point of view of musical calligraphy, if one may so speak - early guitarists clearly patterned themselves at first after* violin *notation. When writing for the violin, one never seriously attempted to denote anything like separate parts by means of the direction of note stems...It is really fascinating to encounter this unmistakable violin notation in "primitive" guitar music...[22]*

Moretti had a hand in changing this situation. In his *Escuela de Guitarra*, Dionisio Aguado acknowledged Moretti's influence:

> *Don Federico Moretti was the first to begin to write guitar music in a manner in which two parts were separated, one part for the melodic line, the other for the accompaniment. After him came Don Fernando Sor and in his compositions he showed us the secret of making the guitar an instrument both harmonic and melodic.[23]*

Brian Jeffery commented in his biography of Fernando Sor:

> *After the somewhat mysterious Padre Basilio, a monk who taught the guitar in Madrid, Federico Moretti was certainly the most important figure in the history of the guitar in Spain... Moretti's music inspired Sor to compose in several real parts or voices, something which he continued to do for the rest of his life.[24]*

28. Guitarists of the Early 19th Century

The expanding guitar repertory at this time involved not only many musicians from Spain, Italy, Germany, Russia, France, etc., but also various kinds of guitar. In Russia, for example, the seven string guitar was popular, while, throughout the rest of Europe, performers often favored guitars quite distinct from the six string instrument:

> *Mertz, like many guitarists of the 19th century, used an instrument with an extended range. Regondi and Legnani both played eight string instruments, Coste a seven string, Makaroff and Carulli ten strings (the latter's was called the* Decachorde) *and in the 1830's Sor and Salomon composed for the twenty- one string Harpolyre.*[25]

Guitarists often view the guitar's achievements of the early 19th century as being represented almost exclusively by Fernando Sor and Mauro Giuliani. But in fact the period is rich in diverse personalities, including the following:

Christian Gottlieb Scheidler (1752-1815):
German guitarist, lutenist, cellist and bassoonist at the court of the Elector of Mainz. He became a celebrated teacher of guitar in Frankfurt in later life. Now known primarily for *Sonata in D major* for violin /guitar or guitar duo.[26]

Simon Molitor (1766-1848):
Molitor studied violin and guitar with his father and continued his education in Vienna with Abbé Vogler. Between 1796 and 1797 he was orchestral director in Venice. After working as a civil servant in Vienna, he retired on a pension in 1831 and dedicated himself to music.[27]

Leonhard von Call (1767-1815):
Austrian composer. His compositions, written mainly for the amateur public, appeared from 1802 onwards in Vienna.[28]

Kaspar Fürstenau (1772-1819):
A flautist and composer whose reputation rests on the works he wrote for guitar and flute. From the age of sixteen he played in the orchestra of the Bishop of Münster, making his first tour of Germany, 1793-1794. In 1794 he joined the orchestra of the Duke of Oldenburg and later toured with his son, Anton, to perform in various European cities.[29]

Wenzel Thomas Matiegka (1773-1830):

After studying law in Prague, Matiegka moved to Vienna, where his solo guitar pieces were published. In 1817 he became Kapellmeister at the Church of St. Leopold. Matiegka's fame rests mainly on Schubert's arrangement of his *Nocturne, Op. 21* for flute, violin and guitar, as a quartet, which includes a genuine Schubertian cello part.[30]

Andrei Osipovich Sychra (1773-1850):

Matanya Ophee commented that Sychra, a leading exponent, teacher and composer of the Russian seven string guitar, published 'during his life time well over a thousand pieces for the Russian seven-string guitar' and left unpublished manuscripts of arrangements (for two guitars) of two complete operas by Glinka. Sychra also wrote a *Theoretical and Practical Method for the 7-String Guitar.* [31]

Francesco Molino (1775-1847):

Molino studied under Pugnani in Turin. His *New and Complete Method for the Guitar* (Florence,1795) appeared while he was in the service of the King of Sardinia. During a career as a travelling virtuoso, he lived in Paris and Spain, performing at the court of Madrid. Later he returned to Paris and also visited London.[32]

François de Fossa (1775-1849):

François de Fossa, born in Perpignan, France, moved to Spain in 1793. Until his retirement in 1844, he pursued an adventurous military career serving in both the Spanish and French armies. The revival of his three Guitar Quartets, Op. 19 has established his reputation as an excellent composer.[33]

Joseph Küffner (1776-1856):

After training as a lawyer, Küffner became a musician in the Bishop of Wurzburg's chapel and later bandmaster in the Bavarian army where he composed a variety of music. Later on he was employed by the Archduke Ferdinand and it has been said that he was well acquainted with Beethoven. In 1825 he visited Paris, publishing several works there.[34]

Mikhail Vyssotsky (1791-1837):

A Russian virtuoso who achieved great fame in his day.[35] It is possible that he met Sor during the latter's stay in Moscow and it has been suggested that in memory of their meeting Sor wrote the duet, *Souvenir de Russie, Op. 63,* for two guitars.[36]

Heinrich Marschner (1795-1861):

Marschner, described 'as the most important composer of German opera in the generation between Weber and Wagner', wrote operas, symphonies, chamber works and over 420 songs. As a leading personality Marschner might well have provided the inspiration the guitar needed. Regrettably his solo guitar works, with their early opus numbers, are essentially juvenilia.[37]

Felix Horetzky (1796-1879):
Few facts of his life are available. His family was Polish and he was brought up in the Duchy of Warsaw. He lived for some time in Vienna before touring Europe (including Germany, Paris, and London), eventually settling in Edinburgh as teacher and composer.[38]

José Broca (1805-1882):
Broca came from Reus, in the province of Tarragona, Spain. From the age of twenty-eight he served in the French army for some years, before moving to Barcelona. In the annals of guitar he is famous for having taught Pedrell and Ferrer. He composed about twenty works for guitar.[39]

Antonio Cano (1811-1897):
Born in Lorca, Murcia, Spain, Cano studied in Madrid and was professionally associated with Aguado. In 1868 he was appointed professor of guitar at the National Conservatoire, Madrid. His *Método para Guitarra* (Madrid, 1852) is available in facsimile.[40]

The following are personalities whose contribution to the guitar is nowadays considered of particular significance, whether in terms of compositional eminence, pedagogic value, or influence on subsequent historical developments:

Ferdinando Carulli (1770-1841)
Fernando Sor (1778-1839)
Mauro Giuliani (1781-1829)
Anton Diabelli (1781-1858)
Nicolò Paganini (1782-1840)
Dionisio Aguado y García (1784-1849)
Luigi Legnani (1790-1877)
Matteo Carcassi (1792-1853)
Marco Aurelio Zani de Ferranti (1801-1878)
Hector Berlioz (1803-1869)
Johann Kaspar Mertz (1806-1856)
Napoléon Coste (1806-1883)
Giulio Regondi (1822-1872)
Julián Arcas (1832-1882)
Francisco Tárrega (1852 -1909)

29. The Art of Ferdinando Carulli

The accepted masters of the guitar at this time explored two vital aspects - the pedagogic and the creative. The great teachers developed technique, methods of study, and theoretical bases of the instrument in a manner similar to Czerny (1791-1857) on the pianoforte or Paganini (1782-1840) on the violin. The foremost performers also composed extended musical structures, including sets of variations, sonatas, études, duo works, and concertos.

Among early maestros who command attention, Ferdinando Carulli (1770-1841), is one of the most eminent.

This Italian guitarist, composer and teacher, settled in Paris in 1808, and was the leading guitarist there for many years until the arrival of Fernando Sor in 1823.[41] Carulli's contribution to the guitar was underestimated for over a century and a half until a publication appeared by the Italian scholar, Mario Torta:

Among the protagonists of these important transformations, Ferdinando Carulli... occupies a prominent place together with his fellow-Italian Mauro Giuliani, the Spaniard Fernando Sor and very few others... The figure that emerges is that of a composer, virtuoso and successful teacher who played a decisive role in moulding the future of his instrument. On a more modest level, he acted as intermediary between the great mainstream repertoire and amateur consumption, acting within the limits of a profession in which he all too frequently had to come to terms with harsh reality.

Yet despite these limitations, the reader will find that it is hard to square the traditional picture of Carulli with the sheer scope and achievement of his production. For alongside the hack work of pieces "pour les commençans", there is a wealth of invention in his finest solo compositions and great instrumental variety and strength in his chamber music.[42]

The vast scope of Carulli's work for guitar is catalogued by Mario Torta up to Op. 366. The output of over 400 pieces included the entire gamut of guitaristic possibilities - concertos, chamber music, sonatas, studies, variations, duets, and transcriptions.

A number of offerings of Carulli's *Guitar Method* in one form or another have remained in print through the generations, though often in editions which have been 'modernized.'[43] Fortunately, the 1822 edition of Carulli's *Méthode complète pour guitare, Op. 27,* has been published in facsimile.[44] This Method, first published 1810/1811, continued with further editions in 1819, 1822, 1824 (?), 1828/1829, and reprintings in various guises throughout the 19th century.[45]

In recent decades, apart from the occasional performance of a Carulli concerto, his works have not merited inclusion in the recital repertoire of major artists.[46] This situation was partially redeemed in the early 1970's, when Julian Bream and John Williams recorded Carulli's *Duo in G, Op. 34*:

In this duet Carulli rather than Sor should be described as the "Beethoven of the guitar", for we unexpectedly find ourselves in the world of an early Beethoven piano sonata. The music is warm and lyrical, and the gentleness, as well as the drama, is brilliantly heightened by the performance.[47]

30. Sor and Giuliani - Rivals in Dominance

In recent years, in terms of the amount of their music played in recitals and recorded, and the volume of research undertaken, Fernando Sor (1778-1839), and Mauro Giuliani (1781-1829), have emerged as the two outstanding guitar personalities of the early 19th century. In particular, the art and lives of both Sor and Giuliani have been thoroughly scrutinized in biographies and achieved the ultimate accolade of having facsimile editions of their complete works published.

Sor, a Catalan, gained his early musical education at the monastery of Montserrat, and later attended the military academy in Barcelona. As a young man he was fortunate to come under the patronage of the Duchess of Alba, who, however, died when Sor was only twenty-two. For some time, following military service, Sor worked in various administrative posts until he finally left Spain in 1813.

Between 1815 and 1823 Sor was in England. He soon achieved the distinction of being elected Associate of the Philharmonic Society and in 1822 was listed as an Honorary Member at the founding of the Royal

Academy of Music. In 1823, Sor travelled to Moscow and proved a great success at the Russian court. Returning to Paris in 1826/1827, he published many compositions in his later years and his *Méthode pour la guitare* appeared in 1830.[48]

Sor's compositions range from easy works for beginners to the virtuosic art of the concert performer.The recitalist's repertoire of Sor includes sets of variations, fantasies, sonatas, and études.[49] His works have become increasingly popular in the concert hall and a number of artists now play his music on early 19th century guitars.

An article in *Harmonicon* (March 1824), summed up his achievements:

Amongst the once favored musical instruments, now for some time neglected, and coming into practice again, is the guitar. To the exquisite and wonderful performances of M. Sor this may be attributed, he makes the instrument "speak so sweetly, and so well," that hundreds fly to "strike the chorded shell," who never before dreamt of what it was capable of producing.[50]

Mauro Giuliani studied cello and counterpoint as well as guitar. After moving to Vienna in 1806, he achieved a reputation there as the finest guitarist of his day. The foremost Giuliani scholar, Thomas F. Heck, has posed the question why so many Italian guitarists were motivated to find artistic fulfilment away from their native country:

...a substantial number of guitar virtuosos of Italian origin emigrated to Austria, France and even the New World in the early years of the 19th century. This phenomenon of voluntary exile has been left unexplained for too long...Giuliani went to Vienna in 1806, and Carulli departed for Paris about the same time. Carcassi left his native Florence for Paris in 1820, and thence London in 1824...Zani de Ferranti (b. Bologna, 1802) settled in Brussels in 1827.[51]

The reasons for these expatriate activities were as follows:

Although Italy provided a climate favorable to the guitar as an accompaniment instrument... she seems not to have rewarded the talented men who chose to play it as a solo chamber instrument. For one thing, the sheer sound level of the classic guitar of c.1800 was diminutive compared to that of other contemporary musical entertainment; to give guitar recitals in festooned, draped and upholstered opera houses was out of the question for reasons of acoustics. Yet solo guitarists had to be heard to make a living!...

The salons of the nobility in Vienna and Paris provided a chance for audition, for appreciation, and for monetary compensation unequalled in their native land, which was then utterly dominated by opera.[52]

In 1808, Giuliani premiered his *Guitar Concerto, Op. 30.* In 1813, he played cello for the premiere of Beethoven's *Seventh Symphony.* He returned to Italy in 1819, living first in Rome, and then Naples, where he died on 8 May, 1829.

Giuliani's prolific compositions include études, sonatas, sets of variations, dances, rondos, potpourris, arrangements, vocal works, three concertos, duos, works for guitar and other instruments, etc.[53]

Once again contemporaries delivered an opinion still relevant to an appreciation of Giuliani's lyrical genius:

> *...The tone of Giuliani was brought to the greatest possible perfection; in his hands the guitar became gifted with a power of expression at once pure, thrilling and exquisite. He vocalized his adagios to a degree impossible to be imagined by those who never heard him... In a word, he made the instrument sing.*[54]

31. The Significance of Anton Diabelli

Diabelli (1781-1858) was an Austrian publisher, composer, pianist and guitarist, whose ultimate niche in musical history was assured when Beethoven wrote his longest and most renowned set of piano variations - *Thirty-three Variations on a Waltz by Diabelli, Op. 120.*[55]

In the guitar world, Anton Diabelli was significant for his close association with Mauro Giuliani, a number of whose later works he published from *Introduction & Variations (Das ist alles eins), Op. 99,* onwards, though there are some shadows round the transactions:[56]

> *...this is the first opus of Giuliani's published by Diabelli, or rather by the firm known at the time as Cappi & Diabelli, created in 1818...It is of Cappi and Diabelli that Giuliani would write, in a letter to his old friend Artaria: "These two super-braggarts who pride themselves on having the best music store in Vienna..." and "Two false businessmen run it...," and "they deserve not only my disdain, but also celestial revenge."*

> *The reason for Giuliani's scorn, evidenced in his letters, was that these men had a reputation for trying to purchase the works of excellent composers for less compensation than any other Viennese publisher would have dared to offer.*[57]

Diabelli's own compositions for guitar, more than 200 in number, include sonatas, sonatinas and serenades, as well as works for guitar and strings, and guitar and piano.[58] His reputation among modern guitarists was enhanced when Julian Bream arranged movements from different sonatas into a single work:

> ...While the guitar writing is extremely good, the musical quality of the sonatas is not uniformly high throughout their four movements, so I have edited and coupled together two specially fine pairs of movements from different sonatas - the first two movements of the F major sonata (transposed to A) and the last two from the A major sonata. This creates a work showing Diabelli at his very best, which will be a welcome addition to the small number of extended guitar works of the classical period. [59]

32. Dionisio Aguado

Dionisio Aguado y García (1784-1849) was first taught the guitar by Padre Basilio, and may also have studied with Moretti. For a few years after the Napoleonic invasion, Aguado lived with his mother at Fuenlabrada, near Aranjuez. Some time after the death of his mother in 1824, Aguado moved to Paris, where his reputation as a guitarist soon flourished.[60] His *Escuela de Guitarra* (Madrid, 1825), was subsequently issued in a French edition, *Méthode complète pour la guitare.*[61]

When Sor returned to Paris from Russia about 1826, Aguado, whom he had met before in Spain, became his good friend and colleague. The two guitarists played concerts together and Sor dedicated *Fantasia No. 7, Op. 30* and *Les Deux Amis, Op. 41* (for two guitars), to him. Aguado returned to Madrid for the last ten years of his life.[62]

Aguado's real achievements were neglected for more than a century after his death as guitarists regarded him as primarily useful for the provision of pedagogic material rather than as a composer worthy of the concert hall. This changed in the 1980's when Julian Bream paid appropriate homage to Aguado with performances and recordings of *Adagio, Op. 2, No 1, Polonaise, Op. 2, No. 2,* and *Introduction and Rondo, Op. 2, No. 3.*[63] Also in the 1980's a definitive edition of Aguado's *Nuevo Método para Guitarra* (1843) was published. Its editor commented that 'the three versions of Aguado's method, along with Sor's *Méthode pour la Guitare* of 1830, are the central texts for the history of the guitar and its technique in the classical period'.[64]

Moreover Aguado's use of the nails as part of his performing technique was recognized in the 20th century as linking up with the predominant Segovian concepts of right hand playing.

I consider it preferable to play with the nails in order to produce from the strings of the guitar a sound which is unlike that of any other instrument. To my way of thinking, the guitar has its own particular nature: it is sweet, harmonious, melancholy; *sometimes it can even be* majestic...*But it does offer very delicate effects, however, and its sounds are susceptible to modifications and combinations which make it* mysterious, *and very appropriate for melody and expression...*

In order better to produce these effects, I prefer to play with the nails, because if they are properly used, the resulting sound is clean, metallic and sweet; *but it must be understood that the strings are not plucked only with the nails, because then the sound would certainly not be very agreeable. The string is first played with the fingertip... and then the string is immediately slid along the nail.[65]*

Thus Aguado can be considered as the far-sighted advocate of techniques accepted and developed by later generations of guitarists.

33. Paganini and Legnani

Nicolò Paganini (1782-1840) is an anomaly in guitar history - an international virtuoso of the violin who also played the guitar and composed for the instrument. He wrote his first work for violin and guitar, *Variazioni sulla Carmagnola* at the age of twelve and continued all his life to find the guitar of great fascination.

Paganini, well acquainted with several leading guitarists of his day, met Giuliani in 1821, Carulli in 1831, and Zani de Ferranti in 1834. In 1836 he met Legnani in Turin, and a contract was drawn up for them to play a series of concerts together.[66]

Paganini's output for solo guitar included *43 Ghiribizzi* (Caprices), *37 Sonate* and a number of sonatinas and miscellaneous short pieces. He wrote works for guitar and string quartet, many duets for guitar and violin, and various trios. His *Grand Sonata* for violin and guitar, has become popular in the concert hall in virtuosic arrangements for solo guitar.

Luigi Legnani (1790-1877), destined to become a close friend of Paganini, made his first public appearance as a guitarist at La Scala, Milan on 2 July, 1819, being advertised as a professor of the *chitarra francese* (French guitar). In October, 1822, he began a tour of Italy, Germany, Austria and France, returning to Vienna for concerts in 1832.[67] At this time he helped guitar makers with their work:

> *When Legnani was in Vienna he visited the most renowned guitar makers; he furnished them with valuable information concerning the acoustic details of the construction of the instrument and also designed several new models and also one of a terz guitar. Those guitars made according to Legnani's instructions by Ries and also by Staufer, both of Vienna, bear labels of which illustrations are reproduced. The labels of Ries are "Model designed by Luigi Legnani, made by Georg Ries in Vienna, at the sign of the lute and violin," and those of Staufer read: "Johann Anton Staufer, in Vienna, after the design of Luigi Legnani;" both these makers' labels bear the seal of Legnani.[68]*

On 29 November, 1835, a concert by Legnani was cancelled when he fell from a carriage and broke an arm. (Sor and Aguado substituted for him.) Unfortunately, the full details of Legnani's musical activities with Paganini are somewhat obscure. It is said that they gave a recital together in the Theater Corignano, Turin, on 9 June, 1837, but the possibility of further concerts was impeded by Paganini's poor health.[69]

In 1838 Legnani performed in Dresden and Munich. In 1842 he visited Spain where Mariano Soriano Fuertes described his concert at the Teatro Principal, Madrid, on 29 May, in glowing terms:

> *The Italian guitar virtuoso, Señor Luigi Legnani, played fantasias and brilliant variations with the full orchestra and solos of his own composition. He displayed a most remarkable agility of execution and produced a tone of infinite depth and rare singing beauty, particularly in his cantabile on the bass strings. He was recalled again and again, after he had already repeated his program.[70]*

Legnani returned to Ravenna in 1850 where he spent the rest of his life making guitars and violins.[71] The final tally of his compositions includes sets of variations, potpourris, rondos, studies, etc.

His music has not found great favor in the concert hall, but the brilliant *36 Caprices, Op. 20*, covering all keys, major and minor have been played with impressive effect by leading recitalists:[72]

> *Although the Legnani Caprices have been part of the repertoire for some time, concert performances and recordings have been sporadic, partly because of their difficulty - many are only truly effective at uncompromisingly fast tempi - and partly because the studies by Coste, Giuliani and, in particular, Sor, have overshadowed them. But the Caprices are quite different in style, coupling grand virtuosity with a melodic character that is rooted in the traditions of Italian opera.[73]*

34. The Contribution of Matteo Carcassi

Matteo Carcassi (1792-1853), is best known for a Guitar Method and his *25 Melodic and Progressive Studies:*

> *In the case of Matteo Carcassi, the popularity of his method with generations of guitarists has somewhat overshadowed his abilities as a performer and composer. Sor, before the recent publication of his complete works, was generally known for only a small percentage of his output.*

Carcassi has suffered the same fate to an even greater degree, with his larger works and many of his studies remaining relatively obscure, and his handful of familiar pieces considered to be only of student quality.[74]

Carcassi moved to Paris at the age of twenty-eight and spent most of his life there. He travelled widely, visiting London in 1822, 1823 and 1828, and Germany in 1824 and 1827. In 1833 Carcassi appeared in an unusual 'historic' concert playing a work by the 17th century lutenist, Johann Strobach, in company with Fernando Sor. The occasion was described by the Belgian musicologist, François-Joseph Fétis:

I presented one of these pieces during one of my historic concerts in the month of March, 1833. The famous guitarist Sor had had the patience to make a special study of the lute, in order to perform the obligato part of the instrument of which I had translated the tablature for him. Carcassi played the mandolin, [Chrétien] Urban the viola d'amore, [Auguste-Joseph] Franchomme the double-bass, and myself the harpsichord.[75]

Carcassi's neglected compositions include fantaisies, valses, nocturnes, songs with guitar, etc. A significant revival of his forgotten works seems unlikely but his pedagogic insights continue to play a role in the development of young players.[76]

35. Zani de Ferranti - End of an Era

The guitar works of Marco Aurelio Zani de Ferranti (1801-1878), may not yet be very well-known outside scholarly circles. But Simon Wynberg, his biographer, has described him as without doubt 'the major guitarist of his generation and one of the greatest of the century.'[77]

Wynberg's biography relates that, as a boy, Ferranti first played the violin, switching to guitar at the age of sixteen. He moved to Paris by 1820, and later to St. Petersburg. After many adventures (including trouble with the authorities of various countries over his political beliefs), he settled in Belgium, where in 1834 he was appointed honorary guitarist to King Leopold I. Over the years he toured Holland, France, England, America and Italy.

In 1859 Hector Berlioz wrote:

I have just heard Zani de Ferranti, the last, yet the foremost, of guitarists. It is truly impossible to imagine the effects Zani de Ferranti draws from that meager instrument which being so limited is therefore so difficult. With a Paganinian technique Zani combines a communicative sensibility and an ability to sing that few, as far as I know, have ever possessed before...[78]

Later in his life, Ferranti endured financial difficulties as the guitar's popularity declined:

A number of Ferranti's concert reviews survive for the late 1850's, but by this time his star was waning and public interest in the guitar had almost evaporated.[79]

36. The Guitar's Decline in Popularity in the 1850's

As we have seen, a distinct decline in the guitar's popularity occurred during the 1850's. The great composer, Hector Berlioz (1803-1869), in his treatise, *Modern Instrumentation and Orchestration,* included a section on the guitar, describing its predicament as he understood it:

The guitar is an instrument suited for accompanying the voice, and for figuring in a few unnoisy compositions, as also for executing singly pieces more or less complicated in several parts, which possess a true charm when performed by really good players... One can hardly, I repeat, without playing the guitar, write for it pieces in several parts, containing various passages, and introducing all the resources of the instrument. In order to form an idea of what the best performers are able to produce in this way, the compositions of such celebrated guitar-players as Zani de Ferranti, Huerta, Sor, &c., should be studied.

Since the introduction of the pianoforte into all houses where the least taste for music exists, the guitar has dropped into somewhat rare cultivation, excepting in Spain and Italy. Some performers have studied it, and still study it, as a solo instrument; in such a way as to derive effects from it, no less original than delightful. Composers employ it but little, either in church music, theatrical music, or concert music. Its feeble amount of sonorousness, which does not admit of its being united with other instruments, or with many voices possessed but of ordinary brilliancy, is doubtless the cause of this.

Nevertheless, its melancholy and dreamy character might more frequently be made available; it has a real charm of its own, and there would be no impossibility in writing for it so that this should be made manifest. The guitar - unlike the majority of instruments - loses by being employed in aggregate. The sound of twelve guitars playing in unison is almost absurd.[80]

Wynberg, taking up Berlioz's point, observed that by the 1850's 'public interest in the guitar had almost evaporated', and 'the guitar moved to the periphery of general music making':

Central to the issue of the instrument's decline was the nature of music itself which became ever more chromatic, harmonically experimental and increasingly difficult for all but the most accomplished guitarists to exploit (as opposed to a pianist of even average ability).[81]

Unfortunately such dilemmas continued to haunt guitar developments for decades. But, over the course of the 20th century, finding solutions to the guitar's abiding problems, whether recital venues, lack of volume, or the paucity of its repertoire, would be the aim of guitarists, composers and luthiers alike.

37. The Music of Mertz and Coste

Johann Kaspar Mertz (1806-1856) and Napoléon Coste (1806-1883) posthumously merited a revival of interest during the 1980's with the publication of multi-volumed editions of their works.[82] Certain compositions by Mertz, in particular, began to attract recitalists in search of extended virtuosic structures involving pyrotechnical display.

Nikolai Makaroff (1810-1890), the Russian guitarist, commented:

Of the guitar virtuosos whom I have come to know, Mertz was certainly the most important. His playing was marked by force, sweep, sensitivity, precision, expression and assurance... I have found in his works everything I had not come across before: a varied message, a profound knowledge of the laws of composition, an interesting alternation of harmonies, bold, never trivial, effects, and finally, an acquaintance with every secret and effect of the guitar.[83]

Mertz, born in Pressburg (later Bratislava, Czech Republic), moved to Vienna by the 1840's. He toured Moravia, Poland and Russia and gave concerts in Berlin and Dresden. For over a year he suffered a severe illness caused by misuse of medication but recovered. In 1855 he played for Ludwig of Bavaria. In 1856 he was posthumously awarded first prize for his guitar pieces in a competition in Brussels.

Mertz performed on various types of guitars, including eight and ten string guitars from the 1840's onwards.[84] His guitar compositions include didactic and easy pieces, extended concert works, arrangements of Schubert songs, duos, and a set of 36 fantasies based on famous opera themes. (Mertz's *Fantaisie hongroise, Op. 65, No. 1,* and *Elégie* have become his most frequently played works in the concert hall.)[85]

The French guitarist/composer, Napoléon Coste (1806-1883), almost thirty years younger than Sor, represents the continuity of the older artist's trail-blazing efforts to extend the concert repertoire for the instrument. Though for some years Coste's family lived in eastern France, they moved to Valenciennes (north east of Paris) when he was eighteen. Here he taught guitar and played for the local Philharmonic Society and made the acquaintance of Luigi Sagrini:[86]

> *In 1828 the guitar virtuoso Sagrini came to Valenciennes in order to give a concert there, heard the young Coste playing and suggested they should play in concert together. Coste accepted the offer and the two played Giuliani's* Variazioni Concertanti, *Op.* 130 *and achieved overwhelming success from the public.*[87]

Coste moved to Paris in 1830, where he studied with Sor, appearing with the master in what was possibly Sor's last concert:

> *...The last concert in which [Sor] is known to have played was in April or early May 1838, organized by Napoléon Coste as a benefit for himself. The* Revue et Gazette Musicale de Paris *(V. 1838, p. 190), reported that the concert began with a duet played by Sor and Coste.*[88]

From 1840 onwards Coste began to publish his compositions. In 1856 he came second in the Brussels competition for guitar composers, his entries being *Les Feuilles d'Automne, Op. 27, Fantaisie Symphonique, Op. 28, La Chasse des Sylphes, Op. 29,* and *Grande Sérénade, Op. 30.* [89]

Coste's playing career ended prematurely in 1863 when he injured his right arm in a fall. But his work as a teacher and composer continued until his death on 17 February, 1883.

Coste generally wrote his compositions for a seven string guitar, an instrument which carried an extra string in the bass, usually tuned to D and extended to twenty-four frets. [90]

38. Giulio Regondi

Giulio Regondi (1822-1872), was among the 19th century maestros whose music was posthumously neglected. His compositions were not generally available until the 1980's,[91] when Simon Wynberg published an edition of the complete works, commenting that Regondi 'conceivably possessed one of the most awesome techniques of his generation.'[92] The virtuosic elements in Regondi's compositions immediately attracted many leading recitalists.

Regondi was a child prodigy who began public concerts at the age of five. His extraordinary gifts were apparently exploited by his father who made him practice many hours a day. After highly acclaimed performances throughout Europe, the boy was taken to England in 1831. At that time a talented young guitarist in England was Catherina Pelzer, (later known by her married name, Madame Sidney Pratten). Frank Mott Harrison, one of her students, wrote in his reminiscences:

> The musical public was, indeed, privileged at this time. The infant prodigies - Catherina Josepha Pelzer and Giulio Regondi - had met, and were brought out together. Such diminutive performers were "lost" on a large platform; so to be seen as well as heard, they were mounted upon a table. Madame Pratten often used to speak of these days when she played duets with Regondi, whose abilities she always highly praised.[93]

One of these duo events took place on 13 March, 1834 at the King's Concert Rooms, Hanover Square, London. About this time it is alleged that Regondi's father absconded with the money earned from concerts. Others remain sceptical about aspects of the romantic stories which surround Regondi's childhood.[94]

Regondi's recitals continued into his maturity. He played in many European cities such as Vienna, Prague, Leipzig, Frankfurt, Darmstadt and Dresden, performing on either seven or eight string guitars and was also acknowledged as a virtuoso of the concertina. Regondi died in London on 6 May, 1872.

His most frequently performed works for guitar include *Rêverie (Nocturne), Op. 19, Fête Villageoise (Rondo Caprice), Op. 20, 1er Air Varié, Op. 21, 2me Air Varié, Op. 22, Introduction et Caprice, Op. 23,* and some *Etudes.*[95]

39. Julián Arcas

In the first half of the 19th century, guitarists (including Sor, Aguado, Carulli, Carcassi and Giuliani), built up reputations away from their own countries. But from 1850 onwards, as the instrument declined in popularity in northern Europe, a dynamic Spanish-based renaissance of the guitar developed and the focus shifted to south of the Pyrenees. One of the founding fathers of the new wave in Spain was Julián Arcas (1832-1882):

> *Julián Arcas was, beyond a doubt, the best guitarist in the world of his time. This magnificent artist, who achieved international recognition through contemporary music authorities and critics, was the link in the chain that ran from Sor and Aguado to Tárrega.*
>
> *The traditional techniques and characteristic effects of the guitar developed up to that time were passed down from J. Arcas to Tárrega, and from the latter to our times by way of many different guitarists (E. Pujol, M. Llobet, P. Roca, J. Robledo, Salvador García, D. Fortea, R. Sáinz de la Maza, A. Segovia, etc.). This unbroken chain of masters makes up the traditional 'School of the Spanish Guitar', recognized by history.*[96]

Arcas's connection with Francisco Tárrega was, of course, especially significant. In February 1862, Tárrega, aged ten, attended a recital by Arcas at Castellón de la Plana and was invited to play for him:

> *Towards the end of February 1862, Arcas's concert in Castellón would have a tremendous impact on the youthful spirit of Francisco Tárrega...*
>
> *Tárrega's father had the chance to speak with Arcas. He asked him if he would be so kind as to listen to his son, and the maestro agreed. The young Tárrega played without vanity, but also without shyness. Being surprised at the young man's skill, Arcas offered to give him lessons, and suggested that he be sent to Barcelona, where Arcas was living at the time. A little later... Tárrega would go to Barcelona... he would be greatly disappointed... Arcas did not welcome him as expected, and the young man from Villarreal had to look for a place to stay in the home of relatives.[97]*

Arcas wrote over fifty compositions for the guitar, most of which were neglected until an edition of his works was published in Madrid in 1993.[98] His concert career flourished between 1860 and 1870. In 1862, Arcas performed concerts in England. After one of his concerts in the Brighton Pavilion (in the presence of members of the royal family), a critic wrote that the guitar, in the hands of Arcas, was 'a miniature orchestra', a description now familiar in guitar history.[99]

40. Antonio de Torres

One of Arcas's most significant contributions to guitar history was his advocacy of the guitars of Antonio de Torres (1817-1892).This master luthier revolutionized guitar construction and gave the world the classic guitar as we now know it with its specific structure, string length, fan-strutting beneath the front of the instrument (as seen below), overall proportions, types of wood used, quality of tone, etc.

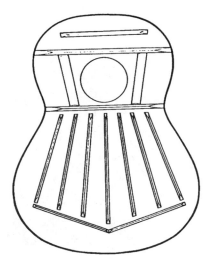

Torres probably made his first guitar between 1836 and 1842 and became a professional luthier on the advice of Arcas:[100]

> ...we know that Torres started his professional career as a guitar maker in Sevilla on the advice of Julián Arcas about 1850... Their first meeting must have taken place in 1856 or earlier... Torres produced the Leona guitar for Arcas in 1856... Arcas continued to play Torres guitars until his death.[101]

During the two vital periods of his life when he was constructing instruments (1852-1869 and 1875-1892), Torres made some 320 guitars, averaging about nine guitars a year.[102] In these creative epochs he set a precedent and a standard of excellence which changed both the theory and the methods of classic guitar construction for ever and offered later generations of luthiers a potent tradition to extend.

41. Francisco Tárrega

Francisco Tárrega, was born at Villarreal, Castellón, on 21 November, 1852. As a boy he studied piano and learned a little about the guitar from a blind player, Manuel González. As we have seen, the turning point may have come when he heard Arcas perform a recital in 1862.

Around 1869, Francisco Tárrega (and his patron, Don Antonio Cánesa Mendayas), visited Torres, in Seville, to acquire a guitar of comparable quality to the one Arcas had played in his performance at Castellón de la Plana. At first Tárrega was shown only cheaper guitars but, after a while, began to play. At this point, Torres, impressed by the young man's skill, brought out one of his finest instruments - a maple wood guitar with a spruce front, cedar neck and ebony fingerboard. Tárrega used that guitar in recitals until 1889.[103]

After military service, Tárrega entered the Real Conservatorio, Madrid, in 1874, to study piano and harmony. He was also invited to perform a guitar recital for the teachers at the Conservatory. Encouraged by this (and other favorable indications), Tárrega soon dedicated his musical energies wholly to the guitar. Before long he established an international reputation as guitarist and teacher.[104]

Tárrega developed many concepts of technical improvement appropriate to the playing of the new Torres guitar. In lessons with his various influential pupils he advocated specific right and left hand positioning guidelines and the precise use of a footstool under the left foot.

Because of the tonal qualities of the Torres instrument, Tárrega took meticulous care to indicate in his written transcriptions, the exact placing of every note and where it was to be played on the fingerboard to achieve the desired effect. As with violinists and cellists, Tárrega was keen to avoid the gratuitous use of open strings, and, in particular, opted where possible for the resonances and tone colors available from notes located among the higher positions of the fingerboard. He carefully indicated the use of slurs and other effects on sound production such as the combined use of open strings with fretted notes.

His own activities soon extended to Paris and London, as well as the cities of Spain, and in 1884 he played in a concert with Isaac Albéniz.[105] The *Enciclopedia Espasa* compared him favorably with Sarasate and Anton Rubinstein.[106]

The following programs performed by Tárrega established precedents for the subsequent shape and content of guitar recitals, the tripartite structure of the first concert often being employed by Segovia, Pujol, Barrios and Llobet:

1) La Real Academia de Santa Cecilia, Cádiz, 10 May, 1888:[107]

Melodía de las Vísperas Sicilianas	Verdi
Fantasía de Marina	Arrieta
Gran Tremolo	Gottschalk
Fantasía Española	Tárrega

Célebre Gavota	Arditi
Polonesa de Concierto	Arcas
Carnaval de Venecia	Tárrega

Motivos Heterogéneos	Tárrega
Scherzo y Minuetto	Prudent
Gran Marcha Fúnebre	Thalberg
Aires Nacionales	Tárrega

2) Palacio Corea, Rome, 7 February, 1903:[108]

Melodía	Verdi
Barcarola	Mendelssohn
Granada (Serenata)	Albéniz
Seguidillas	Chueca
Rapsodia Andaluza	Albéniz
Fantasía Española	Tárrega

Trémolo	Tárrega
Motivo Español	Chueca
Momento musical	Schubert
Tema con variaciones (La Pastoral)	Mozart
Nocturno en Mi bemol	Chopin
Variaciones sobre un tema de Paganini	Tárrega

This mixture of transcriptions and works originally written for guitar provided the central inspiration of guitar recitals for many decades. In particular these programs reveal how Tárrega advocated arranging works from the great composers - Bach, Beethoven, Berlioz, Chopin, Handel, Haydn, Massenet,

Mendelssohn, Meyerbeer, Paganini, Rubinstein, Schubert, Schumann, and Wagner - as well as from a variety of Spanish composers, including Albéniz, Arrieta, Caballero, Calleja, Chueca, Iradier, Malats and Valverde.

Many of Tárrega's transcriptions (with some notable exceptions such as the pianoforte music of Beethoven and Chopin, now usually considered aesthetically inappropriate on the guitar), have been widely performed or re-transcribed ever since. Tárrega's arrangements of Albéniz's *Cádiz, Granada,* and *Sevilla,* set precedents of particular significance.

Tárrega as composer was a quintessential romantic. Whereas Sor, Giuliani, and their followers generally aspired to write in the form of variations, sonatas/sonatinas, fantasias, etc., Tárrega's works convey vividly picturesque images. Titles such as *Recuerdos de la Alhambra, Capricho Arabe, Sueño, Lágrima, Adelita, María, Marieta, Rosita, Pepita, Danza Mora, Las Dos Hermanitas,* and *Alborada,* depict places, moods, or miniature sketches in music of his family members and are representative of his finest work.

Tárrega's characteristic approach to the guitar sets the imagination to work. In this he may have inspired many composers to continue writing in impressionistic terms for the tonal qualities of the guitar with inventive colorful titles. But regrettably Tárrega's approach to composition, though picturesque and evocative at a certain level, remained well in arrears of the adventurousness of the great European composers of his era, and created a limited and conservative precedent for guitar music.

Tárrega's ideals of composition may well have been centered on Chopin. But to imitate certain Chopinesque features on the guitar, though often productive of lyrical miniatures, would inevitably prove retrospective rather than progressive. Thus the guitar entered the 20th century in a condition of romanticized dream with little reference to contemporary mainstream European music. But such was the power of Tárrega's charisma that it would be his music that proved influential for composers such as Agustín Barrios Mangoré, Emilio Pujol, Regino and Eduardo Sáinz de la Maza and Federico Moreno Torroba.

Footnotes to The Classic Guitar

1. José L. Romanillos, *Antonio de Torres, Guitar Maker - His Life and Work* (Shaftesbury: Element Books, 1987), p. 41.

2. Victor Anand Coelho, ed., *Performance on Lute, Guitar and Vihuela, Historical Practice and Modern Interpretation*, Richard Savino, 'Essential issues in performance practices of the classical guitar, 1770-1850,' (Cambridge University Press, 1997), pp. 195-196.

3. Neil D. Pennington, *The Spanish Baroque Guitar, with a Transcription of De Murcia's Passacalles y Obras*, Vol. 1 (Ann Arbor, Michigan: UMI Research Press, 1981), pp. 24-25.

4. Sources for this list include *The Spanish Guitar* (New York: The Metropolitan Museum of Art, Madrid: Museo Municipal, 1991-1992); Tom and Mary Anne Evans, *Guitars, from the Renaissance to Rock* (New York & London: Paddington Press, 1977); Harvey Turnbull, *The Guitar from the Renaissance to the Present Day* (London: Batsford, 1974); *Exposición de Guitarras Antiguas Españolas* (Alicante: Caja de Ahorros Provincial de Alicante, 1990).

5. Alexander Bellow, *The Illustrated History of the Guitar* (New York: Franco Colombo Publications/Belwin-Mills, 1970), p. 157.

6. Brian Jeffery, *Fernando Sor, Composer and Guitarist* (London: Tecla, www.tecla.com, 1977), p. 16.

7. Ferdinand Sor, *Method for the Guitar*, trans. A. Merrick, reprint of the ca. 1850 edition (New York: Da Capo Press, 1980), p. 9.

8. *La Guitarra Española* (New York/Madrid: Metropolitan Museum of Art, 1991-1992), pp. 115-124.

9. François Lesure, ed., *Guitares* (Paris: Collection Eurydice, 1980), pp. 134-135.

10. Sor, *Method for the Guitar*, op. cit., p. 1.

11. Stewart Button, *The Guitar in England 1800-1924* (New York & London: Garland Publishing, 1989), pp. 215 -216.

12. Stanley Sadie, *The New Grove Dictionary of Music and Musicians*, Vol. 2 (London: Macmillan, 1980), p. 826.

13. Matanya Ophee, *Luigi Boccherini's Guitar Quintets, New Evidence* (Columbus, Ohio: Editions Orphée, 1981). Carlo Andrea Giorgetti, notes for Jakob Lindberg's recording with the Drottningholm Baroque Ensemble, *Luigi Boccherini, Quintets with Guitar 1-VI*, BIS CD-597/598, 1992.

14. Mariano Soriano Fuertes, *Historia de la Música Española desde la venida de los fenicios hasta el año 1850* (Barcelona-Madrid: Narciso Ramírez, 1855-1859).

15. Antonio Martín Moreno, *Historia de la música española, Vol. 4, Siglo XVIII* (Madrid: Alianza Editorial, 1985), pp. 256-257.

16. Quoted in Paul Cox, 'Classic Guitar Technique and its Evolution as Reflected in the Method Books ca. 1770-1850,' (Dissertation, Indiana University, 1978), p. 12.

17. Brian Jeffery, ed., *Fernando Ferandiere, Arte de tocar la guitarra española por música (Madrid, 1799)* (London: Tecla, www.tecla.com, 1977), p. 76.

18. From the *Prológo*, quoted in Pennington, op.cit., p. 25.

19. Martín Moreno, op. cit., pp. 334-335.

20. Thomas F. Heck, 'The Role of Italy in the Early History of Classic Guitar', *Guitar Review*, No. 34, Winter 1971, p.1.

21. Sor, op.cit., (footnote b), p. 6.

22. Heck, op.cit., pp. 1-4.

23. Dionisio Aguado, *Escuela de la Guitarra, 2nd Edition*, p. 1. (From original edition in the author's collection. Trans. GW.)

24. Brian Jeffery, *Fernando Sor, Composer and Guitarist* (London: Tecla, www.tecla.com, 1977), p. 16.

25. Simon Wynberg, ed., *Johann Kaspar Mertz, Guitar Works*, Vols 1-X (Heidelberg: Chanterelle, 1985), *Preface*. The harpolyre was a hybrid chordophone invented by Jean-François Salomon (1827). Three necks were attached to a guitar-type body, the central neck had six strings, the other two had seven and eight strings. (Jeffery, op.cit., p. 102.)

26. Karl Scheit, ed., (Vienna: Universal, 1949). Michael Macmeeken, ed., Facsimile edition (Monaco: Editions Chanterelle, 1979).

27. Works by Molitor in print include: *Guitar Method* (with Klingenbrunner, 1799), guitar solos, *Op. 7, 10, 11, 12, 15*, duos for violin and guitar, *Op. 3, 5*, and trio for flute, alto and guitar, *Op. 6; Grosse Sonate, Op. 7*, Matthias Henke, ed., (Wilhelmshaven: Heinrichshofen's Verlag, 1979). For further details see Philip J. Bone, *The Guitar & Mandolin* (London: Schott & Co. Ltd, 2nd Edition, 1972), p. 242.

28. Works by Leonhard von Call in print include: Walter Götze, ed., *Easy Trio in C major, Op. 26*, for three guitars (Mainz: Schott, 1929). For further details see Alois Mauerhofer, *The New Grove Dictionary of Music and Musicians*, Vol.3, op. cit., p. 624.

29. Several of Fürstenau's works have been edited by Siegfried Behrend (Frankfurt: Wilhelm Zimmerman, 1969).

30. Georg Kinsky, ed., Franz Schubert, *Quartett* (New York: C.F. Peters Corporation, 1956). (Matiegka's *Quartet* is often erroneously thought to be composed by Schubert. Charles Osborne, *Schubert and his Vienna*, (London: Weidenfeld & Nicolson, 1985), p. 12: 'Early in the year [1814], for some family occasion or other, he [Schubert] had turned another composer's trio for flute, violin and guitar into a quartet (D.96) by adding a cello part. His manuscript was found in 1918, and published as a guitar quartet by Schubert. The work is a charming piece of Biedermeier domestic music, and not unworthy of the youthful Schubert who never lost his ability to compose pieces of amiable unimportance as well as works of great genius. It was, however, identified

some years after its publication as an arrangement of a piece by Wenzel Thomas Matiegka (1773-1830), a minor Austrian composer who flourished in Vienna at the beginning of the 19th century, and who specialized in music for the guitar.'

31. Matanya Ophee, ed., *Andrei Sychra, Four Concert Etudes, The Russian Collection*, Vol. II (Columbus, Ohio: Editions Orphée, 1992), p. iii. Thomas F. Heck, *The New Grove Dictionary of Music and Musicians*, Vol. 17, op. cit., p. 311.

32. Bone, op.cit., pp. 241-242.

33. Matanya Ophee, *Luigi Boccherini's Guitar Quintets; To which is added, for the first time, a reliable biography of François de Fossa, his portrait, and a checklist of his known compositions* (Boston: Editions Orphée, 1981). Recording: Simon Wynberg, Gabrieli String Quartet, *François de Fossa, Three Guitar Quartets, Op. 19,* Chandos, ABRD 1109, 1985.

34. Bone, op. cit., pp. 197-200.

35. Matanya Ophee, *The Russian Collection*, Vol. 1 (Columbus, Ohio: Editions Orphée, 1986), p. vii.

36. Jeffery, *Fernando Sor, Composer and Guitarist*, op. cit., p. 86.

37. Volkmar Köhler, *The New Grove Dictionary of Music and Musicians*, Vol. 11, op. cit., pp. 700-704. Bone, op. cit., pp. 222-224. Walter Götze, ed., *12 Bagatellen, Op. 4* (Mainz: Schott, 1927). Karl Scheit, ed., *3 Bagatellen, Op. 4* (Vienna: Universal, 1974).

38. Jozef Powrozniak, *The New Grove Dictionary of Music and Musicians*, Vol. 8, op. cit., p. 695.

39. Bone, op. cit., p. 60. Françoise-Emmanuelle Denis, notes for David Russell's recording of Broca's *Fantasía*, Guitare GHA 5256003, 1986.

40. Bone, op. cit., p. 66. Works available include: Melchor Rodríguez, ed., *Antonio Cano, Método para Guitarra* (Madrid: Soneto, 1993); *Antonio Cano, 35 Etudes* (Tokyo: Zen-On Music, c.1995); Rafael Balaguer, ed., *Dos estudios brillantes de concierto, Seguidillas Manchegas* (Madrid: Union Musical Española, 1973).

41. Thomas F. Heck, *The New Grove Dictionary of Music and Musicians*, Vol. 3, op. cit., p. 839.

42. Mario Torta, *Catalogo tematico delle opere di Ferdinando Carulli*, Vols 1 & II (Lucca: Libreria Musicale Italiana, 1993), p. xxxv.

43. e.g. Edgar Hunt, ed., *F. Carulli, Elementary Guitar Method for Self Instruction* (London/Mainz/New York: Schott, 1953).

44. Paolo Paolini, ed., *Ferdinando Carulli, Méthode complète, Op. 27, 61, 71, 192* (Florence: Studio per Edizioni Scelte, 1981).

45. Torta, op. cit, pp. 677-682.

46. Recordings of Carulli's *Concerto in A major:* Karl Scheit/ Kammerorchester der Wiener Festspiele, Wilfried Boettcher, conductor, TURNABOUT TV 34123S, 1968; Marta Zelenka/ Slovak Chamber Orchestra, Bohdon Warchal, conductor *(Favorite Guitar Concertos),* Figaro Classics 99276/3, undated.

47. Notes by Tom Eastwood for *Together, Julian Bream-John Williams,* RCA SB6862, 1972.

48. A greater understanding of Sor's life and music became possible after these publications: Brian Jeffery, *Fernando Sor, Composer and Guitarist* (London: Tecla, www.tecla.com, 1977); Brian Jeffery, ed., *Fernando Sor, Complete Works for Guitar* (New York: Shattinger-International Music Corp., 1977).

49. Vital steps towards recognition of Sor's potential were Bream's recordings: *Introduction and Allegro, Op. 14*, RCA SB 6796, 1969; *Sonata in C, Op. 25*, RCA ARL 1-0711, 1974, *Fantasies, Op. 30* and *Op. 7, Variations on a Theme of Mozart, Op. 9*, RCA RL 14033, 1981.

50. *Harmonicon*, March, 1824, p. 48, quoted in Jeffery, op. cit., p. 71.

51. Thomas F. Heck, 'The Role of Italy in the Early History of Classic Guitar', *Guitar Review*, No. 34, Winter, 1971, p. 1.

52. Ibid; further reasons given for guitarists to leave Italy were the considerable number of players in the main centers, political turmoil wreaked by Napoleon, and the opportunities for publication north of the Alps.

53. Certain publications changed perceptions of Giuliani: Thomas F. Heck, *The Birth of the Classic Guitar and its Cultivation in Vienna, Reflected in the Career and Compositions of Mauro Giuliani*, Vols. 1 & 2 (Ph.D. Dissertation, Yale University, 1970); Thomas F. Heck, *Mauro Giuliani: Virtuoso Guitarist and Composer* (Columbus: Editions Orphée, 1995); Brian Jeffery, ed., *Mauro Giuliani, The Complete Works in Facsimiles of the Original Editions* (London: Tecla, www.tecla.com, 1984-1988). Bream's performances/recordings expanded public awareness: *Grand Overture, Op. 61, Sonata in C, Op. 15*, RCA SB 6796, 1969; *Les Rossinianes, Op. 121 and Op. 119*, RCA ARL 1-0711, 1974.

54. *Giulianiad*, Vol. 1, 1833, facsimile reproduction in *Guitar Review*, No.18, 1955.

55. William Kinderman, *Beethoven* (Oxford University Press, 1995), pp. 253-260.

56. For the full list see Heck, op.cit., (1970).

57. Heck, op. cit., (1995), pp. 97, 115.

58. Guitar compositions by Diabelli still in print include: Arthur Just, ed., *3 Sonatas*, GA 57; Georg Meier, ed., *Very Easy Pieces for Guitar and Piano, Vols 1-4*, GA 22-25; Walter Götze, ed., *24 Easy Old Viennese Ländler*, GA 85 (Mainz: Schott). Heinrich Albert, ed., *Sonatina for guitar and piano, Op. 68* (Frankfurt: Zimmerman). Siegfried Behrend, ed., *Grande Sonate Brillante, for guitar and piano, Op. 102* (Berlin: Bote & Bock).

59. Julian Bream, ed., *Anton Diabelli, Sonata in A Major* (London: Faber Music, 1969), *Preface*. (Recorded on *Classic Guitar*, RCA SB 6796, 1969.)

60. Simon Wynberg, ed., *The Selected Works of Dionisio Aguado* (Monaco: Editions Chanterelle, 1981), *Introduction*.

61. Brian Jeffery, ed., *Aguado - New Guitar Method* (London: Tecla, www.tecla.com, 1981), pp. x-xii.

62. Wynberg, ed., op. cit., *Introduction*.

63. *Julian Bream, Music of Spain, Vol. 4*, RCA RL 14033, 1981.

64. Jeffery, ed., op. cit., p. xix.

65. Ibid., pp. 10-11.

66. Giuseppe Gazzelloni, ed., *Paganini, The Complete Solo Guitar Works* (Heidelberg: Chanterelle, 1987), Vol. I, p. iv.

67. Simon Wynberg, ed., *Luigi Legnani (1790-1877), 36 Caprices, Opus 20 in all major and minor keys* (Heidelberg: Chanterelle, 1986), *Introduction*.

68. Bone, op. cit., pp. 205-206.

69. Wynberg, ed., op. cit., *Introduction*.

70. Quoted in Bone, op. cit., p. 205.

71. Wynberg, ed., op. cit., *Introduction*.

72. Ten of the *Caprices, Op. 20* were recorded by Eduardo Fernández, Decca, LP 414 160-1, CD 414 160-2, 1985.

73. Wynberg, ed., op. cit., *Introduction*.

74. Jim Ferguson, ed., p. 4, in David Tanenbaum, *The Essential Studies, Matteo Carcassi, 25 Estudios, Op. 60* (San Francisco: Guitar Solo Publications, 1992).

75. Marc Van de Cruys, 'Sor The Lutenist & Carcassi The Mandolin Player', *Soundboard*, Vol. XV, No. 3, Fall, 1988, pp. 194 -195.

76. Of particular interest is Simon Wynberg's edition, *Matteo Carcassi (1792-1853), 25 Etudes Mélodiques Progressives opus 60* (Heidelberg: Chanterelle, 1985).

77. Simon Wynberg, *Marco Aurelio Zani de Ferranti, Guitarist (1801-1878)* (Heidelberg: Chanterelle, 1989), p. 61.

78. Ibid., p. 48. Berlioz in *Journal des Débats*, 1859. Quoted in notes for *The Guitar Music of Marco Aurelio Zani de Ferranti and José Ferrer,* Simon Wynberg, guitar, Chandos, ABRD 1222, 1987.

79. Wynberg, op. cit., p. 43.

80. Hector Berlioz, *Grand traité d'instrumentation et d'orchestration modernes, Op. 10* (Paris, 1843): English translation, *Modern Instrumentation and Orchestration* (Novello, 1855), pp. 66-70.

81. Wynberg, op. cit., p. 43.

82. Simon Wynberg, ed., *Johann Kaspar Mertz, Guitar Works,* Vols. 1-X (Heidelberg: Chanterelle, 1985); Simon Wynberg, ed., *The Guitar Works of Napoléon Coste,* Vols. 1-IX (Monaco: Chanterelle, 1981).

83. Márta Sz. Farkas, quoted in notes for recording by László Szendrey-Karper, *Johann Kaspar Mertz, Guitar Music,* HUNGAROTON SLPD 12894, 1988.

84. Wynberg, ed., op. cit., (1985).

85. Selected recordings: David Russell, *Fantaisie hongroise, Op. 65, No. 1, Elégie,* Guitare GHA 5256003, 1986; László Szendrey-Karper, *Johann Kaspar Mertz, Guitar Music, Fantaisie hongroise, Op. 65, No. 1, Fantaisie Originale, Op. 65, No. 2, Barden-Klänge Op. 13, Books 2, 3, 14, Lieder von Schubert, Ungarische Vaterlands-Blüthen, Op.1,* HUNGAROTON SLPD 12894, 1988; Nicola Hall, *Fantaisie hongroise, Op. 65, No. 1,* Decca 440 678-2, 1994; Franco Platino, *Elégie,* Naxos 8 554344, 1999.

86. Simon Wynberg, ed., *The Guitar Works of Napoléon Coste,* Vol. 1 (Monaco: Chanterelle, 1981), *Introduction*.

87. Fritz Buek, *Die Gitarre und Ihre Meister* (Berlin: Schlesinger, 1926), p. 106. (Trans. GW.)

88. Jeffery, *Fernando Sor, Composer and Guitarist,* op. cit., p. 106.

89. Wynberg, *The Guitar Works of Napoléon Coste,* Vol. IV, op. cit., p. 51.

90. Simon Wynberg, ed., *The Guitar Works of Napoléon Coste:* Vol. 1, *25 Etudes de Genre, Op. 38;* Vols II -VI, *Published Solo Works, Op. 2-53;* Vol. VII, *Guitar Duos;* Vol. VIII, *Works for Oboe (violin or flute) & Guitar;* Vol. IX, *Unpublished Solo Works* (Monaco: Chanterelle, 1981-1983). Note also Simon Wynberg's recording (John Anderson, oboe), *Napoléon Coste, Music for Guitar and Oboe,* Chandos ABR 1031, 1981.

91. This lack of appreciation was alleviated with Simon Wynberg's *Giulio Regondi, Complete Works for Guitar* (Monaco: Chanterelle, 1981) and a recording by Leif Christensen, *Giulio Regondi, Guitar Works,* PAULA 10, recorded February, 1981.

92. Wynberg, op. cit., *Introduction.*

93. Frank Mott Harrison, *Reminiscences of Madame Sidney Pratten* (Bournemouth: Barnes & Mullins, 1899), p. 20.

94. Stewart Button, *The Guitar In England, 1800-1924* (New York & London: Garland Publishing Inc., 1989), pp. 108-109: 'The story concerning the disappearance of Giulio's father is difficult to believe. Why did the supposed father abscond with £2,000, when he could have stayed with Giulio and lived a better life both financially and socially? It was enigmatic stories like this that added to the mysterious personality of Giulio.'

95. John Holmquist, ed., *Giulio Regondi, Ten Etudes for Guitar* (Columbus, Ohio: Editions Orphée, 1990).

96. Melchor Rodríguez, ed., *J. Arcas, Obras Completas para Guitarra / Guitar Works* (Madrid: Soneto, 1993), p. 10.

97. Ibid., p. 15.

98. Ibid., p. 10.

99. Ibid., pp. 15-16. For the guitar as a miniature orchestra see: a) Brian Jeffery, ed., *Aguado, New Guitar Method,* op. cit., p. 3: Aguado comments: 'The guitar is an instrument which is not as yet well known. Who would think that of all those used today it is perhaps the most suitable for producing the effect of an orchestra in miniature?' b) Carlos José Melchior (1785-1873), *Diccionario Enciclopédico de la Música* (Lerida, 1859), p. 499: 'Aguado and Huerta... are still artistic nobilities of the guitar. This instrument... is a miniature orchestra.'

100. Romanillos, op.cit., p. 13.

101. Ibid., p. 17.

102. Ibid., p. 119.

103. Emilio Pujol, *Tárrega: Ensayo biográfico* (Lisbon: 1960), pp. 54-56.

104. Ibid., pp. 61-65.

105. Ibid., p. 95.

106. Ibid., p. 89.

107. Ibid., pp. 107-108.

108. Ibid., pp. 168-169.

PART IV: THE 20th CENTURY

42. Guitar Recitals after Tárrega, 1909 - 1919

Following Francisco Tárrega's death in 1909, recitalists continued the precedents set by the Spanish master. In 1909/10, Andrés Segovia (1893-1987), a guitarist who never met Tárrega, made his debut in a career destined to extend until 1987. The details of his first recital have not survived but some time later he gave a concert which reveals the pervasive Tárrega influence:

Real Academia de Santa Cecilia, Cádiz, 19 May, 1914:[1]

Gavotte in A minor	Tárrega
Estudio in A, No. 24	Coste
Capricho Arabe	Tárrega
Bourrée	Bach
Sonata Op. 13, Adagio	Beethoven
Nocturno	Chopin
Granada, serenata	Albéniz
Cádiz, saeta	Albéniz
Sevilla	Albéniz

Also in 1914, one of Tárrega's famous pupils, Miguel Llobet (1878-1938), performed in Munich, Germany:[2]

Minuet in E, Op.11	Sor
Two Studies, Op. 29	Sor
Capricho Arabe	Tárrega
Romanza (transcr. Llobet)	Rubinstein
Two Studies , Op. 38	Coste
Bourrée (transcr. Llobet)	J.S.Bach
Sevilla (transcr. Llobet)	Albéniz
Mazurka - Minuetto	Tárrega
Variations on a Theme by Sor	Llobet

In this era, recitalists (whether guitarists, pianists or violinists), did not necessarily play selected works in chronological order as later generations came to expect. So the logic of how a specific recital developed as a unified entity may not be obvious unless it is understood that all pieces were subject to similar interpretative concepts. Awareness of stylistic features appropriate to different historical periods was not the major concern.

Thus all works sounded somewhat homogeneous and listeners experienced no problems of incongruity when a Baroque dance was juxtaposed with Albéniz's Sevilla. Neither was it apparently disturbing for audiences to hear various pieces by a composer such as Tárrega in separate parts of a recital rather than grouped together. It was usual also to include some of the performer's own compositions, perhaps as a kind of finale.

On 1 August, 1916, the Paraguayan guitarist, Agustín Barrios Mangoré, gave the following recital in Rio de Janeiro, Brazil:[3]

First Part

Marcha Heroica	Giuliani
Chanson de Printemps	Mendelssohn
Recuerdo del Pacifico	Barrios
Rondo brillante	Aguado

Sarabande	Bach
Meditaçao	Tolsa
Concerto in A minor	Arcas

Second Part

Nocturno, Op. 9, No. 2	Chopin
Phantasia sobre motivos de Traviata	Verdi
Andante y Estudio	Coste
Chant du Paysan	Grieg
Bicho feio - Tango humorístico	Barrios
Rapsodia Americana	Barrios
Jota Aragonesa, variations	Barrios

Barrios is a supreme example of the composer/performer, a recitalist whose own works have pride of place. In the 19th century such a role had been paramount but the emphasis on recitalists as composers shifted as players increasingly preferred to demonstrate their artistry in music written by others.

A concert by Emilio Pujol (1886-1980), one of Tárrega's most influential pupils, at the Orfeo Gracienc, Barcelona, on 8 June, 1918, is again characteristic of the Tárrega tradition: [4]

Minuet	Sor
Canço de Bressol - Vals Intim	Pujol
Recuerdos de la Alhambra	Tárrega
Adagio	Haydn
Loure - Minuet	Bach
Moment Musical	Schubert
El Mestre - El Testament d'Amelia	Llobet
Serenata española	Malats
Granada	Albéniz
Danza	Granados

The substance (if not the style), of guitar recitals would soon be subject to radical adjustments and developments. In less than a decade a profound reassessment of what was considered appropriate to be played in concerts would take place.

43. The Expanding Repertoire, 1920-1930

The 1920's was a decade of immense expansion of the guitarist's repertoire. One way of achieving this was for recitalists to ask their favorite composers to write something for them. Andrés Segovia began his work in this area with a request to a Spanish composer:

Then there was a 'first' in the field of the guitar: for the first time, a composer who was not a guitarist wrote a piece for the guitar. It was Federico Moreno Torroba, whose musical poem had just been premiered by the National Symphony under the direction of Maestro Arbós.

Moreno Torroba had been introduced to me by the orchestra's first violin, Señor Francés. It did not take us long to become friends, nor for him to accede to my suggestion: Would he compose something for the guitar? In a few weeks he came up with a slight but truly beautiful Dance in E major.[5]

Writing for guitar grew especially attractive to composers as Segovia's recitals extended throughout the musical centers of the world with debuts in Montevideo and Buenos Aires (1919/1920), Mexico City (1923), Paris (1924), London (1926), Copenhagen (1927), New York (1928), Tokyo (1929), Shanghai (1929), etc.

Manuel Ponce, the eminent Mexican composer, attended Segovia's Mexico City debut in 1923 and was duly invited to write a guitar work. Later that year Segovia wrote to Ponce to express his 'happiness at seeing that the most interesting composers of this old world are collaborating with my eagerness to revindicate the guitar'. His provisional list of composers promising such activity included Roussel, (who wrote 'a small, beautiful work' - *Segovia, Op. 29),* Ravel, Schoenberg, Grovlez, Turina, Torroba and Falla.[6]

That Schoenberg enters Segovia's list may seem unusual but in 1923 the Viennese composer wrote *Serenade Op.24* (for clarinet, bass clarinet, violin, viola, cello, mandolin, guitar, and baritone voice):

> *In this opus 24, which is linked to the light-hearted Viennese tradition, Schoenberg tries to apply the new compositional techniques to a range of older forms like the minuet and the march. In the whole work it becomes clear that Schoenberg desires to carry over twelve-note principles into every aspect of composition including the vertical one, i.e. into chords and accompanying figures...*
>
> *The Serenade is peculiar in that its complexity from the point of view of compositional technique never consciously strikes the listener. He is diverted in this witty gay work by its fire-engine noises (in the dance scene), its potpourri-like improvisations (in the final march), and its Mediterranean chirping sounds evoked by guitar and mandolin. It is not until the score is examined that the amount of artistic craftsmanship and sovereign technique employed becomes apparent.*[7]

Segovia's abiding hatred of dissonant styles and the avant-garde may well have been consolidated by Schoenberg's piece. Nowadays such a work can be regarded as congenial with a certain humor. But the ironic wit of 'fire-engine noises' and 'Mediterranean chirping sounds' would never be acceptable to Segovia. Thus *Serenade* was mainly left to a later generation of guitarists.[8]

Various other composers, writing in more traditional terms, were enlisted to expand Segovia's repertoire. Foremost were Federico Moreno Torroba (1891-1982), destined to achieve international acclaim by way of Segovia's recitals, and Joaquín Turina (1882-1949), one of Spain's most eminent composers, who wrote perennials for the guitar such as *Sevillana, Op. 29* (1923) and *Fandanguillo, Op. 36* (1925).

Non-Spanish composers in Segovia's service included Alexandre Tansman (1897-1986), from Poland, Gustave Samazeuilh (1877 -1967), a French composer, who had studied with Chausson, d'Indy and Dukas,[9] and Cyril Scott (1879-1970), from England, whose *Reverie* Segovia performed at the Teatro Odeón, Buenos Aires on 23 July, 1928.[10]

Segovia at this time began transcribing pieces by J.S. Bach for guitar. On the centenary of Bach's death in 1850, the *Bach-Gesellschaft* (Bach Society), was founded, dedicated to publishing his complete works. Between 1851 and 1899, forty-six volumes were issued. In January, 1900, the *Neue Bach-Gesellschaft* replaced the original *Bach- Gesellschaft,* intending to present Bach's music in practical editions.[11]

Arising from this, *Johann Sebastian Bach, Kompositionen für die Laute* (1921), edited by Hans Dagobert Bruger, provided the complete set (in notation), of Bach's compositions believed to have been written for the lute.[12] This publication was a vital factor in inspiring Segovia to follow Tárrega's precedent of arranging Bach for guitar.

44. Recordings

Agustín Barrios Mangoré is usually considered as the first classical guitarist to make commercial recordings. His early examples, dating from 1913, were produced in Montevideo for the Atlanta/Artigas labels while a later series of sessions between 1921 and 1929 were on the Odeon label of Buenos Aires.[13]

Vahdah Olcott Bickford (1885-1980), the distinguished North American guitarist, commented that during his early tours of the USA (1914-1917), Miguel Llobet 'tried to make a recording at the Bell Lab. in Brunswick, New Jersey, but was dissatisfied with the sound.'[14]

111

Llobet's main solo recording sessions took place around 1925 in Spain and a few years after that he recorded duo music with María Luisa Anido. Altogether Llobet made some fifteen discs appearing on a variety of labels including Parlophon Electric/Parlophon S.A. España (Barcelona), Odeon, Decca, and Decca/Odeon-Parlophone.[14] (Regrettably during these sessions it seems that no recording was made of Manuel de Falla's only work written directly for the guitar, *Homenaje "Le Tombeau de Claude Debussy,"* composed 1920, a piece with which Llobet's name is always closely associated.)

Segovia's early experiences of recording were possibly during a trip to Havana, Cuba, in 1923. But his commercial recordings began in 1927.[15] The prestigious British journal, *The Gramophone*, reviewed its first Segovia disc at that time:

> ***Andrés Segovia** (H.M.V., D.1255, 12in., 6s.6d.) provides us with some truly astonishing playing on the guitar, an instrument which, by the way, appears to record excellently. His rendering of a Bach Gavotte is pleasantly rhythmic and the rubato, though meretricious, is effective. But the result, interesting as it is, is hardly Bach, and the guitar seems more naturally suited to the pleasant, childish prattling of a Thème Varié by Sor, which is most successful. The playing is, of course, the main thing, and this no one should miss.[16]*

45. Publications, 1924 - 1930

In the 1920's Segovia began editing new pieces by contemporary composers and transcriptions from the classics, achieving a remarkable amount of work between 1924 and 1930.[17]

1924: *Sonatina in A* (Edición Musical Daniel, Madrid), Moreno Torroba.

1925: *Segovia, Op.29* (A. Durand et Fils, Paris), Albert Roussel.

1926: Schott Guitar Archive Nos: 102, *Fandanguillo*, Turina: 103, *Nocturne*, 104, *Suite Castellana*, Moreno Torroba: *Sérénade* (Durand, Paris), Samazeuilh.

1927: *Sevillana* (Sociedad Musical Daniel, Madrid), Turina.

1928: G.A.106, *Prelude - Allemande - Minuettos I & II*, 107, *Courante - Gavotte*, 108, *Andante - Bourrée - Double*, J.S. Bach.

1928: G.A. 109, *Thème varié et Finale*, 110, *Sonata III*, 111, *Tres canciones populares mexicanas*, 112, *Preludio*, Ponce: 113, *Burgalesa*, 114, *Preludio*, 115, *Serenata Burlesca*, Moreno Torroba:116, *Mazurka*, Tansman: 117, *Menuet*, Mozart: 118, *Four Short Pieces*, Franck: 119, I. *Lamento*, 120, II. *Página romántica*, 121, III. *Guitarreo*, Pedrell.

1929: G.A. 122, *Sonata clásica*, 123, *Sonata romántica*, Ponce. (Also in 1929, *Douze Etudes* of Heitor Villa-Lobos were written, dedicated to Segovia, unpublished until the 1950's.)

1930: G.A. 124, *Preludes I*, Nos 1-6, 125, *Preludes II*, Nos 7-12, Ponce: 128, *Ráfaga*, Turina: 129, *Fantasía-Sonata, Op. A-22*, Manén.

This expansion of the repertory was supported by research into the history of the guitar. *Cancionero musical popular español* (1918-1922) by Felipe Pedrell (1841-1922), the Spanish musicologist, emphasized the vihuela's significance in 16th century Spain.[18] Soon afterwards came J.B. Trend's influential books, *Luis Milán and the Vihuelistas* (1925) and *The Music of Spanish History to 1600* (1926).[19] Emilio Pujol meanwhile extended his researches into Renaissance and Baroque guitar:

> *In 1926, following advice in line with the teaching received from Felipe Pedrell, and at the request of Lionel de la Laurencie of the Paris Conservatoire, Emilio Pujol began the first investigations into the guitar's historical past...*

The search began among the archives and libraries of the principal European centers dedicated to music and as a result he delivered a historical-didactic study of the guitar from its origins which appeared in Volume XXIV of the Encyclopedia of Music of the Dictionary of the Paris Conservatoire, *1926.*

The task took him to the Pedrell archives and those of Dr. Scheeherer de la Haya, the National Libraries of Madrid, Paris, Brussels and Munich, and the British Museum, London. He brought forward the first transcriptions of the work of the Spanish vihuelistas of the 16th century and guitarists of the 17th century, published later by Editions Max Eschig, Paris, in a series edited by Pujol under the title of "Library of Ancient and Modern Music for Guitar."

These activities were a revelation for guitarists because not only was an unknown past opened up for them but it enabled them to enlarge the content of their programs in an unlimited way, and for our musicology it was the recovery of a historical area which had remained hidden for more than four centuries.

On 6 December, 1927, in the Salle Erard, Rue du Mail, Paris, Emilio Pujol gave a concert which featured for the first time in France the music of vihuelistas, including in the program, for the first hearing, a Pavana of Luis Milán. In this recital, without precedent in contemporary history, a new era began: the glorious names of Milán, Corbetta, Visée and Gaspar Sanz arose to recover the prestige lost in past centuries. [20]

From 1926 onwards, Pujol's transcriptions from tablature appeared from the Parisian publisher, Max Eschig, featuring works by Milán, Narváez, Mudarra, Pisador, Fuenllana, Valderrábano, Besard, Sanz, de Visée, Corbetta, Roncalli, Santiago de Murcia, J.S. Bach, etc. (The series also offered music by contemporary composers for guitar including Rodrigo, Broqua, Grau, Pujol, etc.)

In 1930 Pujol published *El Dilema del Sonido en la Guitarra (The Dilemma of Timbre on the Guitar)*, asserting that the most expressive tone on the guitar is achieved through the fingertips, and not by any use of the nails:

> *The sound produced with the nails strikes one's ear as if each note were a very small, sharp arrow piercing our sensibility. It is conical, pungent and nasal, reminiscent of the lute and the harpsichord... The tone of a string struck with the fingertip possesses an intrinsic beauty, which affects the deepest feelings of our sensibility, just as air and light permeate space.[21]*

Segovia emphatically disagreed. His technique utilized nail and flesh to produce the tonal richness characteristic of his playing. When eventually he wrote his autobiography, Segovia would not forget the prejudice against him on his visit to Valencia early in his career:

> *And so... to Valencia. I bought a third-class ticket and took the train for the city where the loving memory of Tárrega lived in the heart of friends, pupils, and fans, the last ones more interested in the instrument than in music, as I soon discovered. It was curious to see the zeal with which all of them - the pupils for their personal narrow view of the issue, the others for no apparent reason - adhered blindly to the method prescribed by the master in his last years: to pluck solely with the finger pads, avoiding contact of the fingernail with the strings... to the detriment of the full rendering of the guitar's characteristic qualities: variety of tone color and of sound volume.[22]*

Discussion among guitarists and lutenists on nails or fingertips was a perennial issue which had probably occupied players ever since the instruments first came into being. For the guitar, Segovia, by force of example, at last won this particular argument decisively, thereby assuring his great technical influence on subsequent generations of recitalists.

46. Continued Momentum, 1930 - 1935

The guitar's advance, propelled by leading personalities and indicated by an expanded repertory, recordings and numerous recitals, was consolidated during the early 1930's. Segovia, above all, developed his recording activities, concentrating at this time on works by Manuel Ponce:

6 October, 1930: Manuel Ponce: *Suite (in the style of Weiss) (Prelude - Allemande - Gavotte-Sarabande - Gigue):* Joaquín Malats: *Serenata española:* Federico Moreno Torroba: *Nocturno.* 6-7 October, 1930: Manuel Ponce: *Folies d'Espagne - Thème, Variations et Fugue.* 7 October, 1930: Manuel Ponce: *Sonata No. 3 (lst Movement), Canción (2nd Movement), Postlude.*

Issued on 78 rpm, 10 inch recordings: HMV E-569, England: Joaquín Malats: *Serenata española,* Federico Moreno Torroba: *Nocturno.* HMV DA-1225, England: "S.L. Weiss" (M. Ponce): *Sarabande, Gavotte.*

Issued on 78 rpm, 12 inch recordings: HMV DB-1565, England: "S.L.Weiss"(M. Ponce): *Prelude and Allemande, Gigue.* HMV DB-1567, DB -1568, England -Vols 1 & 2: Manuel Ponce:*Folies d'Espagne.*

Miguel Llobet also pursued a successful career, making extended European tours, 1930-1931, with concerts in London, Berlin, Munich, Budapest, Vienna, Bologna, etc.

On 26 January, 1931, Llobet performed at the Sala dell'Instituto Musicale, Adria, Italy:[23]

Minuet - Estudio	Fernando Sor
Andante (from *Don Giovanni)*	Mozart
Prelude	J.S. Bach
Sueño	Francisco Tárrega
Echos du Paysage	Alfonso Broqua
Chanson de Léon	Rogelio Villar
Nocturno	Moreno Torroba
Torre Bermeja (transcr. Llobet)	Isaac Albéniz
Danza (transcr. Llobet)	Enrique Granados
Barcarola (transcr. Llobet)	Felix Mendelssohn
Chanson gitane (transcr. Llobet)	Manuel de Falla
Three Catalan Folk Songs - Jota	Miguel Llobet

In September, 1932, Segovia travelled with Manuel de Falla to Venice. There he met the Italian composer, Mario Castelnuovo-Tedesco (1895-1968), who would be inspired to write a number of substantial works for the guitar, including concertos and chamber music, as well as many solos.

Agustín Barrios Mangoré continued with recitals in Columbia, Panama, Costa Rica, El Salvador, Mexico, etc. He often assumed the *persona* of Nitsuga Mangoré (Nitsuga being Agustín spelled backwards), appearing on stage dressed as a Paraguayan Indian to entice larger audiences into the hall.

On 1 July, 1933, Barrios Mangoré performed at the National Theater, San Salvador:[24]

First Part:	1. *Serenata Morisca*	Barrios
	2. *Cueca*	Barrios
	3. *Vals No. 3*	Barrios
	4. *La Catedral*	Barrios
Second Part:	1. *Gavotte*	Bach
	2. *Minuet*	Beethoven
	3. *Mozart Variations*	Sor
	4. *Nocturne in E♭*	Chopin
Third Part:	1. *Granada*	Albéniz
	2. *Sonatina*	Tárrega
	3. *Un Sueño en la Floresta*	Barrios
	4. *Diana Guaraní*	Barrios

In 1933, the Austrian guitarist, Karl Scheit (1909-1993), was appointed as Professor of Guitar at the Vienna State Academy. Teaching posts in guitar were thus gradually increasing, bringing the instrument into line with traditional aspects of studies at leading conservatoires. Scheit ultimately became not only a well known teacher but also one of the most prolific editors of guitar music this century. His extended series with Universal Edition, Vienna, first appeared in 1940.

Scheit's editions would include *Quatre Pièces Brèves* (1933) by the Swiss composer, Frank Martin (1890-1974). Though originally written for Segovia, the atonal nature of these pieces ensured their neglect for many years. (The work eventually achieved renown following Bream's performances in the 1950's and his subsequent recording):[25]

Martin first explored serial technique himself in two of the four Quatre pièces brèves *for solo guitar, which he composed for Andrés Segovia in 1933 and almost immediately re-arranged in versions for both solo piano and orchestra under the title* Guitare. *Segovia never played the original version of the* Quatre pièces, *ostensibly because they were too difficult.*

118

In fact, it must be admitted that Martin made a serious miscalculation in attempting to experiment with serialism whilst writing for an instrument of which he must have had scant technical knowledge and which hardly seems suited to esoteric intellectualism. Guitare contains a few nods in the direction of Spain, but these sit uncomfortably in the predominantly atonal idiom of the two twelve-note pieces... In his orchestral arrangement... Martin attempted to rectify an incipient tonal dullness through inventive orchestration.[26]

Martin was clearly ahead of his time in terms of guitar composition, and would not be the last composer to experience Segovia's dislike of digressions from traditional tonality.

In 1931 Emilio Pujol published editions of Milán's *Pavanas*. Two years later he put the final touches to the first volumes of *Escuela Razonada de la Guitarra* (Rational School of the Guitar), subtitled 'based on the principles of Tárrega's technique.' For this pedagogic master work Pujol would receive a vivid endorsement from Manuel de Falla:

Since the distant times of Aguado, we lack a complete Method which would communicate to us the technical progress which Tárrega began. You have excellently provided this need, offering your own magnificent personal contribution, and thus of benefit not only to the performer but also to the composer of keen sensibility, who will find in your Method the stimulus to discover new instrumental possibilities.[27]

On 21 February, 1934, Pujol played a concert (in company with his wife, Matilde Cuervas), at the Sala Mozart, in Barcelona:[28]

I

Two Pavanes	Luys Milán (1535)
Gavota (favorite of the Duke of Monmouth)	Fr. Corbetta (1615)
Gallardas y Folias	Gaspar Sanz (1674)

II

Passepied (from a manuscript in the National Library, Paris)	Anon.
Gigue (for lute)	Weiss (1686 -1750)
Minuet	Sor
Preludes and Studies	Tárrega

III

Homenaje a Debussy	M. de Falla
Estudis Criollos	Alfonso Broqua
(first performance)	
Faula	Agustí Grau
(first performance)	
Els Tres Tambors (harmonized for guitar)	Emilio Pujol
(first performance)	
Guajira Gitana	Emilio Pujol

IV

Minuet (from Symphony in E flat)	Mozart
Therezinha de Jesus (Ciranda)	Villa-Lobos
Danza española	Albéniz
Danza de La Vida Breve	M. de Falla

Matilde Cuervas: Emilio Pujol

Also in 1934, Pujol travelled to England to perform one of six Quartets by Paganini for guitar and bowed instruments.[29]

On 3 April, 1934, in Florence, Segovia gave the first performance of Castelnuovo-Tedesco's *Variazioni Attraverso i Secoli* and Manuel Ponce's *Sonatina Meridional* (composed 1932). Segovia's request after this recital for Castelnuovo-Tedesco to write a four-movement work was responded to with the composition of *Sonata (Omaggio a Boccherini), Op. 77*, premiered in Paris in June, 1935.[30]

In July, 1934, in a limited edition of 1605 copies (each signed by the author), Domingo Prat's encyclopedic *Diccionario de Guitarristas*, was published by Romero y Fernández of Buenos Aires.

In a much celebrated recital in Paris, on 4 June, 1935, Segovia performed his transcription of J.S. Bach's *Chaconne* (from *Partita in D minor,* BWV 1004). As early as 1927, Segovia indicated that he was working 'deliriously' on the *Chaconne*.[31] The inclusion of this work in the repertory was to prove a significant advance, setting a mark by which those who aspired to fame could measure their prowess.

Just as the 1920's had changed the range of guitar publications so the steady accumulation of Segovia's editions continued in the 1930's:

Segovia editions published 1930-1935:

1930: J.S. Bach: *Siciliana* (from *Sonata in G minor,* BWV 1001), *Sarabande* (from *Partita in B minor,* BWV 1002).
Schubert: *Three Little Waltzes.*
Beethoven: *Minuetto,* (all publ. Union Musical Española, Madrid).
Ponce: *Preludes 1-6,* Schott, G.A. No.124, *Preludes 7 -12,* G.A. No. 125.
Turina: *Ráfaga,* G.A. No.128. Manén: *Fantasía-Sonata,* G.A. No.129.

1931: Sor: *Variations on a Theme of Mozart, Op. 9,* G.A. No. 130.
Ponce: *Estudio,* G.A. No. 131, *Variations on "Folia de España" and Fugue,* G.A. No. 135.
Moreno Torroba: *Pièces caractéristiques,* Vol. I, G.A. No. 133, *Pièces caractéristiques,* Vol. II, G.A. No. 134.
Mendelssohn: *Romanza sin Palabras, Op. 31, No.3,* Ricordi, Buenos Aires.

1932:   Turina: *Sonatina,* G.A. No.132.
         Castelnuovo-Tedesco: *Variations à travers les siècles,* G.A. No. 137.

1933:   Handel: *Air (Suite X).*
         Schumann: *Canción silvestre, Mayo, buen Mayo.*
         Grieg: *Canto del Campesino.*
         Haydn: *Minuetto.*
         Mendelssohn: *Romanza sin Palabras, Op. 19, No. 4,* (all UMP).

1934:   J.S. Bach: *Chaconne,* G.A. No. 141.

1935:   Haydn: *Minuet from G minor Quartet* (Hoboken III:75),G.A.No.139.
         Castelnuovo-Tedesco: *Sonata (Omaggio a Boccherini), Op. 77,* G.A. No. 149.
         Chopin: *Mazurka, Op. 63, No. 3,* G.A. No. 140.
         J.S.Bach: *Pieces from the Notebook of Anna Magdalena Bach,* G.A. No. 142.
         Kuhnau: *4 Petits Morceaux,* G.A. No. 143.
         Scarlatti: *Sonata in A minor,* G.A. No. 144.
         J.S. Bach: *Prelude and Fugue,* (BWV 998), G.A. No. 145.
         C.P.E. Bach: *La Xénophone, La Sybille,* G.A. No. 146.
         C.P.E. Bach: *Siciliana,* G.A. No. 147.
         Handel: *8 Aylesford Pieces,* G.A. No. 148.

On 6 December, 1935, news of a professorial appointment for Regino Sáinz de la Maza appeared in *Diario de Madrid*:

> *The Ministry of Public Instruction has just created a professorship of guitar at the Madrid Conservatoire, and Regino Sáinz de la Maza has been appointed. The name and prestige of one of our most eminent guitarists serves to justify this ministerial resolution. The Conservatoire acquires with Regino Sáinz de la Maza not only a professor of the highest instrumental quality, but also a musician whose youth gives promise of so many excellent things to come.*[32]

Regino Sáinz de la Maza (1896-1981) studied with Daniel Fortea, a pupil of Tárrega. His close friendship with Falla, Rodrigo, Lorca, and Dalí, establish his centrality in Spanish culture of this era. His reputation as composer, teacher and editor, has been steadily enhanced over the years since his death. On 8 May, 1936, he gave the following recital at the Teatro Español, Madrid:[33]

I

Sarabande, Minueto, Air, Gavotte	Handel
Andantino	Sor
Estudio	Tárrega
Variaciones y fuga sobre el tema de 'Las Folias de España'	M. Ponce

II

Fantasia	Mudarra
Prelude in D	Weiss
Chaconne	J.S. Bach

III

Elegía, homenaje para la tumba de Murnau	Gustavo Pittaluga
Bolero	E. Sáinz de la Maza
Rondeña	R. Sáinz de la Maza
Sevilla	Albéniz

47. Segovia and Hauser

With the outbreak of the Spanish Civil War in 1936, Segovia left Spain not to return for some sixteen years. In 1937 he acquired one of the world's finest guitars, constructed by Hermann Hauser I (1882-1952).

Hauser, the son of a musical instrument maker, made guitars and lutes from 1905 onwards. But during Miguel Llobet's tour of Germany (1913 - 1914), Hauser examined Llobet's Torres guitar of 1859. In so doing he saw the possibilities of the Torres traditions and began a process of intense research. By 1920 he had reached a number of conclusions and patented a design for a new type of guitar table.[34]

In 1924 Hauser was allowed to inspect Segovia's famous Manuel Ramírez/Santos Hernández guitar, a gift from the Ramírez workshop in 1912. From this time Hauser worked to create what Segovia would call 'the greatest guitar of our epoch'. By 1937 Hauser produced an instrument which Segovia was pleased to accept:[35]

Hauser guitars, following the Spanish influence, are divided into two categories: those that followed the Ramírez pattern and those in which he reverted, with subtle innovatory touches, to the basic Torres pattern. In his guitars based on Ramírez's one can see his influence in the choice of the head design, the wide lay-out of the struts and the dimensions. Hauser tried many combinations and shapes for his instruments, even after he had produced Segovia's 1937 guitar. In some of these guitars he introduced an amalgam of both makers using the rounded and more harmonious shape of the Manuel Ramírez instrument and the facets adapted from the Torres guitars, such as the head, scale length and decorations.[36]

Thus Hauser incorporated within his approach the finest elements of guitar design evolved in Spain and became one of the great influences on later generations of guitar makers.[37]

124

48. The Pre-War Years

The two years preceding the Second World War, with their profound disturbances and premonitions of utter disaster, were full of a remarkable creativity among composers for guitar. Several works written in those difficult months proved to be of lasting significance. In contrast, the saddest loss for the guitar was the death of Miguel Llobet from pleurisy on 22 February, 1938, at the relatively young age of fifty-nine.[38]

In 1938, Joaquín Rodrigo (1901-1999), composed his second piece for solo guitar, *En los Trigales*, (his first piece was *Zarabanda lejana*, 1926), to be dedicated, some years later, to Narciso Yepes.[39]

In the same year, Rodrigo and his wife, Victoria Kamhi, on their way back to Paris from northern Spain, stopped overnight at San Sebastián to dine with Regino Sáinz de la Maza. On this occasion the topic of a guitar concerto was first raised. Fascinated by the concept, though facing difficult personal circumstances, the composer began the task. His *Concierto de Aranjuez,* destined to become the world's most popular work for guitar and orchestra, was completed by the time Joaquín Rodrigo returned to Spain in September, 1939.[40]

On 2 May, 1938, Emilio Pujol performed at the Salle Erard in Paris, concentrating on 16th century music. He accompanied Madame Conchita Badia in various songs, and played vihuela solos by Milán, Narváez, Valderrábano and Mudarra.[41]

Prominent among younger guitarists was José Rey de la Torre (1917-1994). Of Cuban origin, he studied as a young boy with Llobet in Barcelona, where he gave a solo recital on 4 July, 1934.

Rey de la Torre eventually emigrated to the USA to become one of the esteemed post-war international recitalists and recording artists:

When Rey... began his career, the present worldwide popularity of the classical guitar, so easy to take for granted, was still many years away. The guitar was, as Rey wrote, 'practically unknown to musical audiences and largely ignored by the classical performers'. Beginning with a New York recital in 1938, for four decades Rey concertized all over North America, in most of Europe, parts of Latin America and the Middle East, and did much to bring the instrument the respect it enjoys today.[42]

In December, 1938, Segovia made his last visit to the Wigmore Hall, London for nine years, including in his recital a special tribute to the late, dearly beloved Miguel Llobet:

I

Aria con Variazioni	G. Frescobaldi
Menuet	J.P. Rameau
Andante	W.A. Mozart

II

Prelude and Mazurka	F. Chopin
Choro No. 1	H. Villa-Lobos
Three Pieces	E. Granados

III

Variations on Folia de España and Fugue	M.Ponce
Six Catalan Folk Songs	arr. M. Llobet
Capriccio Diabolico	M. Castelnuovo-Tedesco

In 1939, Schott published several new Segovia editions:

G.A. 151: Manuel Ponce: *Sonatina meridional*
G.A. 154: Isaac Albéniz: *Tango*
G.A. 155: Georg Benda: *2 Sonatinas*
G.A. 156: Louis Couperin: *Passacaglia*
G.A. 157: Girolamo Frescobaldi: *Aria con Variazioni detta 'La Frescobalda'*
G.A. 158: Girolamo Frescobaldi: *5 Pieces*
G.A. 159: Alonso Mudarra: *Romanesca*
G.A. 160: Jean-Philippe Rameau: *2 Minuetti*
G.A. 161: Christian Friedrich Schale: *2 Minuetti* (with J.F. Wenkel), *Musette*
G.A. 162: Johann Baptiste Vanhall: *Cantabile*
G.A. 163: Johann Baptiste Vanhall: *Minuetto*

In the summer of 1939, Mario Castelnuovo-Tedesco completed his new Guitar Concerto (premiered by Segovia in Montevideo, Uruguay, on 28 October of the same year).[43]

Following the Nazi invasion of Poland on 1 September, 1939, Britain, France, India, Australia and New Zealand declared war on Germany on 3 September, 1939. For a long while, concert activities, publications, and recordings would be subordinated to extraordinary circumstances. But significant developments of guitar history would still occur, in the immediate future, in Spain and South America.

49. The War Years, 1939-1945

During World War II, Segovia lived in Montevideo, Uruguay, though making frequent forays throughout neighboring countries to perform recitals and concertos. In 1940, Heitor Villa-Lobos visited Segovia's house with 'six *Preludes* for guitar.'[44]

The *Preludes* of Villa-Lobos (five in all, one was lost), would soon be renowned as some of the finest guitar music ever written. *Preludes Nos 3 & 4* were premiered by the Uruguayan guitarist, Abel Carlevaro (b.1918) on 11 December, 1943.[45]

On 9 November, 1940, Joaquín Rodrigo's *Concierto de Aranjuez* was premiered in Barcelona, (with subsequent performances in Bilbao and Madrid), the soloist being its dedicatee, Regino Sáinz de la Maza. The Spanish press greeted the work with enthusiasm and in Madrid the composer was carried through the streets of the old city on the shoulders of his admirers.[46]

Rodrigo's composition exploited the guitar's resources with an unprecedented intensity and complexity in an orchestral context. On a technical level the Concerto set fresh challenges while its interpretative demands always require refined artistry of a high order.

Segovia, meanwhile, continued his own personal challenge to the *Concierto de Aranjuez*. On 4 October, 1941, he premiered Ponce's *Concierto del Sur* in Montevideo (the composer conducting).[47] Armed with Guitar Concertos by Castelnuovo-Tedesco and Ponce, Segovia now advanced his cause with major orchestras, performing throughout South America and, later, the USA.[48]

On 22 March, 1944, Segovia gave a recital in San Salvador. This was his last chance to renew acquaintance with Agustín Barrios, who had suffered a major heart attack in 1939 and been ailing ever since. Barrios died a few months later on 7 August, 1944.[49]

On 16, 19 and 21 November, 1945, Segovia demonstrated the extent of his repertoire when he gave three recitals at the Palacio de Bellas Artes, Mexico City:[50]

PRIMER CONCIERTO

Aria 'La Frescobalda'	G. Frescobaldi
Preludio - Sarabande - Bourrée - Double	J.S. Bach
Allegretto grazioso	J. Haydn

Sonata (homenaje a Schubert que amaba la guitarra)	M. Ponce
Capriccio (omaggio a Paganini)	M.Castelnuovo-Tedesco

Mazurca	A. Tansman
Vidala	G. Crespo
Oriental - Torre Bermeja - Sevilla	I. Albéniz

SEGUNDO CONCIERTO

Siciliana - Preámbulo - Allemande - Alegramento	C.Ph.Em.Bach
Ballet - Sarabande - Gavotte - Gigue	S.L. Weiss

Tres Estudios	F. Sor
Variaciones sobre un Tema de Paisiello, y Rondo	F. Sor
Preludio, Canción y Danza	F. Moreno Torroba
Tarantella	M. Castelnuovo-Tedesco

Tema variado y Final	M. Ponce
La Maja de Goya - Danza en sol	E. Granados
Leyenda	I. Albéniz

ULTIMO CONCIERTO

Pavana y Galliard	Luis Milán
Aria variada	G. F. Handel
Preludio - Fuga - Gavotte y Musette	J. S. Bach

Largo assai y Allegretto	J. Haydn
Andante	W. A. Mozart
Minuetto	F. Schubert
Canzonetta	Mendelssohn

Mazurca	M.Ponce
Fantasía	Turina
Mallorca -Granada	Albéniz

130

50. Publications after 1945

Pujol's monumental transcription of the entirety of Narváez's *Los seys libros del Delphin* was published in 1945, followed by similar editions of the music of Alonso Mudarra (1949), and Enríquez de Valderrábano (1965). These publications heralded a great advance in accessibility to the history of the vihuela and another landmark in guitar scholarship.[51]

In 1945, Segovia's *Twenty Studies for the Guitar by Fernando Sor* appeared.This featured studies considered of value both musically and technically, attempting to achieve 'the right balance between the pedagogical purpose and the natural musical beauty.' For generations of recitalists and students this would be a most influential text.[52]

A far-reaching event of guitar history was the founding of *The Guitar Review* (1946) by New York enthusiasts, their intention being to reclaim 'the classic guitar from obscurity and disparagement, so that it may regain its full measure of dignity in the musical world.'[53] The guitar now possessed a formidable periodical through which to express the vitality and aspirations of its players.

The Guitar Review remained closely linked with the promotion of Segovia's vision of music. To counterpoint this further a Segovia Society was formed in Washington D.C., later in the same year, under its secretary, Sophocles Papas. This Society sought 'to widen the circle of those who appreciate the guitar as a serious instrument and a vehicle of the finest music'. To this end a quarterly bulletin was published and assistance given in the promotion of concerts, recordings and publications.[54]

In 1947, excerpts of Segovia's autobiography, *La Guitarra y Yo* were published in Spanish and English in the fourth issue of *The Guitar Review.*[55] The opening episodes (slightly different from those in the autobiography published in book form in 1976), concentrated primarily on Segovia's acquisition of musical knowledge and his early guitar repertoire.

51. Nylon Strings

In 1946, Vladimir Bobri introduced Segovia to Albert Augustine (1900-1967), a guitar-maker of Danish origin, who had emigrated to the United States in the mid-1920's.[56] Before the 1940's, guitarists traditionally used gut treble strings (despite problems of intonation, constant breakages and other difficulties associated with the use of gut), with metal-wound spun silk strings for the bass.

But in the 1940's experiments were made with nylon guitar strings. According to Alexander Bellow these were first tried on stage by Olga Coelho in New York in January, 1944.[57]

In 1946, Segovia asked Augustine to research the development of nylon strings, and the product was eventually copyrighted in 1947.[58] The new kind of string certainly enabled recitalists to have a less anxious life and, in the long run, helped the classic guitar to attain greater popularity than ever before as an inexpensive instrument easy to tune and maintain.

52. The Death of Manuel Ponce

Manuel Ponce, Mexico's foremost composer, died on 24 April, 1948.

Segovia's epitaph evaluated Ponce's contribution:

He lifted the guitar from the low artistic state in which it had lain. Along with Turina, Falla, Manén, Castelnuovo-Tedesco, Tansman,Villa-Lobos, Torroba, etc., but with a more abundant yield than all of them put together, he undertook the crusade full of eagerness to liberate the beautiful prisoner. Thanks to him — as to the others I have named — the guitar was saved from the music written exclusively by guitarists.[59]

Thus, within a few years, several personalities of major importance in contemporary guitar history - Llobet, Barrios, Falla, and now Ponce - had passed on. In his mid-fifties Segovia began to assume a symbolic significance as a representative of the earlier 20th century tradition.

He also continued to achieve a number of distinguished firsts. *The Gramophone,* in June, 1948, announced that Segovia had recorded an all-Bach album for Musicraft, including the *Chaconne.* This was followed by Segovia's debut at the prestigious Edinburgh International Festival, Scotland, with three recitals on 7, 8, and 10 September.

In 1949 he recorded Castelnuovo-Tedesco's *Guitar Concerto No. 1 in D major, Op. 99,* and a number of solos, once again extending the discographical horizons of the guitar.[60]

During the 1940's Segovia had manoeuvred his career into (what was for a guitarist), unprecedented levels of fame and esteem. In the meantime a new generation of recitalists prepared the ground for their own success.

53. Ida Presti

At the end of the war interest was focused on Ida Presti (1924-1967), the prodigiously talented guitarist from France:

Ida Presti was born at Suresnes (just outside Paris) in 1924, and her first introduction to the Spanish guitar was when her father used to play the instrument to induce his little infant daughter to go to sleep. At a very early age her father commenced to give her lessons, and before she had reached the age of six her playing on the concert platforms of Paris was causing music critics to hail her as the "Female Mozart."

While still only thirteen she was made Membre d'Honneur of "Les Amis de la Guitare" and ranked with the most celebrated guitarists. On February 13th, 1938, she was accorded the honor of being the first player of the guitar to be invited to appear before the Société des Concerts du Conservatoire de Paris. The Conservatoire was founded in 1828 and never before had a guitarist appeared in Paris who was considered worthy of playing before this austere gathering of renowned virtuosi — and most of the world's famous guitarists have visited Paris. In 1937 she recorded eight sides for the French H.M.V. label which proved that the young Ida Presti was an outstanding performer on the Spanish guitar and that the Press notices eulogizing her talents were not influenced by her sex or youth. For three years prior to the outbreak of the war she was heard regularly broadcasting from the Paris P.T.T. station, and in 1938 took the leading part in a French film.[61]

After the war, news of Ida Presti's abilities soon circulated. As well as her many solo recitals she appeared with various orchestras in performances of Rodrigo's *Concierto de Aranjuez:*

> *The* Concierto de Aranjuez *was broadcast from France on September 16 last [1948], with Ida Presti and the French National Radio Orchestra. Those of us who heard this broadcast will never forget the thrill of that superb music so brilliantly played. It was a studio performance, but the music lovers of Paris heard Ida Presti repeat her performance on March 24 at the Salle Pleyel, with the Orchestre des Jeunes Universitaires.[62]*

On 1 December, 1951, Presti made her London debut at the R.B.A. Galleries:

> *Ida Presti's program included works of early composers and the more usual compositions of Pujol, Villa-Lobos, Llobet, Tárrega, etc. From her first number it was obvious that here was a soloist of outstanding skill, possessing complete co-ordination of both hands...Her perfect sense of rhythm showed to best advantage in the Spanish pieces, while her wide range of tone colors gave a beauty hitherto unknown to familiar pieces.[63]*

Despite this enthusiastic critical reception, Presti's career changed. After her marriage to Alexandre Lagoya (1929-1999) in 1952, she relinquished the solo recital to concentrate on the Presti-Lagoya Duo, which achieved international acclaim for a musical partnership unique in guitar history.

54. Narciso Yepes

Narciso Yepes (1927-1997), from Lorca, Spain, made his debut in Madrid with Rodrigo's *Concierto de Aranjuez* on 16 December, 1947.[64] Yepes's performances of this work would play a major part in the establishment of his international reputation:

> *Earlier in March - on the 2nd [1949] - a special two-hour program of Spanish music was broadcast by the Swiss Radio. It included orchestral works by Falla, Turina and other Spaniards as well as the "Concierto de Aranjuez" by Rodrigo. The guitarist was Narciso García Yepes and the Orchestre de la Suisse Romande was conducted by Ataulfo Argenta, director of the National Orchestra of Madrid.*

> *A friend, now living in Switzerland, wrote of this broadcast: "Not since Segovia's visit to England have I heard such a masterly performance as the Rodrigo Concerto played by Narciso Yepes. He is in the very first rank. He interpreted this ultra Spanish music with a fiery musicality I have seldom heard equalled. His technique is so effortless that one does not notice it, his tone mellow and crystal clear. He made us live the very spirit of this remarkable modern work. The Adagio movement was particularly beautiful, full of restrained and dignified feeling, and the last movement was playfully sparkling. Altogether a remarkable performance by a remarkable young man." [65]*

On 26 February, 1952, Narciso Yepes gave a recital at the Spanish Institute, Eaton Square, London, before a specially invited audience:

> *In the tapestry lined drawing room, packed to capacity by an enthusiastic audience which overflowed to the landings and staircase, Señor Yepes's program ranged from solos by Bach to modern numbers by Granados and Albéniz. His delicate tone and almost faultless technique were heard to the best advantage in Falla's "Farruca" and Albéniz's "Malagueña," although the impression persisted that Señor Yepes was a little overawed by the occasion with a detrimental effect to his playing.[66]*

In the same year Narciso Yepes's sound track for the French film *Jeux Interdits* (Forbidden Games) achieved a high profile. Yepes played *Romance de Amor,* and a number of other pieces including a dance by Robert de Visée and a Catalan Folk Song.

Narciso Yepes's historic recording of Rodrigo's *Concierto de Aranjuez* nowadays still acclaimed as one of the finest interpretations, was favorably reviewed by *The Gramophone* in March, 1955:[67]

> ...*I must tell you that Rodrigo's Guitar Concerto is a charmer. The outside movements are witty, especially in the orchestra, and the middle movement is most evocative. The problem of balance between orchestra and guitar is brilliantly solved.*[68]

Yepes continued his upward climb, with a South American tour (1957), a debut in Japan (1960), and a first appearance in the USA in 1964.

From 1963, Narciso Yepes performed on a Ramírez ten-string guitar, the first 20th century leading recitalist to depart from traditional concepts about the kind of instrument most suitable for concerts.[69]

55. Julian Bream

On 17 February, 1947, the English guitarist, Julian Bream (b. 1933), made his debut, aged thirteen, with this program, at the Cheltenham Art Gallery:

Romanza	Schumann, arr. Tárrega
Prelude and Minuet	Bach, arr. Segovia
Tonadilla	Granados, arr. Llobet
Chanson	Ernest Shand
Sonata	Paganini
Concert Study	Napoléon Coste
Granada	Albéniz, arr. Tárrega
Theme and Variations	Ferdinand Sor
Sonata in A	Terry Usher

When in December, 1947, Segovia made his first British concert tour for ten years, Bream attended the London recital and years later described the experience:

> *I was simply riveted by his playing. I had never heard such beautiful articulation, such a wealth of tone color, and such wonderful integral interpretation. His technique really is formidable... I think the most remarkable thing on hearing Segovia would be the effect of the sound that he produces and the effect of that sound upon one's sensibilities. It is very clear, it is very fine, and, if one may use the word, aristocratic.*[70]

On 8 December, 1947, the Philharmonic Society of Guitarists provided a reception for Segovia at the Alliance Hall, London:

> *After the interval, Julian Bream played at Segovia's request. His solos received great applause and Segovia declared that in Julian we have a young guitarist of great promise.*[71]

In 1948, Julian Bream played guitar for the sound track of the film, *Saraband for Dead Lovers* (starring Stewart Granger and Joan Greenwood). Nowadays, engaging a fourteen year old to perform for a film may seem improbable. But Bream's playing throughout remained mature and expressive. The young artist was already firmly established in the media, the BBC making frequent calls on him for broadcasts.

Three years later, on 26 November, 1951, Julian Bream, eighteen years old, gave his first recital at the Wigmore Hall, London:

Six Pieces from Thesaurus Harmonicus	Besard
Fantasia - My Lady Hunsdon's Puffe	Dowland
Air -Rondeau	Purcell
Hornpipe-Fantasia	Weiss
Suite No. 3 for Lute	J.S. Bach

Interval

Andantino-Prelude-Andante	F. Sor
Alba - Melodía	Moreno Torroba
Granada	Albéniz
Choros No. 1	H. Villa-Lobos

In 1955, Julian Bream, eminent lutenist as well as guitarist, saw the issue of his first long playing record, *An Anthology of English Song,* with Peter Pears (tenor), followed in 1956 by the solo guitar albums, *Sor, Turina, Falla* (Westminster XWN 18135), and *Villa-Lobos and Torroba* (Westminster XWN 18137). This was the beginning of a remarkable recording career extending over the next forty years.

56. Segovia's Activities, 1950-1956

In 1950, Mario Castelnuovo-Tedesco composed his *Quintetto, Op.143,* for guitar and string quartet and *Fantasia, Op. 145,* for guitar and piano. Very little contemporary chamber music for guitar and strings was available and the composer was 'expanding the accepted notions of the guitar's idiomatic resources.'[72]

In the summer of 1950, Segovia was at Siena, Italy, where, in August, he began a new venture, teaching at the Summer School of L'Accademia Musicale Chigiana. Here for the first time the younger generation was able to study with him. The prospects were further enriched when in December a competition for new guitar music was organized by the Accademia.[73]

Meanwhile, a new age of recording technology was developing with the advent of the long-playing record. By 1952 *The Guitar Review* could advertise 'Long Playing 33⅓ rpm GUITAR RECORDINGS featuring the finest music ever recorded by world-famous concert guitarists,' with albums by Rey de la Torre, Felix Argüelles, Carlos Montoya, Vicente Gómez, Julio Martínez Oyanguren and five LP's by Segovia.[74]

In June, 1952, after an absence of some sixteen years, Segovia returned to Spain to play in the Festival of Music and Dance in Granada. From now on Segovia played occasional concerts at selected venues in Spain, mainly for charity, but did not undertake extended tours of the Iberian peninsula.

Also in 1952, back in New York, Segovia wrote a Preface for the edition of Villa-Lobos's *Douze Études.* Though composed in 1929, it was only in the 1950's that these pieces were published. Segovia described the studies as consisting of 'formulas of surprising efficiency for the technical development of each hand', which have, at the same time, 'a disinterested musical beauty.'[75]

Villa-Lobos completed his *Concerto for Guitar* by 1951, but the work was not premiered until 1956 for a number of reasons:

After Villa-Lobos's long association with Segovia, it is not surprising that the Spaniard eventually commissioned a concerto. Villa-Lobos responded in 1951 with a Fantasía concertante, *which disappointed the guitarist because it contained no cadenza. Segovia refused to play the work for several years, his agitation coming to a head when he heard Villa-Lobos's* Harp Concerto, *complete with cadenza.*

Villa-Lobos was persuaded that he had no option but to provide a cadenza (a separate unit between second and third movements), and re-title his work 'Concerto'. The delighted Segovia gave the work's premiere on 6 February, 1956, in Houston under the baton of the composer.[76]

In 1954, Joaquín Rodrigo, wrote *Fantasía para un Gentilhombre (Fantasia for a Gentleman)*. This full-length work for guitar and orchestra, dedicated to Segovia, is based on themes from Gaspar Sanz.[77] This Concerto's premiere came with Segovia's celebration of the 30th anniversary of his debut recital in the United States (8 January,1928).

Victoria Kamhi de Rodrigo described the occasion:

We left for San Francisco the 27th of February, 1958, and on the 6th, 7th and 8th of March, Segovia presented the Fantasía para un Gentilhombre *in the great Opera House of that city... the success was complete, unanimous, enthusiastic. In all three of the successive concerts, the audience who filled the hall applauded the soloist and the composer with fervor... Several weeks later Segovia recorded the* Fantasía para un Gentilhombre *in New York, with the Orchestra of the Air, under the direction of Jordá.*

From then on, the work began its worldwide career, versions multiplied, and it can now be said to compete with the Concierto de Aranjuez *whose fame has not diminished in all these years.*[78]

57. Developments and Compositions, 1956 - 1959

In 1956, the English composer, Reginald Smith Brindle (b. 1917), wrote
El Polifemo de Oro, four fragments inspired by 'García Lorca's poetic
references to the guitar'. In *Adivinanza de la Guitarra* (Enigma of the
Guitar), the instrument is compared to Polyphemus, the Cyclops, with his
single eye. Smith Brindle commented:

> *Lorca attributes to the guitar occult powers, and returns again and again
> in his poems to the image of its strings spread out like the arms of
> Polyphemus, or the "great star" of a tarantula's web, waiting to trap our
> sighing souls within its "black wooden cistern."*

> *This mystic power of the instrument has always cast a spell over me. It
> seems to possess a life of its own, a supernatural incantatory spirit, which
> defies expression in words.*

> *I have searched to express this elusive spirit in* El Polifemo, *through the
> intangible, fleeting sounds of the first movement, the whirling, intertwining,
> softly dissonant harmonies of the second, the supernatural harmonics and
> tamburo effects of the third, and the ruthless vivaciousness of the finale.* [79]

Despite this Spanish inspiration, the work was well removed in mood,
texture and technique from traditional Iberian guitar music. Julian Bream
premiered the piece in April, 1958, and the composition soon achieved the
status of a classic.

In 1957 *A Bach Recital for the Guitar* (Westminster XWN 18428) by
Julian Bream was issued, the program including the mighty *Chaconne* (from
Partita II in D minor, BWV 1004), *Prelude and Fugue* (from the *Suite in C
minor,* BWV 997) and *Prelude, Fugue and Allegro* (BWV 998). Bream's
recording of the *Chaconne* was a clear signal that the younger generation
had discovered a musical identity strong enough to challenge Segovia on
his own territory.

Moreover, Bream, by concentrating on fewer composers within a record program was subtly changing the accepted format of a guitar album. *The Gramophone* welcomed this:

Julian Bream uses a wide range of tone-color, a superlative technique, and a good sense of 18th century style to present an all-Bach program — a welcome departure from the 37 short pieces chosen from five centuries that so often seem to make up the guitar's LP.[80]

A few months later, Julian Bream, at the age of twenty-four, indicated his own concepts of Segovia's influence:

It is often thought that I was a pupil of Segovia. Even after hearing my playing people have remarked to the effect that they can hear that I was a Segovia pupil! I am sure that Segovia would be the first to state that I was never his pupil for, although I had several 'sessions' with the great Maestro between 1947 and 1950 during which he made general observations on my technique and fingering, I never actually studied with him. All he said then has been of invaluable assistance to me in my pursuit of the guitar. In fact, by and large, I have evolved my own technique. With my right hand I employ a different stroke to that of Segovia, for whereas he habitually plucks the string with the right hand fingers at right angles to the strings, I tend to use a less rigid position for reasons of tonal variety.[81]

Bream also expressed further critical observations:

It has often struck me that guitarists limit musical potential by being too concerned with the instrument and not enough concerned with the expression from it. Whilst I am obviously a firm advocate for the guitar and a great lover of the instrument, my ultimate aim is to project music by using the guitar as just another vehicle for musical expression, the one which I happened to develop in much the same way as a conductor 'takes up' conducting.

At times I feel exasperated with the instrument, especially its seeming lack of sustained sound and rather insignificant repertoire. But no sooner than that mood has arrived, in the next breath I find something which is completely beautiful and captivating. The only way in which the guitar, now lifted to a hitherto unknown point of respectability, can maintain its position in the realm of serious music, is for it to be cultivated by enthusiasts who make a thoroughly musical, as well as practical, approach to its technique and possibilities...[81]

Bream believed the repertoire to be 'rather insignificant.' Throughout his career he has endeavored to correct this and establish a truly contemporary repertoire for the guitar.

Already eminent composers were exploring guitar sonorities on their own terms. The French composer, Darius Milhaud, completed a piece on 26 November,1957, entitled *Segoviana, Op. 366.*[82] In the same year the Austrian composer (and proponent of Schoenberg's serial techniques), Ernst Krenek, composed his one and only solo guitar work, *Suite, Op. 164:*

The Suite *for guitar consists of five miniature movements in the twelve-tone style. Each movement except the third utilizes the row - C Bb B F Eb E D C# F# Ab G A - in its original form. In the third movement the row is inverted. Compositional devices such as tone clusters of major and minor seconds, grace note attacks, and motivic brevity are carefully woven into the twelve-tone fabric of each movement, creating a unified textural foundation throughout the entire work.* [83]

Krenek's *Suite* never became popular among recitalists but the composer's use of guitar timbres continued in various ensemble works.[84]

In 1955, Maurice Ohana (1914-1992), born in French Morocco of Spanish parents, composed *Tiento,* a work of Spanish allegiance set in a modern idiom. It opens with a statement of *La Folía,* leading into the habanera rhythm, the melodic line being nostalgically reminiscent of Falla's *Homenaje,*

Pour le Tombeau de Debussy. A third section hints at a theme from Falla's Harpsichord Concerto. These ideas are skilfully woven together and the work ends on a dominant pedal point with an insistent drum-like beat.[85]

Two years later, Ohana completed *Tres Gráficos (Three Designs)* for guitar and orchestra:

> *The personal voice of Ohana makes itself heard in a world so steeped in tradition, 'folklore' and the same natural kind of sound as that of the guitar. Whereas in* Tiento *for solo guitar he goes deeply into the values of* jondo *music (Andalusian popular song), in the* Tres Gráficos, *to the introspection of the popular* Farruca, Siguirya, Bulería *or* Tiento, *there is added the profile and perspective of an orchestra which creates a space dimension in which the guitar performs its difficult task. A dimension which in turn is suggested by the guitar part with its interval characteristics (including microtones), its harmonic, rhythmic and tonal attributes. We have here a southern Spain experienced from afar - lyrical, serious and brusque in its fundamental Andalusianism; geometrical and exact at times, misty and vague on occasion: sweltering in noonday heat of the sun and hidden in the darkness of the night, alternately.*[86]

Ohana also wrote a seven movement suite, *Si le jour paraît...* (1963), for the ten-string guitar, a work so far neglected because of the comparative rarity of players of that instrument.

In 1959, Goffredo Petrassi (b. 1904), the eminent Italian composer, wrote *Suoni Notturni*:

> Suoni Notturni *(1959) was Petrassi's first work for guitar, and it more than lives up to the nocturnal imagery conveyed by its title...A successful performance must include an exact reading of the colors and dynamics, for in this music gesture and contrast are the materials from which meaning is derived.*[87]

145

Ernesto Bitetti, who recorded *Suoni Notturni* in the 1970's, described the piece as 'a series of tonal and environmental discoveries that give the work an original quality of shadowed mystery'. Yet despite its tonal possibilities, the composition made little appeal to recitalists when published in 1961.[87] It seemed indeed (in terms of the guitar), to be written ahead of its time, some of its effects and moods anticipating Benjamin Britten's *Nocturnal after John Dowland, Op. 70.*

58. The Guitars of Hermann Hauser II

Hermann Hauser II (1911-1988), created between five and six hundred guitars in his lifetime, many played by leading recitalists such as Segovia, Bream, the Romeros, etc. He followed closely the traditions of his father, first at their workshop in Munich but later moving to Reisbach an der Vils, Bavaria. He experimented with different sizes of guitar, including a special Ramírez model with a bigger body than that made by Hauser I. He also tried to discover the effects of varying the position of the struts.

Hauser II sustained head injuries during the war and for the rest of his life was affected by this, eventually succumbing to serious illness. But over the years he communicated to his son, Hauser III, the essential concepts of the family art of guitar making.

One of his finest guitars, made in 1957, can be heard on *The Art of Julian Bream* (RCA RB 16239, issued 1960), where Bream plays music by Frescobaldi, Mateo Albéniz, Scarlatti, Cimarosa, Berkeley, Rodrigo, Ravel, and Roussel. (A picture of this guitar is on the original record cover. Julian Bream played the instrument between 1959 and 1963.)[88]

59. John Williams

In 1958, Segovia returned to Siena to teach. That year, John Williams was invited to present a recital at the Summer School on 10 September, a unique honor for a student. With the passing of the years, Segovia yearned for the continuation of guitar performance at the technical and spiritual levels which he had demonstrated himself. Meanwhile a new generation was emerging and it seemed likely that the torch would be carried forward by the players nurtured in the Academy at Siena.

Older players such as María Luisa Anido (b.1907), Karl Scheit (b.1909), Luise Walker (b.1910), Laurindo Almeida (b.1917), José Rey de la Torre (b.1917) and Abel Carlevaro (b.1918), achieved distinguished international careers. Guitarists born in the 1920's included such eminent figures as Alirio Diaz (b.1923), Ida Presti (b.1924), Narciso Yepes (b.1927), and Alexandre Lagoya (b.1929).

But Segovia was urgently aware of the need for younger players. Among the many gifted students who would visit Siena, John Williams (b. 1941) immediately emerged as the most promising:

In November, 1952, Segovia came to London and John played for him at his hotel, probably the most important performance of his life. With Segovia, a most difficult man to impress, reaction was immediate — 'He

must go to the Summer School at Siena; I shall recommend him.'...It is a measure of his regard for John Williams's talent in that he arranged for him to attend the Siena Academy during August and September 1953, with a scholarship providing free tuition and board... Before leaving London, Segovia gave much of his time to John, taking him through the famous book of twenty Sor-Segovia studies and giving guidance. Finally he left John to work on the Sor book and on his own scale-fingering system which he had written down for him, until such time as they should meet again at Siena.[89]

John Williams's debut at the Wigmore Hall, London, took place on 6 November, 1958, his program revealing Segovia's influence:

Gallardas	Sanz
Gavotte	A.Scarlatti
Suite in A minor	Weiss
Prelude, Allemande, Bourrée	J. S. Bach (arr. Duarte)
Variations on a Theme by Mozart, Op. 9	Sor
Sonatina	Moreno Torroba
Mazurka	Tansman
Tonadilla (La Maja de Goya)	Granados

But even at this early stage in Williams's development it was evident that the young artist did not copy Segovia in any stylistic or interpretative approaches. When John Williams recorded two debut albums in December 1958, Terry Usher commented:

In Suite No. 3 in C *(J. S. Bach, transcribed for guitar by Duarte), John Williams still shows the influence of Segovia, who did so much to help him reach his present place as one of the few great players in the world, but he will quickly grow out of that influence and become himself alone, that is clear: an artist in his own right. Indeed, it is now but rarely any echo of Segovia is heard in his playing ...John Williams makes no attempt to copy the Segovia interpretation and if we cannot have fresh fields and pastures new from our young recording artists of the guitar, at least it is good to hear so fine an interpretation that is not a copy of anyone else's.[90]*

60. The Golden Year, 1959

In 1959, Segovia not only celebrated the Golden Jubilee of his 1909 debut in Granada but also enjoyed one of the most successful years of his career, with 120 recitals and the release of new recordings. At the age of sixty-six, the momentum of his artistic life continued to increase rather than diminish. The *Segovia Golden Jubilee* album which appeared early in 1959 (Brunswick AXTL 1088/1089/1090) represented, at the time, the most comprehensive set of long-playing guitar recordings ever issued, covering the range of Segovia's music, including concertos.[91]

In the summer of 1959, the first International Course was held at Santiago de Compostela, Spain, and Segovia went there instead of Siena. It was to prove the beginning of another pedagogic tradition with long lasting memories for those who attended over the years.

61. Julian Bream, 1959-1964

While Segovia enjoyed the glory of his Jubilee year, far-reaching events occurred elsewhere. In 1959 Julian Bream signed a contract with the RCA record company and embarked on his second USA/Canada tour (September to November), visiting Washington, D.C., Chicago, Berkeley (California), Toronto, and New York.[92]

Audiences now had a point of comparison between Segovia and the younger generation of artists. Interesting differences in repertoire, philosophy, tone color and technique, could be observed.

In 1960, Julian Bream's first RCA recording, *The Art of Julian Bream,* was issued. This included respectful gestures towards Segoviana with *Aria detta La Frescobalda* (Frescobaldi, arr. Segovia), *Sonata in E minor,* K.11

(Scarlatti, arr. Segovia), and *Segovia, Op. 29* (Roussel). Bream's own characteristic identity as performer and arranger was powerfully evident in *Sonata in E minor,* K.87 (Scarlatti, arr. Bream), *Two Sonatas* (Cimarosa, arr. Bream), *Pavane pour une Infante défunte* (Ravel, arr. Bream), and *Sonatina, Op. 51* (Lennox Berkeley, ed. Bream). In the following year came Bream's recording of Malcolm Arnold's *Guitar Concerto, Op. 67* (in company with Giuliani's *Concerto for Guitar and Strings*).

RCA also catered admirably for the other side of Bream's interests with a solo lute record, *The Golden Age of English Lute Music* (released 1961). In 1964, RCA issued *An Evening of Elizabethan Music* by the Julian Bream Consort.[93] Bream founded the Consort to perform Elizabethan ensemble music of Dowland, Morley, Johnson, Byrd, etc:

The close affinity of the Consort *to the early Elizabethan stage drama may well have been instrumental in nourishing the seed which was later to blossom forth as the highly exotic and finely balanced* broken Consort *- a singularly English phenomenon - containing three plucked instruments (two strung with wire, the other with gut), two bowed instruments and one blown. The* broken Consort *could fairly claim to be the origin of the modern orchestra, its highly developed and specialized instrumental character (allowing little tolerance for alternative instrumentation) was, without doubt, a unique achievement in the field of secular music.*

Perhaps the most outstanding feature of the ensemble, was its functional use within the framework of Elizabethan life. For example, its sound could frequently be heard at civic functions, at weddings, feasts, maskes, and in the theater. It also provided music for dancing, was an ideal accompaniment to the singing voice, and not least offered ample sustenance for the connoisseur.[94]

62. José Ramírez III

Many guitar makers naturally wished to place their best instruments in Segovia's hands for his recitals. Foremost among these was the Spanish luthier from the Ramírez dynasty of makers, José Ramírez III (1922-1995), whose great uncle, Manuel Ramírez, provided Segovia with his first concert guitar in 1912.

José Ramírez III had been apprenticed at his father's workshop in 1949 and embarked on research into the guitar's acoustic properties:

He studied the application of the Golden Section, the reflections of sound waves on elliptical bodies, the use of woods that were different from those previously employed for the guitar, such as red cedar (Thuja plicata), *the crystallization of different types of varnishes... the behavior of the sideboards in percussion instruments and resonance boxes, the vibration of masses, string length with respect to box volume...*[95]

One ambition was fulfilled when Segovia put aside his ageing Hauser guitar of 1937 to advocate the cause of Ramírez:

[José Ramírez III] used to be very upset by the fact that since 1937, Maestro Segovia had continued using a German guitar, but, in 1960, he finally succeeded in having him play one of his guitars, and from that date on, until his death, the Maestro used his guitars almost constantly at all his concerts.[96]

Following Segovia's acceptance of these instruments, the best Ramírez guitars were sought after by many leading recitalists, the red cedar soundboard being a characteristic feature. Through innovative means of standardized production and apprenticing promising young luthiers in the first stages of their career, such as Paulino Bernabe (b.1932), and Manuel Contreras (1926-1994), the Ramírez workshop could claim to have produced more than 20,000 concert guitars over the years.[97]

63. Alirio Diaz

On 22 October, 1960, the Venezuelan guitarist, Alirio Diaz, performed at the Wigmore Hall, London:

...the soloist came to grips with what is probably the supreme test in the whole gamut of guitar music: Segovia's transcription of the Chaconne from Bach's D minor Sonata for Unaccompanied Violin. The punishing demands were met with a technique of staggering power and sureness, coupled with the breadth, fullness and flexibility of tone that are the hallmarks of true disciples of Segovia technique... The successful appearance of this great artist, with its promise of repetition, now adds another event to the London guitarists' calendar and a compulsive one too.[98]

Thus Alirio Diaz (b. 1923), now in his late thirties, achieved fame as a mature artist. Though he had studied with Segovia, Diaz's clean, well articulated playing, free from rhythmic exaggeration, was very much in line with contemporary concepts of interpreting music. He was, moreover, the foremost advocate of the compositions of his fellow countryman, Antonio Lauro (1917-1986).

In 1961, Diaz was the dedicatee of Joaquín Rodrigo's *Invocation et Danse (Hommage à Manuel de Falla),* which was awarded first prize in the Coupe Internationale de Guitare, 1961, organized by Radio Télévision Française. This virtuosic work, though recorded by Alirio Diaz (issued 1964), was hardly performed until Julian Bream brought it into his repertoire in 1983. Since then *Invocation et Danse* has been much played.[99]

152

64. New Horizons for Segovia, 1961-1964

In 1961, Segovia's recording of Boccherini's *Concerto for Guitar and Orchestra in E major* coupled with J.S. Bach's *Suite No. 3 in C major for Cello,* BWV1009 (arr. Duarte), was released, the only time Segovia recorded a Bach suite in its entirety.[100]

In October, 1961, Segovia began his first visit to Australia. The schedule at the outset planned concerts in Melbourne, Perth, Adelaide, Hobart, Sydney, and Brisbane. Contrary to expectations, all seats for the concerts were quickly sold out and extra recitals arranged.

On 23 August, 1962, Segovia married for the third time, his bride being Emilia Corral. The daughter of an amateur guitarist, Madame Segovia had begun to play the guitar when she was five years old, studying with José María de la Fuente, a teacher in Madrid, and later with Emilio Pujol. For a wedding present, John W. Duarte dedicated his *English Suite, Op. 31,* 'To Andrés Segovia and his wife on the occasion of their marriage.' (As a result, when Segovia later recorded the work, Duarte became the only English composer since Purcell to be recorded by Segovia.)

On 18 March, 1963, following his seventieth birthday, Segovia performed for the Cabinet of the President of the United States under the honorary chairperson, Mrs. John F. Kennedy, in the State Department Auditorium.

An appreciation of Segovia printed in the program concluded:

By the devotion of a lifetime Andrés Segovia has restored the guitar to its high and proper place as a member of the family of stringed instruments.[101]

Also in 1963 Segovia's edition of Joaquín Rodrigo's *Tres piezas españolas* (composed 1954) was published. His work of extending the repertory was now nearly complete. Rodrigo's *Fantasía para un Gentilhombre* (publ.1964), would be among the last Segovia editions.

65. The Guitars of Bouchet and Rubio

Robert Bouchet (1898-1986) began to play the guitar as a hobby in 1932, acquiring an instrument from the luthier, Julián Gómez Ramírez in Paris, whose shop he frequently visited. Years later Bouchet decided to make a guitar for himself:

> *Bouchet's first guitar was based on a Torres guitar and his fourth one, a flamenco guitar, was intended to be a replica of a Torres guitar made in cypress wood. Bouchet made his first guitar in 1946 and a few years later he had the opportunity of restoring two very interesting Torres guitars which he subsequently used as models for his own guitars.*[102]

Players became eager to acquire one of his guitars and the recordings of Presti and Lagoya demonstrate the greatness of his finest instruments. Bouchet guitars (of 1957 and 1962) can also be heard on Bream's *Popular Classics for Spanish Guitar* (RCA RB 6593, issued 1964). Other owners of Bouchet guitars include Emilio Pujol, Oscar Ghiglia, Turibio Santos, and Manuel López Ramos.

The English luthier, David Rubio (1934-2000), originally planned a career in medicine but instead studied flamenco in Spain. Becoming interested in guitar making, he observed Spanish luthiers at work. In 1961 he decided to live for a while in New York, setting up his first guitar workshop there in 1963. Julian Bream took a Bouchet guitar for him to repair and suggested that he should copy the instrument. The results were successful and Bream and Rubio became friends.

After several years in New York, Rubio returned to England, living first in Wiltshire and occupying a workshop at Bream's house. In a short time Rubio established a reputation as one of the great luthiers, making several guitars and lutes for Bream.[103] In 1969 David Rubio took up residence in Duns Tew, near Oxford, where Paul Fischer, destined to become one of the foremost British luthiers, became his assistant. In the early 1980's Rubio moved his premises to Cambridge, where his extensive and varied instrument making activities continued.

In the 1990's, Rubio designed a radically new type of eight-string guitar for the British guitarist, Paul Galbraith, based on the late 16th century model of the orpharion.

66. New Directions, 1964 - 1976

On 12 June, 1964, in the quiet seaside town of Aldeburgh, Suffolk, England, Julian Bream premiered Benjamin Britten's *Nocturnal after John Dowland, Op.70*. The impact of this piece on the accepted guitar repertory was to be revolutionary, along with other contemporary works carefully harvested by Bream.

The beginning of a new era in the guitar's development could be dated from the premiere of *Nocturnal*. After its publication in 1965 a process of revaluation would be forced upon guitarists who were now presented with a powerful technical and interpretative challenge. The historical significance of Britten's composition soon became clear.

The day after the premiere, Julian Bream, still only in his early thirties, was honored by Queen Elizabeth II with the award of the Order of the British Empire in recognition of his contribution to British musical life.

Elsewhere in the contemporary world were reverberations of a different revolution. The early 1960's saw the rise to fame of the Beatles and a new prominence in the media and public consciousness at every level for popular music. The phenomenon of Beatlemania can be dated from this time. The group's single *Love Me Do*, made the Top Twenty in December, 1962, and *Please Please Me* was top of the charts in early 1963. *I Want to Hold Your Hand* and *She Loves You* were also hits of 1963. A new cultural tidal wave was making its presence felt.

Much to the astonishment of various critics of the 1960's, the passing of the years has given the pop stars of the decade an almost invulnerable status as icons of an era. In 1963 the process of making rock stars into demigods had not yet established itself and many classical and jazz musicians first regarded the Beatles as an essentially ephemeral fashion. It seemed reasonable then to suppose the manifestations of pop had less to do with music and more with haircuts, novelties, images and personalities, as the young pursued their search for appropriate role models.

Meanwhile, at some distance as yet from popular music, John Williams continued his meteoric climb to eminence. Since his Wigmore Hall, London, recital in 1958, Williams had embarked on a rising curve of success with debuts in Paris and Madrid, a tour of the Soviet Union (1962), and a debut in Japan (1963). On 6 December, 1963, he appeared at Town Hall, New York, to enormous critical acclaim. [104]

The following year Williams's recording career opened up with *CBS Records presents John Williams* (CBS 72339). He had previously made three long playing records but now he traversed those subtle boundaries from the realm of the musical prodigy into true artistic maturity:

> *This album brings John Williams before the recording microphones after a considerable time lapse. 'I enjoyed these recording sessions which were my first for several years,' Mr. Williams commented with characteristic enthusiasm. 'It was particularly interesting to hear how technical improvements in recording have brought about more faithful reproduction of the guitar.'*[104]

In 1965, John Williams continued with *Virtuoso Music for Guitar*, featuring *Partita for Guitar* by Stephen Dodgson (b. 1924), a work dedicated to him, which he had premiered at the Cheltenham Festival on 4 July, 1963.[105]

While pop music consolidated its hold on thousands of people world-wide in 1964, the younger classic guitarists were also evolving artistic identities and future ambitions. The storm of pop and rock publicity clamored outside, but the small voice of the unamplified guitar was indisputably a potent force in music, attracting the attention of many eminent composers. At this point those who cared about the guitar as an expressive medium had much to be excited about. The guitar not only possessed a glorious past but also a promising future - a number of outstanding 20th century compositions were still to come and such progress was keenly anticipated by recitalists and the public.

In 1966, *Julian Bream: 20th Century Guitar* appeared, featuring contemporary works such as *El Polifemo de Oro* (Smith Brindle), *Nocturnal, Op. 70* (Britten), *Quatre pièces brèves* (Martin), *Drei Tentos* (Henze), as well as *Études, Nos 5 & 7* (Villa-Lobos). This recording changed the concepts of guitar possibilities for many recitalists and composers.[106]

On 2 April, 1967, Bream played a recital at the Queen Elizabeth Hall, London, which demonstrated the steady forward progress of the instrument. At the same time the program kept its roots in tradition, being a chronological synthesis of many voices of the guitar and various historical periods from 1546 onwards.

La Romanesca - Fantasía (1546)	Alonso de Mudarra
Pavana-Canarios (1674)	Gaspar Sanz
Prelude-Sarabande-Gigue	J. S. Bach
Two Sonatas	Domenico Cimarosa
Sonata in C (Allegro)	Mauro Giuliani

Interval

Four Lyric Pieces	Edvard Grieg
Nocturnal after John Dowland, Op. 70	Benjamin Britten
Fantasia (1957)	Roberto Gerhard
Sevilla	Isaac Albéniz

Bream's development of his recital format was skilfully achieved. While integrating new with well-tried elements, and establishing the centrality of his own transcriptions and editions, he carefully excluded extreme avant-gardism though emphasizing the contemporary. In this he continued the custom of Segovia and earlier guitarists but extended the essential framework to the point where there could be no return to former limitations.

Developments continued with the appearance of the *Faber Guitar Series* (1967), edited Bream, a project comparable to Segovia's Guitar Archive Series of the early 1920's.[107] At the same time as the historical search continued, the contemporary repertoire expanded. Works written for Bream, 1968-1976, include:[108]

1968: *Five Impromptus,* Richard Rodney Bennett.

1969: *Soliloquy,* Thomas Wilson.

1970: *Paseo,* Peter Racine Fricker; *Fantasy,* Malcolm Arnold; *Concerto for Guitar and Chamber Ensemble,* Richard Rodney Bennett; *Theme and Variations,* Lennox Berkeley.

1971: *Five Bagatelles for Guitar,* William Walton; *Elegy,* Alan Rawsthorne.

1974: *Guitar Concerto, Op. 88,* Lennox Berkeley; *Five, Op. 61,* Humphrey Searle.

1976: *Royal Winter Music,* Hans Werner Henze.

In November, 1971, John Williams premiered André Previn's *Guitar Concerto,* a work which includes a symbolic struggle between the classic guitar and the combined forces of the jazz combo:

> *The work justifiably holds a favored place among André's compositions for it contains a great many musical ideas, well planned and well executed. The moods vary considerably from movement to movement, with the central* Adagio *the longest and heaviest in content. The third movement introduces a jazz combo of electric guitar, electric bass, and drummer, which does its best to interrupt the conventional flow of the piece, but in the end the trio is overcome by the unrelenting stream of the classical tradition. It is, in a manner of speaking, an autobiographical composition.[109]*

A development in recitals was the formation of a Duo partnership between Bream and Williams.

This combined their extraordinary performing gifts and indicated that the spirit of past rivalry had modulated into musical togetherness. The sounds produced were fresh and new, but the Duo opted for the shades of traditional guitar history, evoking primarily Spanish warmth, vitality and virtuosity, as their central message.[110]

From 1970 onwards many publications of contemporary music edited by the Italian guitarist and scholar, Angelo Gilardino, emerged from Bèrben of Ancona, Italy. Within a few years over eighty composers from a variety of countries would be represented.[111]

Among the first in Gilardino's series were pieces by John W. Duarte (b. 1919, Sheffield, England) whose compositional activities for the guitar had begun in 1945 and continued prolifically.[112] As virtually all Duarte's music is written for guitar - whether solo or ensemble, virtuosic or material for beginners - its quantity exceeds that of most composers for the instrument and has been made available over the years by many publishers. At the same time Duarte continued to weave a critical, sometimes controversial, exegesis round the instrument by extensive journalism, reviewing, and liner note writing. His other contributions include a host of editions and transcriptions, books and pedagogic material, the organization of Summer Schools and a lifelong teaching input. Over fifty of his pieces have been recorded, often by several artists.

In 1971, Goffredo Petrassi composed *Nunc*, taking the guitar into a complex deployment of colors and timbres:[113]

> *The title* Nunc, *which means 'now, at this time' in Latin, would seemingly relate the music to the realm of 'moment form', a style of composition developed by Stockhausen in the late 1960's. And in fact the score bears this out: each of the five sections of the piece contains like gestures, which display their moods and then suddenly shift to new material...*
>
> *Petrassi's subtle use of instrumental color includes percussive aspects of the guitar, such as the use of left-hand pizzicato... and extensive use of golpe in the two slow sections... Other effects include wide use of tremolo, harmonics, tambora, and rapid arpeggios, all in order to produce the greatest contrast of texture possible. The overall effect is truly kaleidoscopic - images constantly transform, while never repeating, simultaneously giving the viewer impressions that are novel, yet familiar.* [114]

Throughout the 1970's, Leo Brouwer (b. Cuba, 1939), began to attract considerable admiration and attention. He had already written much guitar music, but it was only now that it began to be published.[115] As Brouwer's music emerged from the obscurity of Fidel Castro's Cuba, the composer's imaginative powers were rapidly appreciated. The time lag between Brouwer's writing of compositions and publication would soon diminish. But by the 1970's he had written enough excellent music for guitar to achieve an extraordinary cumulative effect when his work became suddenly available within the space of a few years.

161

On 27 November, 1976, in Washington D.C., Carlos Barbosa-Lima premiered *Sonata Op. 47,* by the Argentinian composer, Alberto Ginastera. This was soon accepted as a virtuosic masterpiece, much to the composer's delight:

When... Mr. Barbosa-Lima suggested that I should compose some music for this instrument, something made me accept, and at this point I realized that the guitar - in contrast to other solo instruments - relied on a repertoire of almost exclusively short pieces without any unity of form. This gave me the idea to compose a work of sizeable proportions, and therefore I wrote this SONATA in four movements, in which the rhythms of South American music recur.

...When the critics at its premiere received this work as one of the most important ever written for the guitar, as much for its conception as for its modernism and its unprecedented imaginative use of sound, I thought that I had not waited in vain for several decades to make the attempt.[116]

67. The Guitars of José Romanillos

José Romanillos (b. Madrid,1932), went to live in England in 1956. Originally a cabinet maker, he constructed his first guitar in 1959 and continued to make more after encouragement from friends. In 1964 he went back to Spain for three years, building three or four guitars while he was there.

On returning to England in 1967 he was soon acknowledged as one of the world's foremost luthiers when Julian Bream began playing Romanillos guitars:

I first met Julian in September '69 when I showed him a guitar I had made. He asked whether I was making any more at the time, and I said that I had three more on the go. Later he telephoned and asked me to take the guitars to show him when they were finished. It was Christmas when

I took them to him. He played all the guitars and kept one for himself. It was after this time that Julian sent me a letter inviting me to go to Semley and work in his studio making guitars. I couldn't say yes quickly enough...

We discuss every aspect of guitar making, and we pool our ideas. There's never any punches pulled between the two of us, and he tries all the guitars and praises them or points out their faults. He has a wonderful intuition for guitars, and he knows what he is talking about...I have always admired his playing. I suppose it's simply that his conception of tone is nearer to mine than anyone else's.[117]

Later, Romanillos made a vihuela, a four-course guitar and a Baroque guitar, all of which were played by Julian Bream in the documentary film on the history of the instrument, *Guitarra.*[118]

Romanillos has also published an influential biography, *Antonio de Torres, Guitar Maker - His Life and Work.*

68. The Music of Agustín Barrios Mangoré

In July 1974, an article by Peter Sensier appeared about Agustín Barrios Mangoré.[119] The music of Barrios had been severely neglected for thirty years since the guitarist's death. Laurindo Almeida and Alirio Diaz had recorded a few pieces, but the public was generally unaware of the nature or extent of his works. A full scale revival of interest began.

In October 1975, John Williams gave a recital at Wigmore Hall, London, the second half consisting entirely of music by Barrios. This was followed, early in 1976, by a television film about the Paraguayan guitarist and the publication of some of his music. (So far only a handful of his works had been published but soon two four-volume editions appeared.)[120] John Williams commented for his Barrios album:

> *Barrios is increasingly appreciated today as the outstanding guitarist-composer of his time, I would say of any time, for the qualities of inventiveness and obvious love of the instrument. He was the first guitarist to make records, from 1909, and the first to play a complete Bach lute suite on guitar. As well as being a virtuoso player, he composed hundreds of pieces... I am very indebted to Carlos Payet of San Salvador for providing me with a lot of the then unpublished music during a visit he made to London in 1969: at that time one or two well-known Barrios pieces had always been published, but the unexpected addition of so many more beautiful pieces has sustained in me a constant enthusiasm for one of our instrument's great personalities.[121]*

From such enthusiasm came a shift in recital content. Barrios Mangoré's music now became a focus for many players until, once again, ever increasing familiarity with a composer's output brought about a certain diminution of interest. In 1992, Richard D. Stover's biography, *Six Silver Moonbeams, The Life and Times of Agustín Barrios Mangoré,* provided the essential background.

69. Shifting Currents of the 1970's

In the 1970's radical changes occurred in the musical world. A concern for scrupulous research of music from the Middle Ages onwards, brought about a new journal, *Early Music*, first appearing in January, 1973 with the following editorial:

Ten years ago a journal such as this would have been impossible: there were then no early music consorts such as those whose reputation now begins to reverberate beyond these shores. There were relatively few instrument makers and those interested in early music tended to be divided into members of the various separate societies for recorder, lute or gamba, or they were readers of specialist journals. Now all is mysteriously changed.

The contents of this first issue make clear our aims and directions. We want those who play or listen to early music to feel that here is an international forum where diverse issues and interests can be debated and discussed. We want to provide a link between the finest scholarship of our day and the amateur and professional listener and performer. At one end of the scale there will be practical help and guidance on techniques, interpretation and instruments: at the other authoritative articles written in such a way that they will stimulate and help the uninitiated as well as those more experienced.[122]

That all was 'mysteriously changed' heralded a new era in linking scholarship with performing musicians. Scholars in all fields began to focus on problems appropriate to instrumental development, history, repertory, and contemporary predicament.

Distinct stirrings were also apparent elsewhere. Traditionally up to this time, the leading personalities of the classic guitar had usually maintained some distance from the world of popular entertainment and jazz. (Guitarists such as Laurindo Almeida, gave classic guitar recitals and participated in jazz, but similar versatility was rare.) In 1972, the British magazine, *Guitar,* was founded, its avowed policy being to unite guitarists of different styles.

John Williams, in the first issue, reinforced the message:

One reprehensible drawback to the development of the guitar as an instrument with a classical background and technique has been the narrow-minded, reactionary and, in many cases, unmusical attitude of its most "pure" advocates. I say "has been" because this attitude is nearly dead and buried; however, any extra pushing towards this end can only be welcomed, and for this reason I wish you all the best on the occasion of your first issue of GUITAR.[123]

Already Williams was developing other sides to his playing, intending to loosen up the classic guitar and to capture a wider audience. Eventually he formed the group Sky, to provide a platform for these explorations.[124] In August, 1973, an interview with John Williams established that he felt 'very differently about music than Segovia,' being 'completely at the other end of the pole':

Segovia thinks pretty vertically in music: there's very little tension in his playing and very little forward drive. It is beautiful sounds and no hurry. It always has been and it's a beautiful style. Whereas my feeling is more urgent and I've always had this inner tension, and no matter how relaxed the music is.[125]

Thus between the new and old generations of guitarists appeared an ideological divide, which could never be resolved. In this changing environment periodicals with perspectives rooted in earlier decades, lost ground. In 1973 *Guitar News* (founded 1951), published its last issue while *BMG (Banjo, Mandolin, Guitar,* founded 1903), encountered financial difficulties though its demise would not come until April, 1976.

In 1974, Harvey Turnbull's *The Guitar from the Renaissance to the Present Day* was published, its concepts (like those of *Early Music*), being precise and to the point:

The present book grew out of the inadequacy of general histories of music to satisfy my own curiosity about the history of the guitar... The unreliability of much of the secondary material made recourse to primary sources a necessity, which in turn entailed an extensive research program... Fortunately, the task has been eased by the appearance of reliable articles and theses, and my debt to these will be obvious.[126]

The scholarly study of the guitar from the Renaissance onwards was the only road to an awareness of the repertory of each era and the realization that four-course guitar, vihuela, Baroque guitar, early 19th century guitar, etc., were individual and specific instrumental types. Thus the post-Torres classic guitar could no longer be considered the superior vehicle for performance of all periods of guitar music.

Analysis of guitar history was furthered by the inauguration of *The Soundboard*, the journal of the Guitar Foundation of America. The first issue (February, 1974), covered *Research in Progress* with a wide range of projects.[127] In November, 1974, *The Soundboard* announced the founding of *Il Fronimo*, 'a new serious guitar journal', edited by the Italian scholar, Ruggero Chiesa.[128] Later periodicals dedicated to classic guitar included *Gitarre und Laute* (Cologne, Germany, founded 1979), the French magazine, *Les Cahiers de la Guitare* (1982) and, in England, *Classical Guitar* (from September, 1982).

One result of this scholarly activity was an increase in well researched editions of all kinds of composers from the 16th to the early 19th centuries, (including new transcriptions of works by J.S. Bach).

But critical attention also began to focus on the familiar Spanish composers. An arrangement by Manuel Barrueco of Albéniz's *Suite Española, Op. 47* (Melville, New York: Belwin-Mills, 1981) brought perennials of the concert hall such as *Granada, Sevilla,* etc., much closer to the original text than the traditional Tárrega/Segovia transcriptions. Thus began a thorough reorientation of how this music could sound on guitar. Barrueco's interpretations of Albéniz and Granados, proved highly influential.[129]

John Williams, who had grown up 'with all the wonderful Segovia recordings of Albéniz and Granados', found them 'overshadowed' by Barrueco's interpretations and was inspired to record an all Albéniz album (1981).[130] The process of revisiting and improving this repertory continued with Julian Bream's recording of his own transcriptions of Granados and Albéniz (1982).[131]

70. The Music of Antonio Lauro (1917-1986)

Antonio Lauro, born in Ciudad Bolívar, Venezuela, studied composition with Vicente Emilio Sojo and guitar with Raúl Borges, the teacher of Alirio Diaz. Originally a pianist, Lauro preferred to write for the guitar:

I was won over by the guitar after hearing one of the greatest guitar virtuosos that the world has ever known - Agustín Barrios Mangoré. He came to Caracas and gave some recitals... His playing moved me so much that I decided to take up the guitar as my instrument of study.[132]

Lauro first attracted world-wide attention with John Williams's recording of *Vals Venezolano No. 3* on his debut album (recorded1958). The subsequent publication of *Quatro Valses Venezolanos, Suite Venezolana* (1963), *El Marabino, Carora, Angostura, María Luisa* (1968) and *Variations on a Venezolean Children's Song* (1969) (ed. Diaz, Broekmans & van Poppel,

Amsterdam), boosted Lauro's popularity to great heights, a process closely identified with the playing of Alirio Diaz.

Other popular pieces included *Sonata* (publ. 1975) and the virtuosic *Seis por Derecho* (1977). The first all-Lauro recording, *David Russell plays Antonio Lauro* (GMR 1001), was released in 1980. Since then the seminal favorites have been much performed and recorded. Though Lauro's compositions, over the years, have lost their capacity to surprise, they represent (as with Tárrega, Barrios Mangoré and Villa-Lobos), an enduring tradition of guitar music appealing directly to the imagination:

> *Lauro, like Stravinsky and Falla, had a "poetic" conception of his art, in refreshing contrast to the long tradition of self-serving "aestheticism" in guitar history... Lauro's proud craftsmanship, the choiceness of his creativity, stands as powerful reproof of the essential "dilettantism" which affects a substantial part of today's guitar literature, amidst a profusion of novel techniques and effects; his music has no gimmicks... its only concern is its intrinsic beauty.[133]*

71. Ignacio Fleta (1897-1977)

The world renowned Catalan luthier, Ignacio Fleta, died on 11 August, 1977, bringing to an end a unique era in guitar making. Fleta, the son of a cabinet maker, began making guitars in the 1930's, modelling his instruments around the revered example of Torres, though he also made bowed and replica instruments. In 1955 Fleta heard Segovia on a radio program and decided to place 'all my efforts in guitar construction.'[134]

After 1957 Segovia would, at different times, own three fine Fleta guitars. Other artists who played Fleta instruments included John Williams, Ernesto Bitetti, Oscar Caceres, Eduardo Falu, Alexandre Lagoya and Alberto Ponce. Over the years Fleta's workshop made some 700 guitars, as well as 87 violins, 7 viols, 39 cellos and 6 vihuelas.[135]

72. The Passing Generation

The early 1980's saw the passing of several major personalities, the old guard of the 20th century guitar. On 15 November, 1980, Emilio Pujol died, the last of Tárrega's pupils. On 26 November, 1981, Regino Sáinz de la Maza (the dedicatee of Rodrigo's *Concierto de Aranjuez)*, died, and on 12 September, 1982, Federico Moreno Torroba passed away at the age of 91. Over six decades, Torroba had become one of the most popular Spanish composers for guitar.

For the last years of his life Segovia pursued an illustrious career honored by monarchs, presidents and universities. On 11 March, 1979, he performed in the White House, Washington D.C., at the request of President and Mrs. Carter.

In 1980, Segovia's early recordings between 1927 and 1939, were issued on LP's, described by John W. Duarte as 'what must be, for those who love the guitar, the most important recording to be released in their lifetime.'[136] In the same year MCA Records, California, reissued various Segovia recordings of more recent years.[137]

On Wednesday, 24 June, 1981, Segovia was granted the title of Marquis of Salobreña by King Juan Carlos I of Spain, 'to reward an exceptional artistic life.' Approaching Segovia's 90th birthday in 1983 great musicians throughout the world contributed greetings:

Segovia is a peerless and unique artist; his art with its rare qualities of sincerity and humanity, is an example to all of us. (Vladimir Ashkenazy.)

In Andrés Segovia there dwells that quiet fire - fierce yet controlled - which is the mark of the Spaniard. Where other people must rekindle their fires whilst yet others cannot govern them, the supreme artistry of a Segovia, of Casals, of Conchita Supervia, of Victoria de los Angeles, or of Placido Domingo, is proof of an eternal flame. (Yehudi Menuhin.)

My very best wishes to Andrés Segovia - certainly the Maestro is responsible for bringing classical guitar 'al massimo dello splendore', and is an artist I have always respected and admired tremendously. (Luciano Pavarotti.)[138]

On 25 May, 1984, a bronze statue of Segovia, sculpted by Julio López Hernández, was unveiled in his birthplace, Linares, Spain. On 2 October, Segovia received the Gold Medal of the Royal Philharmonic Society of London, inaugurated in 1870 to commemorate the centenary of Beethoven's birth. (Other contemporary recipients included Menuhin, Rostropovich, Horowitz, Messiaen, Tippett, Karajan and Lutoslawski.)

On 3 November, 1985, Segovia was awarded the Order of the Rising Sun, an honor direct from Emperor Hirohito of Japan and two days later was granted an audience with Pope John Paul II in the Vatican. On 26 April, 1986, following a tour of North America, he performed for the last time at the Wigmore Hall, London. That summer the University of Southern California organized *A Salute to Segovia, Andrés Segovia Master Classes and Commemorative,* 16-26 July, 1986, with many of the personalities present whose careers had been shaped by his influence.

171

Later that year, on 3 November, 1986, Segovia's friend, Vladimir Bobri, died tragically in a fire in New York, this loss being compounded on 15 November, by the death of the Polish composer, Alexandre Tansman.

Following his 94th birthday in 1987 Segovia gave his final tour of the United States, performing his last recital at the Miami Beach Theater of Performing Arts on 4 April. Shortly afterwards he was taken ill, but was able to return to Spain. Segovia died in Madrid on 2 June, 1987.

Segovia's passing would bring about a searching assessment of his achievements, though this would take time to be formulated. Such an analysis would necessarily explore the wider perspectives of early 20th century guitar development. Segovia's style of playing may have long ceased to be a role model for the younger generations. But his pursuit of a concert career past his 90th birthday provided a sense of historical continuity and imparted considerable charisma to the guitar.

In 1987 the classic guitar appeared to exist in parallel universes - the movement represented by Bream, Williams, and the younger artists and composers at home in the second half of the 20th century, and the gently retrospective atmosphere created by Segovia's recitals and repertoire. Segovia's departure created a profound sense of loss akin to the demise of a great leader or a beloved Founding Father.

Since 1987, as well as scholarly evaluation, attempts have been made to denigrate Segovia's contribution to the classic guitar. But the facts show that Segovia concerts attracted huge audiences between 1909 and 1987, his recordings were the most commercially successful of any recitalist up to the 1970's, the compositions dedicated to him continue to be studied and performed and he had the gift of inspiring many young players. Moreover, Segovia is remembered by his public with a unique affection and admiration.

172

73. Compositions from 1980

The final decades of the 20th century were fertile in guitar composition, many of the works emerging from young guitarist/composers, who blended impressionism with unusual effects and virtuosity.

A characteristic example of imagistic writing was *A l'Aube du Dernier Jour* (At the Dawn of the Last Day), by the French guitarist, Francis Kleynjans (b. 1951), a composition awarded the 22nd Radio France prize in 1980. Here the last hours of a condemned man are evoked, with the sounds of a clock ticking, the walk to the place of execution, heartbeats and the fall of the guillotine blade.[139]

On 24 October 1980, the suite by the Russian composer, Nikita Koshkin (b. 1956), *The Prince's Toys,* was premiered in Paris. This creates images of a young prince whose toys come to life, before they disappear (and the prince with them), at the behest of a mysterious fairy. Ingenious percussive, pizzicato effects and unconventional techniques are exploited to conjure up *The Mechanical Monkey, Toy Soldiers,* etc:[140]

> *The work itself encapsulates Koshkin's response to imagery and fantasy, a depiction of the fairy-tale world of a child... The range of sound-effects is astonishing and some are quite novel, but what is important is that they are not presented as a 'catalogue of gimmicks' but always in a way that enhances the music and the imaginary world it depicts... The Prince's Toys is one of the most remarkable pieces ever written for the guitar; it opens new doors and remains surprisingly fresh after many hearings.[141]*

Also popular was Koshkin's *Usher Waltz,* a homage to Edgar Allan Poe's *The Fall of the House of Usher.* John Williams described the work as 'probably the most musically dramatic piece in the repertoire: in a way reminiscent of Chopin and Shostakovich,' combining 'musical shape and dynamic guitar writing to powerful effect.'[142]

Meanwhile, Leo Brouwer's reputation soared to even greater heights in the 1980's with a prolific output of compositions:

El Decameron Negro (1981) (Editions Musicales Transatlantiques, Paris, 1983)

Preludios epigramáticos (1981) (Editions Musicales Transatlantiques, Paris, 1984)

Danza del Altiplano (Max Eschig, Paris, 1984)

Variations sur un thème de Django Reinhardt (1984) (Editions Musicales Transatlantiques, Paris, 1985)

Paisaje Cubano con rumba, for four guitars (1985) (Ricordi, Milan, 1986)

Retrats Catalans, for guitar and small orchestra (1983) (Eschig, 1987)

Paisaje Cubano con campanas (1986) (Ricordi, Milan, 1988)

Concierto Elegiaco (Concerto No. 3) for guitar and orchestra (1985-86) (Eschig, 1989)

Concerto No. 4 (de Toronto) (1987) (Doberman-Yppan, Quebec, 1990)

Sonata (1990) (Opera Tres, Ediciones Musicales, Madrid, 1991)

Of the above, *El Decameron Negro* (The Black Decameron), dedicated to Sharon Isbin, became one of the most frequently played. The three movements *(The Warrior's Harp, The Flight of the Lovers through the Valley of Echoes, The Ballad of the Maiden in Love)*, based on African stories collected by the anthropologist and writer, Leon Frobenius, elevated guitaristic impressionism to new levels of intensity:

In the first ballad, a warrior (depicted by lively rhythmic sections) is banished from his tribe because he loves to play the harp (slow interludes). When summoned to defeat an invading army, he returns to save his people. After his victory, the warrior is condemned once again to exile... As he flees with his lover, the music invokes a hastening gallop of horses... Finally, the opening motive of the last ballad portrays a beautiful young maiden in love, followed, in rondo form, by episodes of vibrant, passionate energy.[143]

Brouwer's challenging *Sonata* was premiered on 27 January, 1991, at the Wigmore Hall, London, by its dedicatee, Julian Bream, who commented in the program notes:

The three contrasted movements devise their unity from the thematic idea introduced in the first movement... This is a simple motif of eight notes characterized by the interval of the major second and minor third and their relative inversions. Much of the secondary musical material also explores these intervals, and in so doing, the Sonata is largely mono-thematic.

Fandangos y Boleros opens with a short preambulo which serves as an introduction to the first subject...The second subject is in dotted rhythm, accompanied by a double octave pedal. After the development section, the coda quotes fragments from Beethoven's Sixth Symphony, together with echoes of the second subject...

Mr. Skriabin's Sarabande is in many ways a piece of musical surrealism. The theme from the opening movement appears from time to time, in a totally different harmonic guise... by re-tuning the low E string to F, the composer has created a piece of unusual color and musical texture.

Pasquini's Toccata rounds off the Sonata in a truly athletic way... The brilliant figurations and arabesques eventually give way to a momentary return to the slow movement before the opening music with its vigor and gusto is heard again.[144]

Through the 1990's Brouwer's compositional flow continued with several concertos including *Concierto de Helsinki* and *Concierto de Volos* (both 1996), and *Concierto de Havana* (c.1998). The ideas behind his concerto writing were described by the composer:

As is the case for most of the guitar concertos that preceded it, Concierto de Volos *reflects more the personality of the person to whom it is dedicated than the countryside or local culture to which it seems to refer (*Concierto elegiaco *is a portrait of Julian Bream, like* Concierto de Toronto *was written in the image of John Williams). The different parts of* Concierto de Volos, *lento-allegro-lento-allegro, are inspired by the baroque form of the* sonata da chiesa *for the structure, but the melancholy atmosphere and tenderness of the slow movements, as well as the vitality and dancing character of the fast movements, conform to the idea I have of Costas Cotsiolis...*[145]

Other solo guitar pieces by Brouwer published in the 1990's include *Rito de los Orishas* (publ. 1993), *HIKA, In Memoriam Toru Takemitsu* (1996), and *Paisaje cubano con tristeza* (1999).

In 1981, the English composer, Peter Maxwell Davies, wrote *Hill Runes,* dedicated to Bream, his first solo guitar work since *Lullaby for Ilian Rainbow* (1972):

Hill Runes *was written early in 1981 for Julian Bream, for the opening concert of the Dartington Summer School of Music. Its composition followed that of the* Second Symphony, *to which it is related thematically, and consists of five interlinked movements, played without a break. I set myself the problem of writing a guitar solo quietly evocative in my mind of the almost 'lunar' Scottish landscape in which I live, without overtones of Spain, so often evoked by the guitar, while at the same time writing idiomatically for the instrument.* [146]

After *Hill Runes* came another ambitious work for guitar, *Sonata* (1984), premiered by Timothy Walker in Orkney in 1987. Once again the composer wished to avoid any Spanish echoes:

> *This is the third of a set of three solo sonatas...the others were for organ and for piano. Of all these, that for guitar was the most challenging to write, not only in the avoidance of any unintended Spanish connotations, but in making the available tone colors varied and colorful enough to sustain the abstract form.*

> *The original inspiration came from the harpsichord sonatas of Domenico Scarlatti - clearest in the first movement, an allegro moderato following a slow introduction, where the basic B minor tonality and the thematic core are established.The second movement explores the darkest colors of the instrument, while the Finale is rhythmic and brittle.[147]*

In contrast to Maxwell Davies's northern European austerity, another South American ingredient was added to recital possibilities in 1981. This was the appearance of *Cinco Piezas* by the Argentinian composer, Astor Piazzolla (1921-1992), soon to be well publicized in a recording by his countryman, Roberto Aussel.[148]

Piazzolla had studied with Nadia Boulanger in Paris before going on to breathe fresh life and some controversy into contemporary concepts of composing Argentinian tangos. After hearing Aussel perform Walton's *Five Bagatelles,* Piazzolla began writing directly for the guitar and his subsequent contributions include *Tango Suite* for guitar duo (1984), and *Histoire du Tango* for flute and guitar (c.1986).[149] Moreover, various recitalists, (most notably Baltazar Benítez and Agustín Carlevaro), made guitar arangements of some of his finest pieces, including *Verano Porteño, Milonga del Angel, La Muerte del Angel,* and *Adios Nonino.*

In 1981, the Italian composer, guitarist, editor, and teacher, Angelo Gilardino, wrote *Dodici Studi* (Twelve Studies), subtitled 'of virtuosity and transcendency'. Each study was a tribute to a composer, poet, or painter who had influenced Gilardino. Four subsequent sets of *Twelve Studies* (1983, 1984/5, 1986/7, 1988) provided similar technical and expressive challenges. Gilardino also published two books, *La Tecnica della Chitarra* (1980), and *Manuale di Storia della Chitarra, Vol. 2, La Chitarra moderna e contemporanea* (1988), as well as these compositions:

1985: *Sonata No. 1*

1986: *Sonata No. 2, "Hivern Florit"*

1989: *Variazioni sulla Follía*

1991: *Musica per l'angelo della Melancholia*

1991: *Variazioni sulla Fortuna (studi da John Dowland)*

1992: *Concerto d'estate,* guitar and string quartet

1993: *Concierto de Córdoba,* solo guitar and guitar quartet

1994: *Poema d'inverno,* solo guitar and guitar duo

1995: *Concerto d'autunno,* solo guitar and small guitar orchestra

1996: *Leçons de Ténèbres,* Concerto for guitar and orchestra

1997: *Preghiere per gli innocenti,* voice and guitar; *Fiori di novembre,* Concerto for mandolin, guitar and orchestra

1998: *Concerto Italiano,* four guitars and orchestra

1999: *Forgotten Songs,* Seven melodies on a popular Russian-Spanish Romanza, to be played in duo with guitar and different instruments; *Sonatina-Lied,* bassoon and guitar; *La casa delle ombre,* Concerto for flute, guitar and strings

In 1982, the virtuosic French performer/composer, Roland Dyens (b. 1955), wrote *Libra Sonatine,* a work with an unusual story behind it:

Roland Dyens was born in Tunis in 1955, but is as French as the Eiffel Tower. With the sensibility of a Marcel Proust, he achieves a refinement and cleverness - so typical of French artists - in his compositions through cleverly placed and often difficult playing instructions. The Libra Sonatine *- 'Libra' stands for a sign of the zodiac, and was composed originally by Dyens in 1982 for guitar, double bass, and percussion.*

Only the later solo version became one of his most successful pieces. The three movements, India, Largo *and* Fuoco, *tell the story of a heart operation that Roland Dyens was obliged to undertake.* India, *with its constant change of meter and various styles, depicts the restless beats of a sick heart. The* Largo *depicts the narcotic state during the operation, and in the last piece,* Fuoco, *the power of the 'new' heart breaks out like an explosion.*[150]

Though a prolific composer, Dyens became best known for his *Tango en Skaï,* begun as an improvisation in 1978 and not published until 1985. This work soon assumed the role that Villa-Lobos's *Choros No.1* or Lauro's *Venezuelan Waltz No. 3,* once occupied in recitals - a pleasing and witty encore. Dyens said of the piece:

Skaï in French means imitation leather, maybe worse than bad plastic! It has to be played with a lot of humor, a maximum of dynamics and a minimum of rubato. Not at all 'classico-seriously'![151]

In 1983, Elliott Carter (b. 1908), the eminent American composer, became attracted to guitar sonorities and wrote *Changes* for guitar solo:

Changes, *for guitar solo, is music of mercurial contrasts of character and mood, unified by its harmonic and rhythmic structure. Various aspects of the basic harmony are brought out in the course of the work, somewhat like the patterns used by bell-ringers in ringing changes. The score was written during the summer of 1983 and is dedicated to David Starobin who commissioned it and generously gave me advice about the guitar. He performed its première in New York at a concert given on my 75th birthday, December 11, 1983.*[152]

179

On 9 November, 1983, Julian Bream premiered Sir Michael Tippett's *The Blue Guitar,* a sonata for solo guitar, at the Ambassador Auditorium, Pasadena, California. The inspiration for this work came from a poem by Wallace Stevens, a meditation on Picasso's painting, *The Man with the Blue Guitar.* The three movements express themes of transformation, dreaming and juggling, and how perceptions of reality are subtly changed through the medium of art.

In New York City between 23 November and 10 December, 1983, Richard Rodney Bennett composed *Sonata,* for solo guitar. This was premiered by its dedicatee, Julian Bream, on 17 July, 1985, at the Town Hall, Cheltenham. The sonata, in four movements, has no overall imagistic program but (as the composer explained in an interview), was influenced by Spanish music at certain points:

'At the end of 1983 I began a serious big guitar piece... The first 18 notes became a kind of series from which all the material is derived. I hadn't known it was to be a sonata in four movements, but now it felt like a sonata movement because of its form...'

The second movement...is different in every way from the first movement. Here the composer thought of Spanish flamenco, 'dark rather austere passionate feeling... then a flowing section to relieve the darkness, relieve the tension.'

The third movement again needed a different contrast - again thinking of Spain but 'in a lighter mood'. 'The last movement, novel for me, is a kind of fantasia, like a collage, a picture cut up, all the bits from the other movements pieced together, the themes and ideas lead into each other in a different order.'[153]

In the summer of 1984, Stepan Rak, (b. 1945), emerged from communist Czechoslovakia to play in England.

It was immediately apparent that Rak was a performer/composer of formidable talent, unique both in explosive impressionism and imaginative virtuosity, as well as fluent in expressing concepts of composition:

> *Everything I do in music is affected by my years of painting studies, before I took up the guitar... So now, in harmony and chords I visualize different colors; and melodies are the lines in the painting. Sometimes the color combinations come before the sounds, sometimes the other way round...*

> *My way of composing at present is such that I would like to do in music what is done in Surrealist painting, not so much Dalí as the early 16th century painter Bosch. He puts ideas together which have practically no relationship...*

> *As in Surrealism they might paint a normal room with ordinary furniture, and then place in that scene something very abnormal. In the center of that room is a flame, just on its own. It doesn't belong at all to that house, but to other fire. But now it comes very strange and so it has impact. I believe the same about music, that I put into classical melody or romantic... deliberately placed wrong notes. This happens with me all the time, to place the wrong note in an otherwise harmonious surrounding for new combinations, new atmospheres.* [154]

As with Brouwer, Rak's musical compositions were numerous by the time he became well known, and, similarly, many of his finest works were published within a short time.[155] Rak was also not averse to attempting musical portrayal of huge themes more usually equated with orchestral than guitaristic dimensions (such as his epic work for solo guitar, *Hiroshima).* Over the next few years the prolific nature of his compositions fascinated the guitar public.[156]

The expressive involvement of the Japanese composer, Toru Takemitsu (1930-1996), with the guitar came to prominence in the 1980's. Various of his compositions from the early 1960's featured guitar timbres but it was not until 1974 that Takemitsu produced his first solo work, *Folios,* dedicated to Kiyoshi Shomura.[157]

> The Folios *are three small pieces that fit the folio format of the sheet music. They are composed tonally, which makes them exceptional among Takemitsu's works of this period; dispensing with special experimental techniques they present the guitar's beauty and versatile means of expression with romantic flair.*
>
> *At the end of* Folio III *there appears a well known melody which is taken from the chorale,* Wenn ich einmal soll scheiden, *of Johann Sebastian Bach's* St. Matthew Passion.[158]

Takemitsu's next guitar work was entitled *12 Songs for Guitar* (1977), transcriptions of songs such as Gershwin's *Summertime* and several Lennon-McCartney pieces.[159]

Takemitsu's fame as a guitar composer intensified throughout the 1980's, as recitalists became captivated by his music. Premieres and recordings multiplied including *Toward the Sea,* (February, 1981, Robert Aitken and Leo Brouwer), *To the Edge of Dream,* (March, 1983, Ichiro Suzuki), and *Vers, l'arc-en-ciel, Palma,* (2 October, 1984, John Williams).[160]

In 1988, Julian Bream premiered *All in Twilight, Four Pieces for Guitar,* in New York. The pieces have no titles, merely metronome markings, though No. II is indicated as 'Dark' and No. IV as 'Slightly Fast.' Takemitsu explained that 'An impression from a pastel-touch picture of the same title by Paul Klee is expressed through four different melodic lines in this music.' [161]

In the Woods, Three Pieces for Guitar, written at the end of the composer's life, has thus assumed a poignant significance:

The premiere of the first piece, Wainscot Pond - after a Painting by Cornelia Foss - *took place on the occasion of the funeral service for Toru Takemitsu on February 29, 1996 in Tokyo performed by Norio Sato. The third piece,* Muir Woods, *was premiered by Julian Bream on October 4, 1996 in London. The work in its entirety as well as the second piece,* Rosedale, *was premiered by Kiyoshi Shomura, on October 15, 1996 in Tokyo.* [162]

Takemitsu's art involved many influences:

'Music is Life,' says Takemitsu. For him, the ultimate goal in composing is accomplished when music causes listeners to discover their inner selves. His compositions as a whole are not a conclusion of his personal ideal or thought, but merely stages in the continuing process of the human creative cycle. The extra- musical influences - the literary, artistic and philosophical sources - define reality and universality by representing effectively, and unboundedly, the world surrounding Takemitsu...

Through his attainment of spirituality, established upon non-Western philosophy and aestheticism, Takemitsu has conceived cosmopolitanism and the quality which determines prominence in art by its ability to relate to human sensibility, in any age and place. [163]

In 1985 the Italian guitarist, Carlo Domeniconi (b. 1947), wrote *Koyunbaba, Suite for Guitar, Op. 19,* a virtuosic composition in four movements. Domeniconi had taught at the Istanbul Conservatoire between 1977 and 1980, in the process absorbing many influences from Turkish music. 'Koyunbaba,' means 'shepherd' but also refers to a 13th century holy man after whom an area of southwest Turkey is named:

The two are brought together in Domeniconi's concept, that a shepherd is uniquely given both the time and insight to contemplate and understand the vastness and immense power of Nature...

Each of the four movements develops a separate mood in the hypnotic fashion of eastern music and on a time-scale that reflects the unhurried life of both shepherd and mystic, using a wide range of the guitar's available devices and textures.[164]

Throughout the 1990's Domeniconi's *Koyunbaba* became exceedingly popular among recitalists and was brilliantly celebrated in various recordings.[165]

Later another ambitious work by Domeniconi appeared in the form of *Sindbad, A Tale for Guitar* (1991). Lasting some ninety minutes, this evokes in three cycles and twenty-one movements, the adventures and atmospherics of Sindbad the sailor.[166]

In 1986, Sérgio Assad (b.1952), internationally famous for the phenomenal duo partnership with his younger brother Odair Assad (b.1956), wrote *Aquarelle,* dedicated to the Scottish guitarist David Russell. This work achieved success in both recitals and recordings:

The three-tone motif at the beginning defines the entire first movement as a Divertimento *and is again taken up in the third movement,* Preludio e toccatina, *but here, however, with a greater rhythmic drive.*

The impressionistic, shimmering atmosphere is created by compositional means such as the use of the whole-tone scale at the beginning of the work and through bi-tonality. Thus at the end of the intermezzo-like second movement, Valseana, *Assad combines C sharp with the key note D.* [167]

Steve Reich's minimalist work *Electric Counterpoint* was written in 1987. Here the soloist plays with a pre-recorded multitrack, performing against as many as twelve guitar parts and two bass parts:

The composition has three movements: fast, slow and fast, which seamlessly link together. The slow movement is half the tempo of the fast. After the introduction in the first movement, a theme appears and grows into an eight voice canon.[168]

Certain guitar pieces, such as Brouwer's *La Espiral Eterna* and his *Cuban Landscape* series, Domeniconi's *Koyunbaba,* etc., are strongly influenced by minimalism (a term referring to the repetition of short figures rather than indicating an austere use of few notes).[169]

On 20 April, 1988, Luciano Berio's *Sequenza XI,* was premiered by Eliot Fisk at Rovereto, Italy:

> *Berio's* Sequenzas *(as of this writing there are 13 works bearing this title) are virtuoso pieces for various solo instruments in which the multiple personalities of the instruments in question are brought to expression in novel and fascinating ways through Berio's unique 20th century language.*
>
> *The guitar* Sequenza *is inspired by the Spanish folk tradition of flamenco. Perhaps there is also a breath of the Bach* Ciaccona, *the first work I ever played for Berio when we met in 1987.*
>
> *Berio says that he does not like to write against the instrument, and indeed his* Sequenza XI *is remarkable particularly for a non-guitarist composer in that its considerable technical difficulties are somehow still idiomatic.*
>
> *The work begins quietly,* come preludiando, *before all hell breaks loose* (improvisamente violento). *This starts the work on a magical mystery tour through the guitar's gamut of expressive possibilities.*[170]

In December, 1988, the Cuban-born guitarist, Ricardo Iznaola, recorded *Sonata* by Antonio José (1902-1936), a Spanish composer of great promise executed by Falangist militia during the Civil War:

> *The* Sonata *is made up of four harmonically and thematically linked movements. It is heavily influenced by the French School: the Impressionists, and also d'Indy and Franck. Technically, its demands are staggering. The toccata-like Finale is one of the most rending movements in all of guitar music. One is easily tempted to interpret the music's relentless drama as a premonition of José's own tragic end.*[171]

185

Two editions of José's *Sonata* have now been published,[172] and the work has been performed by a number of recitalists including Julian Bream.[173] Its revival demonstrates the continuity of 20th century guitar history. Regino Sáinz de la Maza, the work's dedicatee, premiered the first movement in Burgos in 1934.[174] Over fifty years later, a neglected masterpiece belatedly entered the repertory.

74. The Guitars of Greg Smallman

In 1989, John Williams concluded an innovative decade in somewhat retrospective mood with a recording of music by Barrios, Piazzolla, Ponce, Lauro, Brouwer, Villa-Lobos, Crespo, etc.[175] These works from the traditional heartland of the repertory, were performed on a guitar made by Greg Smallman (b. 1947), an Australian luthier. His instruments differed radically not only from the usual exemplary Torres prototypes but also from many other structural precedents, especially in terms of fan-strutting:

> *[Smallman] has very definite views on the manner in which guitars produce and emit sound. He likens the box of the guitar to a drum, the front acting as a diaphragm. When the note is plucked, the front being excited moves up and down and because of the bridge and its use, causes a rippling motion across the lower bout.*

> *He considers that in order for the front to act as a diaphragm, it must be thus. Having decided on that, he set about devising an extremely elaborate but strong and light strutting system which would provide necessary support to the front, yet without impeding its flexibility... the fronts of his guitars are unbelievably thin... tapering away at the edges to a wafer.[176]*

Smallman thus invented an intricate lattice system of strutting, bringing in carbon fibers as in aeroplane construction to achieve strength as well as flexibility. The results were outstanding and, within a few years, John Williams's advocacy of Smallman guitars made the luthier internationally famous and his instruments greatly in demand.

75. John Williams and Julian Bream in the 1990's

John Williams's recording career throughout the 1990's continued to be extremely prolific with a wide ranging repertoire:

John Williams plays Vivaldi Concertos, Sony SK 46556, recorded Budapest, Hungary, May 21-25, 1990, released 1991.

Takemitsu played by John Williams, Sony SK 46720, recorded London, September 11-14, 1989, released 1991.

Iberia (Granados, Rodrigo, Llobet, Albéniz), Sony SK 48480, recorded London, 1989-1991, released 1992.

John Williams, The Seville Concert (Albéniz, Bach, Scarlatti, Vivaldi, Yocoh, Koshkin, Barrios Mangoré, Rodrigo), Sony SK 53359, recorded Seville, Spain, 10-18 November, 1992, released 1993.

From Australia (Sculthorpe, Westlake), Sony SK 53361, recorded London 1990, 1994, released 1994.

The Great Paraguayan, John Williams plays Barrios, Sony SK 64396, recorded London, 20-28 June, 1994, released 1995.

The Mantis and the Moon, John Williams-Timothy Kain (Falla, Granados, Soler, Westlake, Houghton, O'Carolan, Brouwer, Madlem, Verdery, Hand, Bellinati, Takemitsu), Sony SK 62007 1, recorded London, 17-20 August, 1995, released 1996.

John Williams Plays the Movies, Sony S2K 62784, recorded London, June-July, 1996, released 1996.

The Black Decameron, The Guitar Music of Leo Brouwer (Concerto de Toronto, Elogio de la Danza, El Decameron Negro, Hika, "In Memoriam Toru Takemitsu"), Sony SK 63173, recorded London, 20-21, 25-27 May, 1997, released 1997.

The Guitarist, John Williams (Theodorakis, Domeniconi, Satie, Williams, Houghton, etc.), Sony SK 60586, recorded London, March 17-21, 1998, released 1998.

John Williams Plays Schubert & Giuliani (Giuliani, *Guitar Concerto,* Schubert, *Arpeggione Sonata),* Australian Chamber Orchestra, Leader, Richard Tognetti, Sony SK 63385, recorded New South Wales, Australia, 9-10 December, 1998, released 1999.

Williams favored combining traditional and contemporary music in concerts, as in this program performed at the Bridgewater Hall, Manchester, England, on 3 May, 2000:

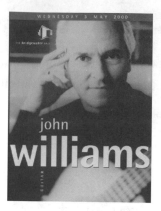

Concerto in D major, Op. 3, No. 9, RV230	Antonio Vivaldi
Medieval Suite	Anon (arr. John Williams)
Two Sonatas *(E major, K.380, A minor, K.175)*	Domenico Scarlatti
Córdoba, Op. 232, No. 4	Isaac Albéniz
El Decameron Negro	Leo Brouwer

Interval

Three Pieces *(La ultima canción, Vals No. 3, Choro da saudade)*	Agustín Barrios Mangoré
Three Epitafios, Nos 3, 4, 5	Mikis Theodorakis
Koyunbaba, Op. 19	Carlo Domeniconi

On 1 March, 1990, Julian Bream signed an exclusive contract with EMI Classics, following 31 years with RCA. Bream commented that his career had now reached a 'turning point':

It's a turning point in your career when you make a move like that. And the great thing is, you have to think of new projects to do. I think it's a good time to do that. I think the guitar has quite an interesting modern repertory now, one that can stand proudly next to the repertory of any other instrument.

And in a way I'm happy to see that the instrument's cult following is levelling off. The cult of the instrument is O.K. for people who are mad about the guitar. But I love music. The guitar is just the instrument I happen to play.[177]

188

In a unique edition, RCA issued a boxed set of 28 compact discs covering Bream's recordings 1959-1990 and offering a panoramic retrospective on guitar history since 1959.

Pursuing his new contractual interests with EMI, Julian Bream produced four significant recordings in the 1990's:

To the Edge of Dream (Rodrigo, *Concierto de Aranjuez*, Takemitsu, *To the Edge of Dream*, Arnold, *Guitar Concerto*), EMI Classics 7 54661 2, recorded 1990-1992, released 1993.

Nocturnal, Julian Bream (Martin, Britten, Brouwer, Takemitsu, Lutoslawski), EMI Classics 7 54901 2, recorded September-October, 1992, released 1993.

J.S. Bach/Julian Bream (*Prelude, Fugue and Allegro*, BWV 998, *Suite in E minor*, BWV 996, *Chaconne* from *Partita in D minor*, BWV 1004, *Partita in E major*, BWV 1006a), EMI Classics 5 55123 2, recorded October-November, 1992, released 1994.

Sonata (Antonio José, Paganini, Castelnuovo-Tedesco), EMI 5 55362 2, recorded November, 1993, released 1995.

In 1997 Bream marked the anniversary of his professional debut with a recital in Cheltenham, England where he had begun his climb to the summit fifty years before:

Suite No. 6 in C minor	Robert de Visée
Suite in E minor, BWV 996	J.S. Bach
Largo , Op. 7 - Minuet, Op.25	Sor

Interval

Five Pieces for Guitar	Manuel Ponce
(Campo - Canción popular mexicana, No. 2 -	
Mazurka - Scherzino mexicano -Valse)	
In the Woods	Toru Takemitsu
(Wainscot Pond - Rosedale - Muir Woods)	
Sonata	Leo Brouwer
(Fandangos y Boleros - Sarabanda di Skyrabin	
- La Toccata de Pasquini)	

On 20 May, 2000, Bream performed a characteristic synthesis of compositional styles at the Blandford Festival, Dorset, England:

Four Pieces	Gaspar Sanz
Pavanas	
Gallardas	
Passacalles	
Canarios	
Three Sonatas	Domenico Cimarosa
Suite No. 6 in D major, BWV 1012	J.S. Bach

Interval

Sonatina for Guitar, Op. 51	Lennox Berkeley
Four Pieces	Federico Moreno Torroba
Allegretto (from Sonatina in A)	
Nocturno	
Madroños	
Fandanguillo	
Valse, Op. 17 - Segovia, Op. 29	Albert Roussel
Four Pieces	Isaac Albéniz
Capricho Catalan, Op. 165, No. 5,	
Zortzico, Op. 165, No. 6,	
Tango, Op. 165, No. 2,	
Rumores de la Caleta (Malagueña) Op. 71, No. 6	

76. The Future of the Classic Guitar

At the turn of the century the great players of the world continued their global journeys. For those at the top of guitar achievement the glittering prizes of fame and esteem are theirs for the asking. One such performer at the pinnacle is Manuel Barrueco, whose itinerary of concerts and many recordings demonstrate the world-wide demand for the finest the guitar has to offer:

Manuel Barrueco's schedule of concerts 1999 -2001:

1999: September: 30, New Brunswick, NJ.

October: 1, Trenton, NJ • 2, Newark, NJ • 3, Newark, NJ • 8, Trieste, Italy • 9, Pordenone, Italy • 10, Trieste, Italy • 11, Ljubljana, Slovenia • 14, Bubenreuth, Germany • 16, Ansbach, Germany • 17, Munich, Germany • 21, Garden City, New York • 22, Washington, DC • 23, Hartford, CT • 25, Charleston, SC.

November: 6, Columbia, MD • 7, Atlanta, GA • 8-14, San Francisco, CA • 16, Cuernavaca, Mexico • 26, Tokyo, Japan • 29, Taipei, Taiwan.

December: 1, Seoul, Korea.

2000: January: 13-15, Indianapolis, IN • 27, Las Palmas, Spain • 28, Tenerife, Spain.

February: 8, Rochester, NY • 23 - **March** 4, San Francisco CA, • 12, Baltimore, MD.

April: 3, Rome, Italy • 7, Rotterdam, Holland • 10, Bari, Italy • 22, Los Angeles, CA.

June: 7-11, Baltimore, MD.

July: 15, Oporto, Portugal,• 21, Ludwigsburg, Germany • 23, Rheingau, Germany • 27, Nurtingen, Germany.

August: 4, Caramoor, NY • 17, Hollywood Bowl, Los Angeles, CA.

September: 23, South Bend, IN.

October: 7, Minneapolis, MN • 12, New York, NY • 28-29, Fresno, CA.

November: 2, La Coruña, Spain • 3, Madrid, Spain • 4, Lerida, Spain.

December: 2, Los Angeles, CA.

2001: January: 12-14, Valencia, Spain • 28, Munich, Germany.

February: 18, Ann Arbor, MI.

March: 5, Milan, Italy • 11, Argonne, IL • 18, Overland, KS

April: 6-8, Barcelona, Spain • 19-21, Delaware.

May: 13-23, Japan Tour.[178]

In addition, Barrueco has recording sessions, teaching programs (including a post at the Peabody Conservatory, Baltimore), and further concerts fitted in over the months. The modern artist needs extraordinary stamina to endure the constant pressures of professional life.

Over recent decades the achievements of performers, composers, scholars and luthiers have established the classic guitar as a creative force to be reckoned with. Moreover, the expansion of guitar teaching at all levels has provided an unprecedented supply of younger performers of virtuosic ability. The following selection of the new generation of recitalists (born after 1960), indicates the abundance of gifted players around the world:

Hugo Germán Gaido (Argentina/Germany), Alexander Swete (Austria), Slava Grigoryan, Craig Ogden (Australia), Denis Azabagic (Bosnia), Cristina Azuma, Marcelo Kayath, Fabio Zanon (Brazil), Remi Boucher, Jeffrey McFadden (Canada), Wang Yameng (China), Ricardo Cobo (Colombia), Zoran Dukic, Ana Vidovic (Croatia), Vladislav Blaha, Pavel Steidl, Marek Veleminsky (formerly Czechoslovakia), Kaare Norge (Denmark), Timo Korhonen (Finland), Frédéric Zigante (France), Franz

192

Halász (USA/Germany), Tilman Hoppstock, Irina Kircher, Thomas Kirchhoff, Susanne Mebes, Martin Pramanik, Stephan Schmidt, Friedemann Wuttke (Germany), Alexander-Sergei Ramírez (Peru/ Germany), Antigoni Goni, Elena Papandreou (Greece), Jozsef Eötvös, Peter and Zoltan Katona (Hungary), Leonardo de Angelis, Tania Chagnot, Flavio Cucchi, Aniello Desiderio, Carlo Marchione, Franco Platino, Emanuele Segre (Italy), Kaori Muraji, Kazuhito Yamashita (Japan), Matthew Marshall (New Zealand), Trond Davidsen (Norway), Berta Rojas (Paraguay), Krzysztof Pelech (Poland), Margarita Escarpa, José María Gallardo del Rey, Ricardo Gallén, María Esther Guzman, Ignacio Rodes, Marco Socias, Carlos Trepat (Spain), Mats Bergström (Sweden), Tom Kerstens (Holland/UK), Mark Ashford, Simon Dinnigan, Tom Dupré, Paul Galbraith, Richard Hand, Nicola Hall, Jonathan Leathwood, Allan Neave, Gary Ryan (UK), Lily Afshar (Iran/USA), Philip Hii (Malaysia/USA), Kevin Gallagher, Adam Holzman, Steve Kostelnik, Scott Tennant, Jason Vieaux (USA), Goran Listes, Istvan Römer (formerly Yugoslavia).[179]

As with creative writers, athletes and actors, the world of the young concert guitarist is precarious. The ascent up the greasy pole of fame, whether slow or rapid, depends not only on outstanding ability, but on a combination of perseverance, forceful character, luck, and the avoidance of incapacitating injury or setbacks. The continuance of a mature progressive career after the label of 'prodigy' has become well worn, demands endurance and management skills in addition to a distinctive musical identity.

For years there has been a decline in attendances at recitals of classical music. Thus emerging soloists (whether guitarists, pianists, violinists, etc.), can sometimes scarcely establish a foothold, let alone a worthwhile income. A playing career is never easy, but rapid cultural changes have increased difficulties confronting musicians.

Regrettably, fine recitalists and excellent new compositions often make little impact on the general public. Powerful commercial interests in the media demand a predominant focus on international rock music, its culture and idols. The quiet voice and subtly expressive repertoire of the unamplified

193

solo guitar does not attract television producers, who, in the main, prefer more exciting images. The classic guitar, imparting its concepts of gentle introversion, is generally at odds with rock music's massive amplification and frenetic dance routines.

Yet surprising resurgences of the guitar occur with the advent of personalities able to offer a broad public a fresh vision of instrumental possibilities. This happened in flamenco guitar when the innovative playing of Paco de Lucía was duly rewarded with a large following.

Similarly, from the 1960's onwards, Los Romeros, the quartet acclaimed as the 'Royal Family' of the guitar - Celedonio Romero (1913-1996) and his sons, Celín (b. 1936), Pepe (b. 1944), and Angel (b. 1946) - achieved immense popularity for virtuosity, musicianship, and their overall charisma, whether in ensemble or as soloists.

Los Romeros, based in the USA, proved capable of capturing the high ground of public interest for four decades in concerts, television and a host of recordings while maintaining the highest standards of the traditions of the classic guitar.

Thus in times of radical changes in public awareness of music and culture, the poetic qualities of the nylon-strung guitar remain at the heart of its appeal. The inherited treasury of five hundred years of music, much of it recently reclaimed from obscurity, indicates that here is a realm of art too precious ever to be lost again. The sonorities of unamplified plucked strings present an eternal poignancy, an intimacy between player and audience of a unique kind. As one of the supremely expressive musical voices of humanity, the classic guitar continues to fascinate and persuade.

Footnotes to The 20th Century

1. Program kindly provided by Alberto López Poveda, from his Segovia Archives, Linares, Spain.

2. Bruno Tonazzi, *Miguel Llobet, Chitarrista dell'Impressionismo* (Ancona/Milan: Edizioni Bèrben, 1966), p. 17.

3. Richard D. Stover, *Six Silver Moonbeams, The Life and Times of Agustín Barrios Mangoré* (Clovis, California: Querico Publications, 1992), p. 49.

4. Juan Riera, *Emilio Pujol* (Lerida: Instituto de Estudios Ilerdenses, 1974), pp. 81-82. (Trans. GW.)

5. Andrés Segovia, *Segovia: an Autobiography of the Years 1893-1920* (New York: Macmillan, 1976), p. 194.

6. Miguel Alcázar, ed., *The Segovia-Ponce Letters,* trans. Peter Segal (Columbus, Ohio: Editions Orphée, 1989), letter of 1923, p. 3.

7. H.H.Stuckenschmidt, *Arnold Schoenberg* (London: John Calder, 1959), pp. 87-88.

8. John Williams recorded Schoenberg's *Serenade, Op. 24*, on L'Oiseau-Lyre, SOL 250, 1962.

9. Gustave Samazeuilh's *Sérénade* (Paris: Durand, 1926), recorded by Segovia on *Andrés Segovia, The Intimate Guitar 2*, RCA ARL1-1323, 1976.

10. Domingo Prat, *Diccionario de Guitarristas*, (Buenos Aires: Romero y Fernández, 1934, reprinted Columbus, Ohio: Editions Orphée, 1986), p. 289. A manuscript of Cyril Scott's composition for guitar, a *Sonatina* in three movements (previously believed lost),was discovered among Segovia's papers in Linares by Angelo Gilardino in 2001. ('*Reverie*' was actually the first movement.)

11. Malcolm Boyd, *Bach (The Master Musicians)*, (London: Dent, 1983), p. 219.

12. Hans Dagobert Bruger, ed., *Johann Sebastian Bach, Kompositionen für die Laute* (Wolfenbüttel/ Zürich: Möseler Verlag, 1921).

13. Stover, op. cit., pp. 46-47, pp. 219-226. Barrios's recordings are on *Agustín Barrios, The Complete Guitar Recordings 1913-1942*, CHR002-1-2-3 (Heidelberg: Chanterelle, 1993).

14. Ronald C. Purcell, notes for *Miguel Llobet, The Guitar Recordings, 1925-1929*, CHR001 (Heidelberg: Chanterelle, 1991), quotes Vahdah Olcott Bickford's comment that the classical guitar with its gut strings was 'more difficult to record' than the banjo or mandolin.

15. Segovia's first commercial recordings were: i) 2 May, 1927: J.S. Bach: *Gavotte en Rondeau (Partita No. 3 for solo violin in E major,* BWV 1006), *Courante (Cello Suite in C major,* BWV 1009); F. Sor: *Thème varié, Op. 9.* ii) 20 May, 1927: Torroba: *Allegretto (Sonatina in A major);* Tárrega: *Recuerdos de la Alhambra.* 15 May,1928: J.S. Bach: *Prelude in C minor* (BWV 999), *Allemande (Lute Suite,* BWV 996), *Fugue in G minor (Sonata No.1 for solo violin,* BWV 1001); Torroba: *Fandanguillo (Suite Castellana);* Turina: *Fandanguillo.* The following titles were issued on 78 rpm: a)12 inch recordings: HMV D.1255, England (also Victor 6766): J.S. Bach: *Gavotte en Rondeau;* F. Sor: *Thème Varié, Op. 9.* HMV D. 1395, England (also Victor 6767): Tárrega: *Tremolo Study;* Turina: *Fandanguillo.* b)10 inch recordings: HMV D. 1536, England (also Victor 1824): J.S. Bach: *Prelude & Allemande, Fugue.* HMV E. 475, England (also Victrola 1298): Torroba: *Allegretto;* J.S. Bach: *Courante.*

16. Peter Latham, *The Gramophone,* Vol. V, No. 3, August, 1927, p. 102.

17. Most of these are in the Guitar Archive Series, publ. Schott. Here Guitar Archive number and publication dates are indicated.

18. Felipe Pedrell, *Cancionero musical popular español,* Vols 1-4 (Barcelona: Boileau, 1958. Originally publ., Valls: 1918-1922).

19. J.B. Trend, *Luis Milán and the Vihuelistas* (Oxford University Press, 1925), *The Music of Spanish History to 1600* (O.U.P., 1926).

20. Riera, op. cit., pp. 41-42.

21. Emilio Pujol, *El dilema del sonido en la guitarra -The Dilemma of Timbre on the Guitar* (Buenos Aires: Ricordi Americana, 1960), pp. 55-56.

22. Segovia, op. cit., pp. 87-88.

23. Tonazzi, op. cit., pp. 17-18.

24. Stover, op. cit., p. 145.

25. Jan J. de Kloe, 'Frank Martin's *Quatre Pièces Brèves,* A Comparative Study of the Available Sources', *Soundboard,* Summer, 1993.

26. Mervyn Cooke, 'Frank Martin's Early Development', *The Musical Times,* September, 1990, p. 476.

27. Foreword by Manuel de Falla, December, 1933, Granada, in Emilio Pujol, *Escuela Razonada de la Guitarra* (Buenos Aires: Ricordi Americana, 1934).

28. Riera, op. cit., p. 83.

29. Ibid., p. 139.

30. Corazón Otero, *Mario Castelnuovo-Tedesco, su vida y su obra para guitarra* (Lomas de Becares, Mexico: Ediciones Musicales Yolotl, 1987), p. 51.

31. Alcázar, ed., op. cit., letter dated 20 July, 1927, p. 13. This transcription was published by Schott in 1934.

32. Paloma Sáinz de la Maza, *Regino Sáinz de la Maza, Semblanza de mi Padre* (Ayuntamiento de Burgos, 1982), p. 74. (Trans. GW.)

33. Ibid., pp. 179-180.

34. Fritz Jahnel, *Manual of Guitar Technology,* trans. J.C. Harvey (Frankfurt: Verlag Das Musikinstrument, 1981), pp. 43, 163.

35. John Morrish, ed. *The Classical Guitar, A Complete History Based on the Russell Cleveland Collection*, Graham Wade, 'Hermann Hauser,' (London: Balafon, 1997), pp. 36-39.

36. José L. Romanillos, *Antonio de Torres, Guitar-Maker - His Life and Work* (Shaftesbury: Element Books, 1987), pp. 56-57.

37. Ibid., p. 59. Examples of Hauser guitars are on: *Julian Bream plays Villa-Lobos*, RCA SB 6852, 1972, where Bream plays instruments dating 1936 and 1950; *Together,* in duo with John Williams, RCA SB 6862, 1972, where a 1936 Hauser is played, the instrument being depicted on the record sleeve. A later recording, *Julian Bream: Villa Lobos,* RCA RL12499, 1978, was played on a 1944 Hauser. For Bream's guitars on recordings see Tony Palmer, *Julian Bream, A Life on the Road* (London & Sydney: Macdonald, 1982), pp. 204-216.

38. Tonazzi, op. cit., p. 12.

39. Graham Wade, *Distant Sarabandes, The Solo Guitar Music of Joaquín Rodrigo* (Leeds: GRM Publications, 1996), pp. 8-14.

40. Victoria Kamhi de Rodrigo, *Hand in Hand with Joaquín Rodrigo,* trans. Ellen Wilkerson (Pittsburgh, Pennsylvania: Latin American Literary Review Press, 1992), pp. 105-109.

41. Riera, op. cit., p. 85.

42. Anthony Weller, Introduction to Rey de la Torre's edition, *Matteo Carcassi, 25 Melodious Studies, Op. 60* (Columbus, Ohio: Editions Orphée, 1996), p. iii.

43. Richard Burbank, *Twentieth Century Music* (London: Thames and Hudson, 1984), p. 193.

44. Alcázar, ed., op. cit., letter dated 22 October, 1940, p. 214. Though Segovia recorded two *Preludes* in the 1950's, he disliked them at first, describing them as 'vulgar'. Villa-Lobos changed the dedication of the *Preludes* from Segovia to Mindinha, (the composer's wife) when the pieces were published by Eschig (1954).

45. Andrade Muricy, *Villa-Lobos-Uma Interpretação* (Rio de Janeiro: Ministerio da Educação e Cultura, 1961), p. 146.

46. Graham Wade, *Joaquín Rodrigo and the Concierto de Aranjuez* (Leeds: Mayflower Enterprises, 1985), p. 16.

47. Burbank, op. cit., p. 203.

48. The North American premiere of Ponce's *Concierto del Sur* was on 13 January, 1946, at Carnegie Hall, New York, Segovia's first appearance with an orchestra in the USA. (Castelnuovo-Tedesco's *Guitar Concerto* was also performed.) Graham Wade, Gerard Garno, *A New Look at Segovia, His Life, His Music,* Vol. 1 (Pacific, Missouri: Mel Bay, 1997), pp. 122-123.

49. Stover, op. cit., pp. 171-174. After Barrios's death, his compositions were neglected until John Williams launched a Barrios revival in the 1970's.

50. Details of recitals in Mexico were kindly supplied by Alberto López Poveda from his archives in Linares, Spain.

51. Emilio Pujol, ed., *Luys de Narváez, Los seys libros del Delphin* (1945), *Alonso Mudarra, Tres libros de música en cifra para vihuela* (1949), *Enríquez de Valderrábano, Libro de música de vihuela, intitulado Silva de Sirenas* (1965) (Barcelona: Consejo Superior de Investigaciones Científicas, Instituto Español de Musicología).

52. Andrés Segovia, ed., *Twenty Studies for the Guitar by Fernando Sor* (New York: Edward B. Marks Music Corporation, 1945), *Preface.*

53. Editor's *Preface, The Guitar Review,* Vol. 1, No. 1, October-November,1946, p. 3.

54. *The Chronicle, The Guitar Review,* Vol. 1, No.2, 1947, p. 38.

55. *The Guitar Review,* Vol. 1, No. 4, 1947, pp. 77-86.

56. Ivor Mairants, *My Fifty Fretting Years* (Newcastle upon Tyne: Ashley Mark Publishing Company, 1980), p. 333.

57. Alexander Bellow, *The Illustrated History of the Guitar* (New York: Belwin-Mills, 1970), p. 193.

58. The DuPont Chemical Company supplied monofilament nylon (used in the manufacture of fishing lines) though they did not produce strings themselves for the guitar trade. Maurice J. Summerfield, *The Classical Guitar, Its Evolution, Players and Personalities Since 1800* (Newcastle upon Tyne: Ashley Mark Publishing Company, 1996), p. 345.

59. Andrés Segovia, 'Manuel M. Ponce, Sketches from Heart and Memory,' *The Guitar Review,* No. 7, 1948, p. 4.

60. The sessions in the studio (1948), produced these 78 rpm/12" records:
Two Studies: Villa-Lobos (27 June)	COLUMBIA CAX 10567, LX 1248
Arada, Fandanguillo: Torroba (27 June)	COLUMBIA CAX 10568, LX 1248
Fandanguillo: Turina (27 June)	COLUMBIA CAX 10569, LX 1248
Norteña: Crespo (22 June)	COLUMBIA CAX 10569, LX 1248
Tarantella in A minor:	
Castelnuovo-Tedesco (30 June)	COLUMBIA CAX 10570, LX 1404-6
Sonatina Meridional: Ponce (29/30 June)	COLUMBIA CAX 10574-5, LX 1275
Allegro (Rondo) (from *Sonata Clásica):* Ponce	COLUMBIA 21151, LB 130
Guitar Concerto No.1 in D major,Op. 99:	
Castelnuovo-Tedesco (Alec Sherman, conductor,	
New London Orchestra) (11/12 July, 1949)	COLUMBIA CAX 10582-87, LX 1404-6

61. *BMG,* Vol. XLII, No. 478, February, 1945, p. 114. Between 1934 and 1936 Presti recorded solos from Segovia's repertoire including *Sonatina in A* (Torroba), *Serenata* (Malats), *Two Popular Mexican Folk Songs* (Ponce), *Courante* (Bach), *Spanish Dance No. 5* (Granados), *Rumores de la Caleta* (Albéniz), and works by Paganini and Fortea.

62. Wilfrid M. Appleby, *BMG,* Vol. XLVI, No. 529, May, 1949, p. 166. Presti also played the *Concierto de Aranjuez* in Lille, Tunis, Algiers, Luxembourg, Monte Carlo and other European cities. Deric Kennard, *BMG,* Vol. XLIX, No. 560, December, 1951, p. 56.

63. A.P. Sharpe, *BMG,* Vol. XLIX, No. 561, January, 1952, p. 98.

64. This performance by Narciso Yepes was at the Teatro Español, Madrid, with Ataulfo Argenta conducting the Madrid Chamber Orchestra, *BMG,* Vol. XLV, No. 521, September, 1948, p. 237.

65. Wilfrid M. Appleby, *BMG,* Vol. XLVI, No. 529, May, 1949, p. 166.

66. *BMG,* Vol. XLIX, No. 564, April, 1952, p. 167.

67. Yepes's recording of Rodrigo's *Concierto de Aranjuez* with the Madrid Chamber Orchestra, conductor Ataulfo Argenta, first issued on London International TW91019.

68. Trevor Harvey, *The Gramophone*, Vol. XXXII, No. 382, March, 1955, p. 437.

69. Summerfield, op. cit., p. 261.

70. Julian Bream, BBC Radio, August, 1974.

71. Wilfrid M. Appleby, *BMG,* Vol. XLV, No. 513, January, 1948, p. 73.

72. Robert Offergeld, notes for recording by Manuel López Ramos of Castelnuovo-Tedesco's *Quintetto, Op. 143,* RCA VICS 1367, 1968.

73. Hans Haug (1900-1967) of Switzerland won the chamber music award with *Concertino for Guitar:* Alexandre Tansman gained the solo prize with his suite, *Cavatina.*

74. Long playing records advertised were: Rey de la Torre, *The Music of Francisco Tárrega,* SMC 516, *The Music of Fernando Sor,* SMC517, *Grand Sonata, Op. 22 by Fernando Sor,* AL76: Felix Argüelles, *Spanish Composers Series,* Vols. 1 & 2, SMC506,507: Carlos Montoya, *Flamenco Inventions,* SMC 512: Vicente Gómez, *Vicente Gómez Plays a Guitar Recital,* DL8017: Julio Martínez Oyanguren, *Latin-American Folk Music,* DL8018. Five Segovia long playing records were advertised, each entitled *An Andrés Segovia Recital:* DL 8022, DL 9633, DL 9638, DL 9647, MGM 123.

75. Heitor Villa-Lobos, *Douze Etudes* (Paris: Max Eschig, © 1953), *Preface.*

76. Simon Wright, *Villa-Lobos* (Oxford University Press, 1992), p. 123.

77. See Chapter 15. At this time, Rodrigo also wrote *Tres piezas españolas (Fandango, Passacaglia, Zapateado).*

78. Kamhi de Rodrigo, op. cit., pp.174-175.

79. Reginald Smith Brindle, *Preface, El Polifemo de Oro* (London:Schott, 1982).

80. Malcolm Macdonald, *The Gramophone,* Vol. XXXVIII, No. 446, July, 1960, p. 74.

81. A. McIntosh Patrick, 'Conversation with Julian Bream', *Guitar News,* No. 43, July-August, 1958, pp. 12-13.

82. Segovia did not play the work and the premiere was by Siegfried Behrend in Strasbourg, November, 1969.

83. David F. Marriott, 'Ernst Krenek', *Soundboard,* Vol. VIII, No. 4, November, 1981, p. 267.

84. David F. Marriott, 'Ernst Krenek', *Soundboard,* Vol. IX, No. 2, Summer, 1982, pp. 124-127. Other works by Krenek with a guitar part include *Kleiner Symphony, Op. 58* (1928), *Sestina, Op. 161* (1957), *Quaestro Tiempo, Op. 170* (1959), and *Hausmusik, Op. 179* (1959), *Quintina, Op. 191* (1965), *Exercises of a Late Hour, Op. 200* (1967) and four operas of the 1960's.

85. Maurice Ohana, *Catalogue of Works* (Paris: Gérard Billaudot, 1992), p. 10. *Tiento* by Maurice Ohana, ed. Yepes (Paris: Gérard Billaudot, 1968).

86. Enrique Franco, trans. Gwyn Morris, notes for recording of *Tres Gráficos,* Narciso Yepes, London Symphony Orchestra, conductor Rafael Frühbeck de Burgos, DG 2530 585, 1975.

87. John Wager-Schneider, 'The Contemporary Guitar', *Soundboard,* Vol. VIII, No. 2, May, 1981, p. 92. Goffredo Petrassi, *Suoni Notturni,* published in *Antologia per Chitarra,* M. Ablóniz, ed., (Milan: Ricordi, 1961). Quote from Ernesto Bitetti in liner notes for his recording, *Four Centuries of Italian Music for the Guitar,* Vox Turnabout TV 34680, 1975.

88. Morrish, ed., op. cit., Graham Wade, 'Hermann Hauser II', pp. 60-61.

89. John W. Duarte, 'John Christopher Williams,' Len Williams, ed., *The Spanish Guitar Today, A Short History and Handbook of Reference* (London: Spanish Guitar Center, c.1955), p. 19.

90. Terry Usher, 'John Williams Guitar Recital,' *BMG*, Vol. LVII, No. 655, November, 1959, p. 34.

91. *SEGOVIA GOLDEN JUBILEE:*

    Vol. I: Brunswick AXTL 1088: *Concierto del Sur,* Manuel Ponce: (with the Symphony of the Air, conductor: Enrique Jordá), *Fantasía para un Gentilhombre,* Joaquín Rodrigo: (Symphony of the Air, Enrique Jordá).

    Vol. 2: Brunswick AXTL 1089: *Prelude,* S. L.Weiss-Ponce (with Rafael Puyana, harpsichord): *Pièces caractéristiques,* Torroba: *Antaño,* Esplá: *Allegro in A major,* Ponce: *The Old Castle (Pictures at an Exhibition),* Mussorgsky: *Segovia,* Roussel: *Study,* Segovia: *Three Pieces,* Tansman: *Tonadilla,* Granados-Llobet.

    Vol. 3: Brunswick AXTL 1090: *Prelude and Allegro,* de Murcia:*Study No.1 in C, Study No. 9 in A minor,* Sor: *Sonata, Homage to Boccherini,* Castelnuovo-Tedesco: *Fandango,* Rodrigo: *Passacaglia, Gigue, Gavotta,* Roncalli: *Study No. 20 in C major, Two Minuets,* Sor: *Spanish Dance No. 10 in G,* Granados.

92. *BMG*, Vol. LVI, No. 653, September, 1959, p. 301.

93. Julian Bream's first RCA recordings were: *The Art of Julian Bream,* RCA RB 16239, 1959; *Guitar Concertos* (Malcolm Arnold, *Guitar Concerto, Op. 67,* Mauro Giuliani, *Concerto for Guitar and Strings), RB16252,* 1960; *The Golden Age of English Lute Music,* RB16281, 1961; *An Evening of Elizabethan Music,* RB 6592, 1962.

94. Program notes by Julian Bream for recital by the Julian Bream Consort at the Wigmore Hall, London, 26 September, 1961. Anthony Gishford, ed., *Tribute to Benjamin Britten on his Fiftieth Birthday* (London: Faber and Faber, 1963), p. 92.

95. José Ramírez III, *En Torno a la Guitarra/Things about the Guitar* (Madrid: Soneto, 1993), p.93.

96. Ibid., p.93.

97. John Morrish, ed., op. cit., Tim Miklaucic, 'José Ramírez III,' pp. 55-59.

98. John W. Duarte, 'Alirio Diaz', *BMG,* Vol. LVIII, No. 668, December, 1960, pp. 66-67.

99. Diaz's recording of Rodrigo's *Invocation et Danse (Hommage à Manuel de Falla)* was first released on RCA RB 6599 (1964), Bream's recording on RCA RL 45548 (1983).

100. Segovia's recording of Boccherini's *Concerto for Guitar and Orchestra in E major* (arr. Cassadó), with the Symphony of the Air under Enrique Jordá, and J.S. Bach's *Suite No. 3 in C major for Cello,* BWV1009, (arr. Duarte), was issued on Decca DL-710043/MCA MUCS 125, 1961.

101. Quoted in *Guitar News,* No. 72, July-August, 1963, pp. 11-12.

102. Romanillos, op. cit., p. 53.

103. A Rubio guitar (1965) can be heard on Bream's *20th Century Guitar,* RCA SB 6723, 1966. A 1966 Rubio guitar was played on *Julian Bream and his Friends,* RCA SB 6772, 1968, and *Classic Guitar,* RCA SB 6796, 1968. Rubio's 1967 lute can be heard on *Elizabethan Lute Songs,* RCA SB 6835, 1970, *The Woods so Wild,* RCA SB 6865, 1973, *Concertos for Lute and Orchestra,* RCA ARL1 1180, 1975, and *Lute Music of John Dowland,* RCA RL 11491, 1976. A 1968 Rubio lute was used for *Music of Spain,* Vol. 1, RCA RL 13435, 1979. Palmer, op. cit., pp. 204-216.

104. Kay Jafee, notes for *CBS Records presents John Williams*, CBS 72339, 1964-1965: *Fourth Lute Suite* (J.S. Bach), *Sevilla* (Albéniz), *Recuerdos de la Alhambra* (Tárrega), *Fandanguillo, Soleares, Ráfaga* (Turina), *El Testamen de Amelia* (arr. Llobet), *Scherzino Mexicano* (Ponce), and *El Colibri* (Sagreras).

105. Stephen Dodgson, *Partita for Guitar* (Oxford University Press, 1965). John Williams *Virtuoso Music for Guitar*, CBS 72348, 1965, included *Sonata in A major* (Paganini), *Spanish Dance No. 5* (Granados), *Etude No. 8* (Villa-Lobos), *Homenaje* (Falla), *Vivo ed energico* (from Castelnuovo-Tedesco's *Sonata).*

106. *Julian Bream: 20th Century Guitar* was first released on RB 6723, 1966.

107. Bream's first publications for Faber were: *Suite in E minor* (Buxtehude), *Three Lyric Pieces* (Grieg), *Suite for Two Guitars* (Lawes), *Suite in E minor* (J.S.Bach), *Three Sonatas* (Cimarosa). *Suite in A minor* (Froberger) followed in 1968.

108. Bream's uniquely authoritative interpretations are on *Julian Bream '70s*, RCA SB 6876, 1973 *(Concerto for Guitar and Chamber Ensemble*, Richard Rodney Bennett, *Elegy,* Alan Rawsthorne, *Five Bagatelles,* William Walton, *Theme and Variations,* Lennox Berkeley), and *Dedication,* RCA RL254190, 1982 *(Five Impromptus,* Richard Rodney Bennett, *Five Bagatelles,* William Walton, *Hill Runes,* Peter Maxwell Davies, *Royal Winter Music,* Hans Werner Henze).

109. Martin Bookspan, Ross Yockey, *André Previn, A Biography* (London: Hamish Hamilton, 1981), p. 279. Ponce, *Concierto del Sur;* Previn, *Guitar Concerto,* John Williams, London Symphony Orchestra, with André Previn, conductor, CBS 73060, 1972.

110. The Duo's recordings:

Together, RCA SB6862, 1972: *Suite* (Lawes, arr. Bream), *Duo in G, Op. 34* (Carulli), *Córdoba* (Albéniz, arr. Pujol), *Goyescas: Intermezzo* (Granados, arr. Pujol), *La Vida Breve, Spanish Dance No. 1* (Falla, arr. Pujol, rev. Bream), *Pavan for a Dead Princess* (Ravel, arr. Bream).

Together Again, RCA ARL 1 0456, 1974: *Serenade in A, Op. 96* (Carulli, ed. Bream/Williams), *Danza Española No. 6 (Rondalla Aragonesa)* (Granados, transcr. Llobet), *Bajo la Palmera (Canto de España No. 3, Op. 232)* (Albéniz, transcr. Llobet), *Danza Española No. 11* (Granados, transcr. Llobet), *Variazioni Concertante, Op. 130* (Giuliani, ed. Bream/Williams), *Evocación* (Albéniz, transcr. Llobet).

Live, RCA RL 03090 2, recorded on USA tour (Symphony Hall, Boston, 15 October, 1978, Lincoln Center, New York, 18 October, 1978): *Pavan and Galliard* (Johnson, arr. Bream), *Partie Polonoise* (Telemann), *Fantasie, Op. 54* (Sor), *Theme and Variations, Op. 18* (Brahms, arr. Williams), *Dolly, Op. 56* (Fauré, arr. Bream), *Rêverie* (Debussy, arr. Batchelar), *Golliwog's Cakewalk* (Debussy, arr. Bream), *Clair de Lune* (Debussy, arr. Bream/Williams), *Castilla* (Albéniz, arr. Llobet), *Spanish Dance No. 2 (Oriental)* (Granados, arr. Bream/Williams).

111. Composers in Gilardino's Bèrben series include: Jean Absil, Hermann Ambrosius, Pierre Ancelin, Denis Aplvor, Vicente Asencio, Henk Badings, Herbert Baumann, Chiara Benati, Lennox Berkeley, Bruno Bettinelli, Gilbert Biberian, Carey Blyton, Dusan Bogdanovic, Jarmil Burghauser, Otello Calbi, Mario Castelnuovo-Tedesco, Luciano Chailly, Sergio Chiereghin, Gian Paolo Chiti, Ernesto Cordero, Enrico Correggia, Ettore Desderi, Stephen Dodgson, David Dorward, John W. Duarte, Thomas Eastwood, Mikael Edlund, Ferenc Farkas, David Farquhar, Victor Fox,

Johan Franco, Terenzio Gargiulo, Emilio Ghezzi, Antonio Giacometti, Angelo Gilardino, Barbara Elena Giuranna, Luis Jorge González, Friedrich Karl Grimm, M. Camargo Guarnieri, Hans Haug, Douglas Jamieson, Bryan Johanson, Antonio José, Bernardo Juliá, Armin Kaufmann, Harrison Kerr, Jacques Leduc, Herbert Lumby, Ruggero Maghini, Tomás Marco, Franco Margola, Edward McGuire, Jost Meier, Josep M. Mestres Quadreny, Miroslav Miletic, Carlo Mosso, Erich Opitz, Juan Orrego Salas, Aurelio Peruzzi, Astor Piazzolla, Manuel M. Ponce, Sergio Prodigo, Giuseppe Radole, Gardner Read, Joaquín Rodrigo, Giuseppe Rosetta, Antonio Ruiz Pipó, Arturo Sacchetti, Vincenzo Saldarelli, Peter Sander, Guido Santórsola, Henri Sauguet, Gary M. Schneider, Reginald Smith Brindle, Bernard Stevens, Richard Stoker, Robert Strizich, Fernando Sulpizi, Alexandre Tansman, Federico Moreno Torroba, Giulio Viozzi, Arthur Wills, Thomas Wilson, Pierre Wissmer.

112. Duarte's publications in Bèrben's list include: *Fantasia and Fugue on 'Torre Bermeja', Op. 30* (1960), *Variations on a French Nursery Song, Op. 32* (two guitars) (1965/7), *Five Quiet Songs, Op. 37* (high voice/guitar) (1968), *Prelude, Canto and Toccata, Op. 38* (1968), *Greek Suite, Op. 39* (two guitars) (1968), *Suite Piemontese, Op. 46* (1970), *Suite Ancienne, Op. 47* (1969), *Sonatina Lirica, Op. 48* (1971), *Etude Diabolique, Op. 49* (1969), *All in a Row (of Webern's), Op. 51* (1972), *Sua Cosa, Op. 52* (1972), *Mutations on the Dies Irae, Op. 58,* (1973/74), *Suite Française, Op. 61* (two guitars) (1974), *Insieme, Op. 72* (guitar/harpsichord) (1978), *Greek Suite No. 2, Op. 89* (1981).

113. *Nunc* followed Petrassi's *Suoni Notturni* (1959) and *Seconda Serenata-Trio* (1962) for harp, mandolin and guitar.

114. John Wager-Schneider, 'The Contemporary Guitar,' *Soundboard,* Vol. VIII, No. 2, May, 1981, p. 93.

115. Brouwer's works published in the 1970's include: *Preludio* (composed 1956; publ. Eschig, 1972), *Danza Caracteristica* (1957; Schott, 1972), *Micro Piezas* (1957-1958; Eschig, 1973), *Etudes simples Nos 1-10* (1959-1961; Eschig, 1972), *Deux Airs Populaires Cubains (Guajira criolla-Zapateo),* (Eschig, 1972), *Elogio de la Danza* (1964; Schott, 1972),*Canticum* (1968; Schott, 1972), *La Espiral Eterna* (1971; Schott, 1973), *Guitar Concerto* (1972), *Parabola* (1973; Eschig, 1975), *Tarantos* (Eschig, 1977), *Deux Thèmes Populaires Cubains (Berceuse-Les Yeux Sorciers)* (Eschig, 1978).

116. Alberto Ginastera, *Preface* to *Sonata, Op. 47* (Boosey & Hawkes, 1978).

117. George Clinton, interview with Romanillos, *Guitar,* Vol. 1, No.5, December, 1972, p. 24.

118. *Guitarra, A Musical Journey through Spain,* devised and presented by Julian Bream, © 1985, Virgin Classics VVD 513-514. A 1973 Romanillos guitar can be heard on these Bream recordings: Giuliani and Sor, RCA ARL1 0711; Rodrigo, *Concierto de Aranjuez,* Berkeley, *Guitar Concerto,* RCA ARL1 118; *The Music of Spain* Vol. IV, Sor and Aguado, RCA RL 14033; *Dedication,* RCA RL 25419; *The Music of Spain,* Vol. V, Albéniz & Granados, RCA RL 14378. See Palmer, op. cit., pp. 213-216.

119. Peter Sensier, 'Agustín Barrios,' *Guitar,* Vol. 2, No. 12, July, 1974, pp. 22-23.

120. Works of Barrios published before 1978 include: Laurindo Almeida, ed.: *Preludio, Op. 5,No. 1* (1957) (Ricordi Americana), *Aconquija* (undated), *La Catedral* (1968), (Sherman Oaks, California: Brazilliance Music Publishing). Alirio Diaz, ed.: *Oración* (1972), *Medallón antiguo* (1974) (Padua: Zanibon). Pierluigi Cimma, ed.: *Choro da Saudade* (Ancona, Milan: Bèrben, 1970). Complete editions: Richard D. Stover, ed., *The Guitar Works of Agustín Barrios Mangoré,* Vols 1-4 (Melville, New York: Belwin-Mills, 1976-1985); Jesús Benites R., ed., *A. Barrios Mangoré,* Vols 1-4 (Japan: Zen-On,1977).

121. John Williams, notes for *John Williams-Barrios*, CBS 76662, 1977.

122. J.M. Thomson, ed., *Early Music*, Vol. 1, No. 1, January, 1973, p.1.

123. John Williams, *Guitar*, Vol. 1, No. 1, August, 1972, p. 1.

124. Recordings include: *Changes*, Cube Records, Toofa 12/1, 1971; *The Height Below*, Cube Records, Toofa 12/2, 1973; *John Williams and Friends*, CBS 73487, 1976; *Best Friends, Cleo Laine - John Williams*, RCA RS 1094, 1976; *Travelling*, Pye, Cube Hifly 27, 1978; *Bridges*, Lotus, WH 5015, 1979; *The Guitar is the Song*, CBS 73679, 1983.

125. George Clinton, interview with John Williams, 'The Guitar doesn't need great players', *Guitar*, Vol. 2, No.1, August, 1973, pp. 20-22.

126. Harvey Turnbull, *The Guitar from the Renaissance to the Present Day*, (London: Batsford, 1974), p. 1.

127. Research subjects included guitar technique, c.1780-1850, Leonhard von Call, an edition of Sanz's *Instrucción de música sobre la guitarra española*, Corbetta's guitar music, etc. The periodical was eventually titled *Soundboard* rather than *The Soundboard*.

128. Guitar periodicals in 1976 included: *Soundboard* (California, USA), *Guitar Review* (New York, USA), *Gitarre* (Munich, Germany), *Gendai Guitar* (Tokyo, Japan), *Il Fronimo* (Milan, Italy), *Creative Guitar International* (Texas, USA), *BMG* (London, England), *Guitar* (London, England), *Guitar & Lute* (Honolulu, Hawaii), *Guitar Player* (California, USA), *Frets* (Gifu City, Japan). *The Soundboard*, Vol. III, No. 1, February, 1976, p. 14.

129. Manuel Barrueco: Albéniz, *Suite Española, Op. 47*, Granados, *5 Spanish Dances, Op. 37*, Turnabout TV 34738, recorded May, 1978, released 1979. Manuel Barrueco, ed., *Isaac Albéniz, Suite Española, Op. 47* (Melville, New York: Belwin-Mills, 1981).

130. John Williams, *Classical Guitar*, Vol. 18, No. 7, March 2000, p. 54. John Williams, *Echoes of Spain-Albéniz*, CBS 36679, recorded October/November 1980, issued 1981. All arrangements by John Williams.

131. *Julian Bream plays Granados & Albéniz*, RCA RS 9008, 1982. All arrangements by Julian Bream.

132. Henry Adams, 'Interview: Antonio Lauro,' *Guitar & Lute*, Issue No. 12, January, 1980, pp. 8-12.

133. Ricardo Iznaola, Tribute to Antonio Lauro, *Guitar International*, Vol. 15, No. 1, Issue 169, August, 1986, pp. 35-36.

134. J. Massó, 'Ignacio Fleta', *Guitar*, Vol. 8, No. 3, October, 1979, pp. 10-11.

135. Siegfried H. Hogemuller, 'In Memoriam Ignacio Fleta', *Guitar*, Vol. 6, No. 11, June, 1978, pp. 3-5.

136. John W. Duarte, notes for *The Art of Segovia, The HMV Recordings 1927-39*, HMV RLS 745, 1980 & EMI CDH 761048 2, 1988.

137. MCA records included:

Segovia España, MCA 2533: *Fandango* (Rodrigo), *Tonadilla, Spanish Dance No. 10 in G* (Granados), *Leyenda, Sevilla* (Albéniz), *Étude No. 1* (Villa-Lobos), *Homage to Aguirre* (Crespo), *Valse* (Ponce), *Albada, Allegretto* (from *Sonatina*) (Torroba), *Sevillana* (Turina).

The Unique Art of Andrés Segovia, MCA 2501: *Allemande in A minor, Sarabande in A minor, Gigue in A minor* (J.S. Bach), *Prelude No. 1 in E minor* (Villa-Lobos), *Mallorca* (Albéniz),

Pavanas, No.1 in A minor, No. 6 in D , No. 3 in C, No. 5 in D, No. 2 in B minor, No. 4 in D (Milán), *Prelude* (from *Suite 'Homage to Chopin'*) (Tansman), *Variations and Fugue on a Theme of Handel* (Harris).

Joaquín Rodrigo, Fantasía para un Gentilhombre, Andrés Segovia, MCA 1-202418: *Fantasía para un Gentilhombre (Villano-Ricercare-La Españoleta-Toques de la Caballería-Danzas de las Hachas-Canario* (Joaquín Rodrigo), *Concierto del Sur (Allegretto-Andante-Allegro moderato e festivo)* (M.Ponce).(Orquesta Symphony of the Air conducted by Enrique Jordá.)

138. Graham Wade, *Segovia -A Celebration of the Man and His Music* (London: Allison & Busby, 1983), pp. 21-34.

139. Françoise-Emmanuelle Denis, notes for *Guitare d'hier et d'aujourd'hui,* Roberto Aussel playing Kleynjans, Ponce, Rodrigo and Ginastera, Guitare GHA 5256002, 1985. Summerfield, op. cit., p. 134.

140. Nikita Koshkin, *Foreword, Suite: The Prince's Toys* (Tokyo: Gendai Guitar, 1983), pp. 4-5.

141. John W. Duarte, notes for Vladimir Mikulka's recording, BIS LP-240, 1983.

142. John Williams, notes for *The Seville Concert,* Sony, SK53359, 1993.

143. Sharon Isbin, dedicatee of *El Decameron Negro,* notes for *Road to the Sun, Latin Romances for Guitar,* Virgin Classics VC791128-2, 1990.

144. Program note by Julian Bream.

145. Leo Brouwer, notes for recording of *Concierto de Volos* by Costas Cotsiolis, with the Orquesta de Córdoba, conducted by Leo Brouwer, GHA 126.025, 1998.

146. Peter Maxwell Davies, quoted in John W. Duarte's notes for *Dedication, Julian Bream,* RCA RL25419, 1982.

147. Peter Maxwell Davies, composer's note from *Sonata* (London: Chester Music Ltd., 1990).

148. Astor Piazzolla: Angelo Gilardino, ed., *Cinco Piezas (Campero-Romántico-Acentuado-Tristón-Compadre),* (Ancona, Italy: Bèrben, 1981). Recorded on *Récital de guitare, Roberto Aussel,* Disques Circé, CIR 822, 1982.

149. Summerfield, op. cit., p. 315.

150. Augustin Wiedemann, trans. Lawrence Brazier, notes for his recording, *All in Twilight, Guitar Music of the 80's* (works by Dyens, Assad, Zawinul, Brouwer, Takemitsu), Arte Nova Classics 74321 58961 2, 1998. *Libra Sonatine* by Dyens, also recorded by Aniello Desiderio on *20th Century Sonatas,* Frame FR9509-2, 1995.

151. Quoted in John W. Duarte's notes for Elena Papandreou's *Guitar Recital,* Naxos, 8.554001, recorded 1996, issued 1998, pp. 2-3.

152. Elliott Carter, *Preface, Changes* (Hendon Music/Boosey & Hawkes, 1983). Recorded by David Starobin, Bridge Records, BDG 2004, 1984.

153. Graham Wade, 'Richard Rodney Bennett and the Classical Guitar', *Classical Guitar,* Vol. 4, No. 1, September, 1985, pp. 49-50.

154. Stepan Rak, interview with Lance Bosman, *Guitar International,* Vol. 13, No. 6, January, 1985, p. 12.

155. Works by Rak include: *Variations on a Theme by Jaromir Klempir* (composed 1969, publ. Prague: Panton, 1977), *Toccata* (1970, Panton, 1977), *Suita* (1974, Panton, 1977), *Variations on a Theme of Nikita Koshkin* (Panton, 1977), *Rumanian Dance* (1979), *Moorish Dance* (1979), *Czech Hymn* (1979), *Crying Guitar* (1979), *Petit Nocturne* (Helsinki, Finland: Chorus Publications, 1980), *Temptation of the Renaissance* (1980) (Chorus Publications, 1984), *Elegy* (1981), *La Guitarra (Homage to Lorca)*, *Farewell Finland* (Chorus Publications, 1984), *First Love* (rev. 1984), *Hiroshima* (c.1984), *Romance* (Chorus Publications, 1984),*Voces de Profundis* (Inspired by the film, *Psycho*) (1984) (Shaftesbury: Musical New Services, 1985), *The Sun, Homage to Tárrega, The Last Disco* (Musical New Services,1985), *Five Studies* (1985) (Chorus Publications, undated, Panton,1991), *Czech Fairy Tales, Rumba-Tango* (Shaftesbury: Montacute Publishing Company, 1985), *Sonata Mongoliana* (1986), *Remembering Prague* (written 1981, Chorus Publications, 1987), *Variations on a Theme by John W. Duarte* (1987), *Spanish Suite* (1988).

156. Rak's compositional reputation went into recession during the early 1990's, perhaps because of an appreciation that Rak himself was the best interpreter of many of his works.

157. John Wager-Schneider, 'The Contemporary Guitar - Toru Takemitsu,' *Soundboard,* Vol. VIII, No. 3, August, 1981, pp. 169-171.*Ring* (1961, flute, terz guitar and lute), *Valeria* (1965, 2 piccolos, guitar, cello and electric organ), *Stanza I* (1969, voice, piano, guitar, harp and vibraphone).

158. Yukiko Sawabe, trans. Griffin Anderson, notes for *Takemitsu played by John Williams,* Sony, SK46720. *Folios,* Toru Takemitsu (Paris: Editions Salabert, 1974).

159. *12 Songs for Guitar,* Toru Takemitsu (©1977, publ. Japan: Schott,1991): Irish Folk Song, *Londonderry Air,* Arlen, *Over the Rainbow,* Gershwin, *Summertime,* Nakada, *A Song of Early Spring,* Kosma, *Amours Perdus,* Converse, *What a Friend,* Fain, *Secret Love,* Lennon/McCartney, *Here, There and Everywhere, Michelle, Hey Jude, Yesterday,* Degeyter, *The International.*

160. Premieres:

    i) February, 1981, *Toward the Sea* (1st movement), for alto flute and guitar, Robert Aitken (alto flute), Leo Brouwer (guitar), Toronto.

    ii) March, 1983, *To the Edge of Dream,* for guitar and orchestra, Ichiro Suzuki (guitar), L'Orchestre Philharmonique de Liège, Liège, Belgium.

    iii) 2 October, 1984, *Vers, l'arc-en-ciel, Palma,* for guitar, oboe d'amore and orchestra, John Williams (guitar), Peter Walden (oboe d'amore), City of Birmingham Symphony Orchestra conducted by Simon Rattle, Birmingham, England.

    Recordings include:

    Takemitsu played by John Williams, John Williams, London Sinfonietta conducted by Esa-Pekka Salonen, *To the Edge of Dream, Toward the Sea, 4 Pieces from 12 Songs for Guitar, Vers, l'arc-en-ciel, Palma,* Sony, SK46720, recorded 11-14 September, 1989, released 1991.

    To the Edge of Dream, Julian Bream, City of Birmingham Symphony Orchestra conducted by Simon Rattle, Rodrigo, *Concierto de Aranjuez,* Takemitsu, *To the Edge of Dream,* Arnold, *Guitar Concerto,* EMI Classics 7 54661 2, recorded 1990-1992, released 1993.

161. Quoted by Gareth Walters in notes for *Nocturnal,* Julian Bream, EMI Classics 7 54901 2, recorded 1992, released 1993.

162. *Introduction* to Toru Takemitsu, *In the Woods*, Three Pieces for Guitar: *Wainscot Pond-after a Painting by Cornelia Foss*, to John Williams; *Rosedale*, to Kiyoshi Shomura; *Muir Woods*, to Julian Bream (Japan: Schott, 1996).

163. Noriko Ohtake, *Creative Sources for the Music of Toru Takemitsu* (Aldershot, England/Brookfield, Vermont: Scolar Press, 1993), p. 98.

164. John W. Duarte, notes for Antigoni Goni's recording of Carlo Domeniconi's *Koyunbaba*, Naxos 8.553774, 1997.

165. Recordings include, *The Guitarist, John Williams*, Sony SK 60586, 1998; Antigoni Goni, Naxos 8. 553774.

166. The composer offered his own performances: Carlo Domeniconi, *Sindbad, Ein Märchen für Gitarre*, Gema, undated; *To Play or Not to Play, Domeniconi plays Domeniconi*, Classic Studio Berlin, LC8716, recorded Leipzig 1992, issued 1993.

167. Augustin Wiedemann, trans. Lawrence Brazier, notes to *All in Twilight, Guitar Music of the 80's*, Arte Nova Classics 74321 58961 2, 1998.

168. Seppo Siirala, trans. Leslie Hyde, notes for *Electric Counterpoint*, Minima Mini 301, 1991.

169. Paul Griffiths, *The Thames and Hudson Dictionary of 20th Century Music* (London: Thames and Hudson, 1986), p. 121.

170. Eliot Fisk, notes for *Sequenza!*, Music Masters Classics 01612-67150-2, recorded 2-3 May, 18-20 September, 1994, Weston, Herts, England, issued 1995.

171. Ricardo Iznaola, notes for *Iznaola, The Dream of Icarus*, IGW 22874, recorded December, 1988, issued 1990.

172. Antonio José, *Sonata, para guitarra*, Angelo Gilardino and Juan José Sáenz Gallego, eds., (Ancona, Italy: Bèrben, 1990). Antonio José, *Sonata, para guitarra*, Angelo Gilardino and Ricardo Iznaola, eds., (Ancona, Italy: Bèrben, 1998).

173. Julian Bream's recording of Antonio José's *Sonata* is on *Sonata*, EMI Classics 5 55362 2, 1995.

174. Antonio José, *Sonata, para guitarra*, Angelo Gilardino and Juan José Sáenz Gallego, eds., op. cit., *Introduction*, p. 7.

175. *John Williams, Spirit of the Guitar, Music of the Americas*, CBS MK 44898, 1989.

176. Julian Byzantine, 'Greg Smallman', *Guitar International*, Vol. 17, No. 1, August, 1988, pp. 20 -22.

177. Julian Bream, quoted by Allan Kozinn, in 'Julian Bream Sets Off in a New (Old) Direction,' *Guitar Review*, Spring, 1990, p. 19.

178. Asgerdur Sigurdardottir, ed., *The Barrueco Times*, Issue #4, 1999-2000, p. 3.

179. List compiled from sources including Maurice J. Summerfield, op.cit., Eduard Wolff and Heinrich Zelton, *Gitarren Lexikon* (Hamburg: Nikol Verlagsgesellschaft MBH, 1996), recordings, agents, etc. Catherine Dickinson and Andrew Liepins of the Spanish Guitar Center, Nottingham, England, kindly assisted with advice. (Where two countries are listed for a player, the first country signifies the place of birth while the second country indicates that the person is believed to have spent some time there, perhaps in a teaching or performing capacity, though not necessarily becoming a citizen of that country.)

SELECT BIBLIOGRAPHY

General Histories of the Guitar

Aviñoa, Xose. *La Guitarra*. Barcelona: Ediciones Daimon, 1985.

Azpiazu, José de. *La Guitare et les Guitaristes*. Basle: Editions Symphonia-Verlag, 1959.

Bellow, Alexander. *The Illustrated History of the Guitar*. New York: Franco Colombo Publications: Belwin-Mills, 1970.

Buek, Fritz. *Die Gitarre und Ihre Meister*. Berlin: Schlesinger, 1926.

Carfagna, Carlo and Caprani, Alberto. *Profilo Storico della Chitarra*. Ancona: Bèrben, 1966.

Dell'Ara, Mario. *Manuale di Storia della Chitarra, Vol. 1: La Chitarra, Antica, Classica e Romantica*. Ancona: Bèrben, 1988.

Evans, Tom and Mary Anne. *Guitars, From the Renaissance to Rock*. New York & London: Paddington Press, 1977.

Giertz, Martin. *Den Klassiska Gitarren*. Stockholm: P.A. Norstedt & Söners Förlag, 1979.

Gilardino, Angelo. *Manuale di Storia della Chitarra, Vol. 2: La Chitarra Moderna e Contemporanea*. Ancona: Bèrben, 1988.

Grunfeld, Frederic V. *The Art and Times of the Guitar, An Illustrated History of Guitars and Guitarists*. New York: Macmillan, 1969.

Kozinn, Allan; Welding, Pete; Forte, Dan; Santoro, Gene. *The Guitar, The History, The Music, The Players*. Bromley: Columbus Books, 1984.

Lesure, François, ed., *Guitares*. Paris: Collection Eurydice, La Flûte de Pan, 1980.

Miteran, Alain. *Histoire de la Guitare*. Bourg-la-Reine: Zurfluh, 1997.

Moldrup, Erling. *Guitaren, Et eksotisk instrument i den danske musik*. Copenhagen: Kontrapunkt, 1997.

Morrish, John, ed. *The Classical Guitar, A Complete History Based on the Russell Cleveland Collection*. London: Balafon, 1997.

Päffgen, Peter. *Die Gitarre*. Mainz: Schott, 1988.

Ragossnig, Konrad. *Handbuch der Gitarre und Laute*. Mainz: Schott, 1978.

Schmitz, Alexander. *Das Gitarrenbuch*. Frankfurt am Main:Wolfgang Krüger Verlag, 1983.

Turnbull, Harvey. *The Guitar from the Renaissance to the Present Day*. London: Batsford, 1974.

Wade, Graham. *Traditions of the Classical Guitar*. London: John Calder, 1980.

Reference Books

Bone, Philip J. *The Guitar & Mandolin*. London: Schott & Co. Ltd, 2nd Edition, 1972.

Chaîné, Jacques, compiled by; Ophee, Matanya, ed. *The Orphée Data-Base of Guitar Records*. Columbus, Ohio: Editions Orphée, 1990.

Jape, Mijndert, ed. *Classical Guitar Music in Print*. Philadelphia: Musicdata, Inc., 1989.

Liepins, Andrew. *The Guitarist's Repertoire Guide*. 3rd Edition. Nottingham: Spanish Guitar Center, 2000.

McCreadie, Sue. *Classical Guitar Companion*. Shaftesbury: Musical New Services, 1982.

McCutcheon, Meredith Alice. *Guitar and Vihuela, An Annotated Bibliography*. New York: Pendragon Press, 1985.

Powrozniak, Jozef. *Leksykon Gitary*. Krakow: Polskie Wydawnictwo Muzyczne, 1979.

Prat, Domingo. *Diccionario de Guitarristas*. Buenos Aires: Romero y Fernández, 1934. Reprinted, Columbus, Ohio: Editions Orphée, 1986.

Schwarz, Werner. *Guitar Bibliography*. Munich: K.G. Saur, 1984.

Summerfield, Maurice. *The Classical Guitar, Its Evolution, Players and Personalities since 1800*, 4th ed. Newcastle upon Tyne: Ashley Mark Publishing Company, 1996.

Wolff, Eduard and Zelton, Heinrich. *Gitarren Lexikon*. Hamburg: Nikol Verlagsgesellschaft, 1996.

The Renaissance

Brown, Howard M. *Instrumental Music Printed before 1600, A Bibliography.* Harvard University Press, 1965.

Music in the Renaissance. Englewood Cliffs, New Jersey: Prentice Hall, 1976.

Coelho, Victor Anand, ed. *Performance on Lute, Guitar and Vihuela, Historical Practice and Modern Interpretation.* Cambridge University Press, 1997.

Dart, Thurston. *The Interpretation of Music.* London: Hutchinson, 1954.

Green, V.H.H. *Renaissance & Reformation, A Survey of European History between 1450 & 1660.* London: Edward Arnold, 1974.

La Guitarra Española. The Metropolitan Museum of Art, New York, 1991-1992.

Pujol, Emilio, ed. *Luys de Narváez, Los seys libros del Delphin.* 1945. *Alonso Mudarra, Tres libros de música en cifra para vihuela.* 1949. *Enríquez de Valderrábano, Libro de música de vihuela, intitulado Silva de Sirenas.* 1965. Barcelona: Consejo Superior de Investigaciones Cientificas, Instituto Español de Musicologia.

Schrade, Leo, ed. *El Maestro, Luys Milán.* Hildesheim: Georg Olms/ Wiesbaden: Breitkopf & Härtel, 1976.

Soutelo, Rudesindo F., ed., *Bermudo, Declaración de instrumentos musicales.* Madrid: Arte Tripharia, 1982.

Trend, J.B. *Luis Milán and the Vihuelistas.* Oxford University Press, 1925. *The Music of Spanish History to 1600,* Oxford, 1926.

Tyler, James. *The Early Guitar, A History and Handbook.* Oxford University Press, 1980.

Wyndham Lewis, D.B. *Emperor of the West, A Study of the Emperor Charles the Fifth.* London: Eyre and Spottiswoode, 1932.

The Baroque

Baron, Ernst Gottlieb. *Study of the Lute.* Trans. Douglas Alton Smith. California: Instrumenta Antiqua Publications, 1976.

Benoist, Luc. *Handbook of Western Painting.* London: Thames and Hudson, 1961.

Bukofzer, Manfred F. *Music in the Baroque Era.* London: J.M. Dent, 1947.

Company, Alvaro and Saldarelli, Vincenzo, eds. *Robert de Visée, Suite in Sol minore.* Milan: Edizioni Suvini Zerboni, 1975.

David, Hans T. and Mendel, Arthur. *The Bach Reader, A Life of Johann Sebastian Bach in Letters and Documents.* New York: Norton, 1966.

Hall, Monica, ed. *Joan Carles Amat's Guitarra española.* Monaco: Editions Chanterelle, 1980.

Hudson, Richard. *Passacaglio and Ciaccona, From Guitar Music to Italian Keyboard Variations in the 17th Century.* Ann Arbor, Michigan:UMI Research Press, 1981.

Jeffery, Brian, ed. *Francisco Guerau, Poema Harmónico.* London: Tecla, www.tecla.com, 1977.

Kirkpatrick, Ralph. *Domenico Scarlatti.* Princeton University Press, 1953.

Moreno, Antonio Martín. *Historia de la música española, Vol. 4, Siglo XVIII.* Madrid: Alianza Editorial, 1985.

Pennington, Neil D. *The Spanish Baroque Guitar, with a Transcription of De Murcia's Passacalles y Obras,* Vols 1 & 2. Ann Arbor, Michigan: UMI Research Press, 1981.

Pinnell, Richard T. *Francesco Corbetta and the Baroque Guitar,* Vols 1 & 2. Ann Arbor, Michigan: UMI Research Press, 1980.

Rangel-Ribeiro, Victor. *Baroque Music, A Practical Guide for the Performer.* New York: Schirmer, 1981.

Russell, Craig H., ed. *Santiago de Murcia's "Codice Saldívar No. 4", A Treasury of Secular Guitar Music from Baroque Mexico,* Vols 1 & 2. Urbana & Chicago: University of Illinois Press, 1995.

Strizich, Robert W., ed., *Robert de Visée, Oeuvres Complètes pour Guitare.* Paris: Heugel, 1969. *The Complete Guitar Works of Gaspar Sanz.* Saint-Nicolas, Québec: Doberman-Yppan, 1999.

Wade, Graham. *The Guitarist's Guide to Bach.* Cork: Wise Owl, 1985.

The Classic Guitar

Berlioz, Hector. *Grand traité d'instrumentation et d'orchestration modernes, Op. 10.* Paris, 1843: English translation, *Modern Instrumentation and Orchestration.* London: Novello, 1855.

Button, Stewart. *The Guitar In England, 1800-1924.* New York/London: Garland Publishing Inc., 1989.

Gazzelloni, Giuseppe, ed. *Paganini, The Complete Solo Guitar Works.* Vols 1-3. Heidelberg: Chanterelle, 1987.

Harrison, Frank Mott. *Reminiscences of Madame Sidney Pratten.* Bournemouth: Barnes & Mullins, 1899.

Heck, Thomas F. *The Birth of the Classic Guitar and its Cultivation in Vienna, Reflected in the Career and Compositions of Mauro Giuliani,* Vols 1 & 2. Ph.D. Dissertation: Yale University, 1970. *Mauro Giuliani: Virtuoso Guitarist and Composer.* Columbus, Ohio: Editions Orphée, 1995.

Holmquist, John, ed. *Giulio Regondi, Ten Etudes for Guitar.* Columbus, Ohio: Editions Orphée, 1990.

Jeffery, Brian. *Fernando Sor, Composer and Guitarist.* London: Tecla, www.tecla.com, 1977.

Jeffery, Brian, ed. *Fernando Ferandiere, Arte de tocar la guitarra española por música (Madrid, 1799).* London: Tecla, www.tecla.com, 1977. *Fernando Sor, Complete Works for Guitar.* New York: Shattinger-International Music Corp., 1977. *Aguado - New Guitar Method.* London: Tecla, www.tecla.com, 1981. *Mauro Giuliani, The Complete Works.* London: Tecla, www.tecla.com, 1988. *Complete Guitar Works of Dionisio Aguado,* Vols 1-4. Heidelberg: Chanterelle, 1994.

Kinderman, William. *Beethoven.* Oxford University Press, 1995.

Moser, Wolf. *Francisco Tárrega, Werden und Wirkung.* Göttingen: Saint-George, 1996.

Ophee, Matanya. *Luigi Boccherini's Guitar Quintets, New Evidence.* Columbus, Ohio: Editions Orphée, 1981.

Ophee, Matanya, ed. *Andrei Sychra, Four Concert Etudes.* The Russian Collection, Vol. II, Columbus, Ohio: Editions Orphée, 1992.

Osborne, Charles. *Schubert and his Vienna.* London: Weidenfeld & Nicolson, 1985.

Piris, Bernard. *Fernando Sor, Une guitare à l'orée du Romantisme.* Arles: Éditions Aubier, 1959.

Pujol, Emilio. *Tárrega: Ensayo biográfico.* Lisbon: 1960.

Rodríguez, Melchior, ed. *J. Arcas, Obras Completas para Guitarra.* Madrid: Soneto, 1993.

Romanillos, José L. *Antonio de Torres, Guitar Maker - His Life and Work.* Shaftesbury: Element Books, 1987.

Sor, Ferdinand. *Ferdinand Sor, Method for the Guitar.* Trans. A. Merrick, reprint of the c. 1850 edition. New York: Da Capo Press, 1980.

Tanenbaum, David. (Ferguson, Jim, ed.) *The Essential Studies, Matteo Carcassi, 25 Estudios, Op. 60.* San Francisco: Guitar Solo Publications, 1992.

Torta, Mario. *Catalogo tematico delle opere di Ferdinando Carulli,* Vols 1 & II. Lucca: Libreria Musicale Italiana, 1993.

Wynberg, Simon, ed. *The Selected Works of Dionisio Aguado.* Monaco: Editions Chanterelle, 1981. *The Guitar Works of Napoléon Coste,* Vols 1-IX. Monaco: Chanterelle, 1981. *Giulio Regondi, Complete Works for Guitar.* Monaco: Editions Chanterelle, 1981. *Johann Kaspar Mertz, Guitar Works,* Vols 1-X. Heidelberg: Chanterelle, 1985. *Matteo Carcassi (1792-1853), 25 Etudes Mélodiques Progressives opus 60.* Heidelberg: Chanterelle, 1985. *Luigi Legnani (1790-1877), 36 Caprices.* Heidelberg: Chanterelle, 1986.

Wynberg, Simon. *Marco Aurelio Zani de Ferranti, Guitarist (1801-1878).* Heidelberg: Chanterelle, 1989.

The 20th Century

Alcázar, Miguel, ed. *The Segovia-Ponce Letters.* Trans. Peter Segal. Columbus, Ohio: Editions Orphée, 1989.

Bobri, Vladimir. *The Segovia Technique.* New York: Macmillan, 1972.

Bookspan, Martin and Yockey, Ross. *André Previn, A Biography.* London: Hamish Hamilton, 1981.

Boyd, Liona. *In My Own Key, My Life in Love and Music.* Toronto: Stoddart, 1998.

Burbank, Richard. *Twentieth Century Music.* London: Thames and Hudson, 1984.

Button, Stuart W. *Julian Bream, The Foundations of a Musical Career.* Aldershot: Scolar Press, 1997.

Clinton, George, ed. *Andrés Segovia, An Appreciation.* London: Musical New Services, 1978.

Duarte, John W. *Andrés Segovia, As I Knew Him.* Pacific, Missouri: Mel Bay, 1998.

Gavoty, Bernard. *Segovia, (Great Concert Artists)*. Geneva: René Kister, 1955.

Griffiths, Paul. *The Thames and Hudson Dictionary of 20th Century Music*. London: Thames and Hudson, 1986.

Jahnel, Fritz. *Manual of Guitar Technology*. Trans. J.C. Harvey. Frankfurt: Verlag Das Musikinstrument, 1981.

Mairants, Ivor. *My Fifty Fretting Years*. Newcastle upon Tyne: Ashley Mark Publishing Company, 1980.

Muricy, Andrade. *Villa-Lobos-Uma Interpretação*. Rio de Janeiro: Ministerio da Educação e Cultura, 1961.

Ohtake, Noriko. *Creative Sources for the Music of Toru Takemitsu*. Aldershot, England/Brookfield, Vermont: Scolar Press, 1993.

Otero, Corazón. *Manuel M. Ponce and the Guitar*. Trans. J.D. Roberts. Shaftesbury: Musical New Services, 1980. *Mario Castelnuovo-Tedesco, su vida y su obra para guitarra*. Lomas de Becares, Mexico: Ediciones Musicales Yolotl, 1987.

Palmer, Tony. *Julian Bream, A Life on the Road*. London & Sydney: Macdonald, 1982.

Pedrell, Felipe. *Cancionero musical popular español*, Vols 1-4. Barcelona: Boileau, 1958. (Originally publ. Valls: 1918-1920.)

Pérez-Bustamante de Monasterio, Juan Antonio. *Tras la Huella de Andrés Segovia*. Cádiz: University of Cádiz, 1990.

Pinnell, Richard. *The Rioplatense Guitar: The Early Guitar and its Context in Argentina and Uruguay*. Westport, Connecticut: The Bold Strummer, 1993.

Pujol, Emilio. *Escuela Razonada de la Guitarra*. Buenos Aires: Ricordi Americana, 1934. *El dilema del sonido en la guitarra - The Dilemma of Timbre on the Guitar*. Buenos Aires: Ricordi Americana, 1960.

Purcell, Ronald C. *Andrés Segovia, Contributions to the World of Guitar*. New York: Belwin-Mills, 1975.

Ramírez III, José. *En Torno a la Guitarra/Things about the Guitar*. Madrid: Soneto, 1993.

Riera, Juan. *Emilio Pujol*. Lerida: Instituto de Estudios Ilerdenses, 1974.

Rodrigo, Victoria Kamhi de. *Hand in Hand with Joaquín Rodrigo, My Life at the Maestro's Side*. Trans. Ellen Wilkerson. Pittsburgh, Pennsylvania: Latin American Literary Review Press, 1992.

Sáinz de la Maza, Paloma. *Regino Sáinz de la Maza, Semblanza de mi Padre*. Ayuntamiento de Burgos, 1982.

Santos, Turibio. *Heitor Villa-Lobos and the Guitar*. Trans. V. Forde and G. Wade. Cork: Wise Owl, 1985.

Segovia, Andrés. *Segovia: an Autobiography of the Years 1893-1920*. New York: Macmillan, 1976, London: Marion Boyars, 1977.

Stover, Richard D. *Six Silver Moonbeams, The Life and Times of Agustín Barrios Mangoré*. Clovis, California: Querico Publications, 1992.

Stuckenschmidt, H.H. *Arnold Schoenberg*. London: John Calder, 1959.

Takemitsu, Toru. *Confronting Silence, Selected Writings*. Trans. and ed. Yoshiko Kakudo and Glenn Glasgow. Berkeley, California: Fallen Leaf Press, 1995.

Tonazzi, Bruno. *Miguel Llobet, Chitarrista dell'Impressionismo*. Ancona, Milan: Edizioni Bèrben, 1966.

Wade, Graham. *Segovia-A Celebration of the Man and his Music*. London: Allison & Busby, 1983. *Maestro Segovia*. London: Robson Books, 1986. *Joaquín Rodrigo, Concierto de Aranjuez*. Leeds: Mayflower Enterprises, 1985. *Distant Sarabandes, The Solo Guitar Music of Joaquín Rodrigo*. Leeds: GRM Publications, 1996. *John Mills, Concert Guitarist - A Celebration*. Leeds: GRM Publications, 1997.

Wade, Graham, and Garno, Gerard. *A New Look at Segovia, His Life, His Music*, Vols 1 & 2. Pacific, Missouri: Mel Bay, 1997.

Walker, Luise. *Ein Leben mit der Gitarre*. Frankfurt am Main: Musikverlag Zimmermann, 1989.

Williams, Len, ed. *The Spanish Guitar Today, A Short History and Handbook of Reference*. London: Spanish Guitar Center, c.1955.

Wright, Simon. *Villa-Lobos*. Oxford University Press, 1992.

Index

B

Bach, J.S., 29, 45, 50, 54, 56, 111, 112, 114, 121, 133, 142, 148, 152, 153, 185
Bach Society, 111
Bach-Gesellschaft, 111
Badia, Conchita, 125
Ballard, Robert, 27
Barberiis, Melchiore de, 26
Barbosa-Lima, Carlos, 162
Baron, Ernst Gottlieb, 54, 55, 56
Barrios Mangoré, Agustín, 98, 100, 107, 108, 111, 117, 118, 129, 164, 169, 186
Barrueco, Manuel, 168, 191, 192
Bartolotti, Angelo Michele, 38
Basilio, Padre, 68, 71, 81
Battute, 36, 39, 43, 44
BBC, 139
Beatles, 156
Beethoven, Ludwig van, 73, 76, 79, 80, 98, 175
Bell Lab., Brunswick, New Jersey, 111
Bellère, Jean, 27
Bellow, Alexander, 132
Benavente-Osuna, Marquis of, 67
Benedid, Josef, 63, 64, 65
Benítez, Baltazar, 177
Bennett, Richard Rodney, 159, 180

Bèrben, 160
Bergström, Mats, 193
Berio, Luciano, 185
Berkeley, Lennox, 146, 150, 159
Berlioz, Hector, 74, 87, 88, 98
Bermudo, Juan, 25, 30
Bernabe, Paulino, 151
Besard, Jean Baptiste, 114
Bickford, Vahdah Olcott, 111
Bitetti, Ernesto, 146, 170
Blaha, Vladislav, 192
BMG, 166
Bobri, Vladimir, 132, 172
Boccherini, Luigi, 67, 68, 153
Borges, Rául, 168
Bosch, Hieronymus, 181
Boucher, Remi, 192
Bouchet, Robert, 154
Boulanger, Nadia, 177
Brayssing, Gregoire, 27
Bream - Williams Duo, 159
Bream Consort, 150
Bream, Julian, 76, 81, 82, 138, 139, 142, 143, 144, 146, 149, 150, 152, 154, 155, 158, 159, 162, 163, 168, 172, 175, 176, 180, 182, 186, 187, 188, 189, 190
Briceño, Luis de, 33
Bridgewater Hall, Manchester, 187
Brighton Pavilion, 94

Colascione, 19
Colonna, Giovanni Ambrosio, 35
Consonancias, 25
Contreras, Manuel, 151
Corbetta, Francesco, 37, 40, 41,
42, 43, 44, 46, 49, 114
Corelli, Arcangelo, 53
Corral, Emilia, 153
Coste, Napoleón, 72, 74, 85, 89,
90, 91
Coupe Internationale de Guitare,
152
Covarrubias, Sebastián de, 33
Craft guilds, 61
Crespo, Jorge Gómez, 186
Cucchi, Flavio, 193
Cuervas, Matilde, 120
Cutting, Francis, 55
Czerny, Carl, 75

D

Dalí, Salvador, 123, 181
Dall'Aquila, Marco, 18
Dangeau, Comte de, 45
Davidsen, Trond, 193
Davies, Peter Maxwell, 176, 177
Daza, Esteban, 21
Decachorde, 72
Decca, 112
Décima, 30
Desiderio, Aniello, 193

Diabelli, Anton, 74, 80, 81
Diario de Madrid, 122
Dias, Belchior, 26
Diaz, Alirio, 147, 152, 164, 168,
169
Dinnigan, Simon, 193
Dodgson, Stephen, 157
Dolmetsch Collection, 63
Domeniconi, Carlo, 183, 184, 185
Domingo, Placido, 171
Dowland, John, 55, 150
Dowland, Robert, 55
Duarte, John W., 148, 153, 160,
161, 170
Dukas, Paul, 111
Dukic, Zoran, 192
Dupré, Tom, 193
Dyens, Roland, 179

E

Early Music, 165, 167
Edinburgh International Festival,
133
Elizabeth II, 155
EMI, 188, 189
Enciclopedia Espasa, 97
Eötvös, Jozsef, 193
Escarpa, Margarita, 193
Eschig, Max, 114
Espinel, Vicente Martínez de, 30

215

Gómez, Vicente, 140
Goni, Antigoni, 193
González, Manuel, 96
Gorlier, Simon, 27
Gramophone, 112, 133, 137, 143
Granados, Enrique, 136, 168
Granata, Giovanni Battista, 37, 43, 44
Granger, Stewart, 138
Granjon, Robert, 27
Grau, Agusti, 114
Greenwood, Joan, 138
Grigoryan, Slava, 192
Grovlez, Gabriel, 109
Guerau, Francisco, 49, 50, 52
Guerra, Dionisio, 63
Guitar International, 166
Guitar News, 166
Guitar Review, 131, 132, 140
Guitarra, 25
Guitarra latina, 13
Guitarra morisca, 13
Guiterne, 25, 41
Guiterre, 25, 41
Guzman, María Esther, 193

H

Hade, 11
Halász, Franz, 193
Hall, Nicola, 193
Hand, Richard, 193

Handel, George Frideric, 50, 98
Harmonicon, 78
Harpolyre, 72
Harpsichord, 86
Hauser guitar, 151
Hauser I, Hermann, 124, 146
Hauser II, Hermann, 146
Hauser III, Hermann, 146
Haydn, Franz Joseph, 98
Heck, Thomas F., 78
Henri II, 26
Henze, Hans Werner, 158, 159
Hernández, Julio López, 171
Hernández, Santos, 124
Hii, Philip, 193
Hildebrand, Zacharias, 56
Hinterleithner, Ferdinand, 54
Hirohito, Emperor, 171
Holzman, Adam, 193
Hoppstock, Tilman, 193
Horetzky, Felix, 74
Hornbostel, E. M., 10, 11
Horowitz, Vladimir, 171
Huerta, Trinidad, 87

I

Idiophones, 10
Indy, Vincent d', 111
Infante Don Luis, 67
Instrument Museum, Leipzig University, 64

216

218

Mudarra, Alonso, 21, 26, 114, 125, 131
Muñoa, Manuel, 64
Münster, Bishop of, 72
Muraji, Kaori, 193
Murcia, Gabriel de, 52
Murcia, Santiago de, 50, 52, 53, 54, 114
Musée Jacquemart-André, Paris, 22
Museo de la Festa, Elche, Alicante, 63
Museu de la Música, Barcelona, 62, 63, 64

N

Narváez, Luis de, 21, 114, 125, 131
National Conservatoire, Madrid, 74
National Library, Paris, 120
National Orchestra of Madrid, 136
National Theater, San Salvador, 118
Neave, Allan, 193
Neue Bach-Gesellschaft, 111
Nitsuga, 117
Norge, Kaare, 192
Nylon strings, 132

O

Odeon, 111, 112
Ogden, Craig, 192
Ohana, Maurice, 144, 145
Oldenburg, Duke of, 72
Oliveira, Pedro Ferreira, 63
Opera House, San Francisco, 141
Ophee, Matanya, 73
Orchestra of the Air, 141
Orchestre de la Suisse Romande, 136
Orchestre des Jeunes Universitaires, 135
Order of the British Empire, 155
Order of the Rising Sun, 171
Orfeo Gracienc, Barcelona, 108
Oyanguren, Julio Martínez, 140

P

Paganini, Nicolò, 74, 75, 83, 84, 99, 120
Pagés, Juan, 64, 65
Palacio de Bellas Artes, Mexico City, 129
Panormo, Joseph, 67
Papandreou, Elena, 193
Papas, Sophocles, 131
Parlophon Electric, 112
Pavarotti, Luciano, 171
Payet, Carlos, 164

219